S0-BWU-704

Older
Workers

Choices and Challenges:
An Older Adult Reference Series
Elizabeth Vierck, Series Editor

Housing Options and Services for Older Adults,
Ann E. Gillespie and Katrinka Smith Sloan

Mental Health Problems and Older Adults,
Gregory A. Hinrichsen

Older Workers, Sara E. Rix

Paying for Health Care after Age 65,
Elizabeth Vierck

Volunteerism and Older Adults, Mary K. Kouri

Forthcoming

Legal Issues and Older Adults,
Linda Josephson Millman and Sallie Birket Chafer

Travel and Older Adults, Allison St. Claire

Older Workers

Sara E. Rix

Choices and Challenges: An Older Adult Reference Series
Elizabeth Vierck, Series Editor

ABC-CLIO
Santa Barbara, California
Oxford, England

Cover Design/Graphein

Library of Congress Cataloging-in-Publication Data
Rix, Sara E.
    Older workers / Sara E. Rix.
      p. cm.—(Choices and challenges)
    Includes bibliographical references.
    Includes index.
    1. Age and employment—United States. 2. Retirement age—United States. I. Title. II. Series.
    HD6280.R57   1990   331.3'98'0973—dc20   90-46349

ISBN 0-87436-259-8 (alk. paper)

97 96 95 94 93 92 91 90   10 9 8 7 6 5 4 3 2 1

ABC-CLIO, Inc.
130 Cremona Drive, P.O. Box 1911
Santa Barbara, California 93116-1911

Clio Press Ltd.
55 St. Thomas' Street
Oxford, OX1 1JG, England

This book is Smyth-sewn and printed on acid-free paper ∞ .
Manufactured in the United States of America

Contents

Figures and Tables

Foreword

Loyal, dedicated, stable, experienced, committed to quality, able to get along with coworkers, prompt, and dependable—this is how employers generally describe older workers. However, as Sara Rix has stated in this comprehensive reference book, far too many employers still harbor negative stereotypes of older workers. These stereotypes must be reversed in order for older workers to gain their fair share of the job market.

Examples of the most common stereotypes are:

Stereotype #1: The productivity of workers declines with age.

Stereotype #2: The performance of skilled and semiskilled workers is higher for younger persons than older persons.

Stereotype #3: The performance of clerical workers declines with age.

Stereotype #4: "You can't teach an old dog new tricks," in other words, older workers do not do well in training and retraining.

Compare these stereotypes with some of the facts that Rix reports in this book:

Fact #1: *No* pattern of higher or lower productivity characterizes any particular age group, and many older workers actually do better on many jobs than younger ones.

Fact #2: The performance of skilled and unskilled workers in their 60s *is often superior* to that of younger workers.

Fact #3: Older clerical workers are *as productive* as younger ones.

Fact #4: Older workers learn tasks *as well as* younger workers, although they may take longer. In fact, recent studies have shown that older individuals can master new computer technology.

Clearly, older persons who are able to work, and wish or need to, have much to offer employers. And, happily, more and more employers, facing a shrinking and increasingly unskilled work force, are overthrowing the stereotypes and beginning to realize the value of older workers. In response, they are beginning to offer creative work options to attract them. McDonald's, for example, now offers older workers "new-concept" part-time work, which means that employees get better wages, fringe benefits, and opportunities for advancement than is usually the case with such work; Aerospace Corporation hires its own retirees and allows them to work for 999 hours per year without giving up benefits; Control Data Corporation now offers older workers "flextime and flexplace" programs, which means that employees can work flexible hours in an alternative work site such as home; and the Polaroid Corporation offers its retirees a variety of retirement options such as rehearsal retirement and phased retirement. Such creative programs are, hopefully, the vanguards of an end-of-the-decade revolution in employment opportunities for older adults.

It is easy to see why one of the most dynamic topics in gerontology today is "older workers." This comprehensive reference book covers a wealth of material on the topic that will provide interested readers with the necessary facts to rethink personal and public retirement policies. Part One of the book is an overview of the subjects that are essential to a basic and up-to-date understanding of the issue. The author does not present a Polyanna view of the topic but lays out the hard facts about such subjects as the seemingly intransigent trend toward early retirement and the painful reality of age discrimination. Other examples of the topics covered in Part One are: the labor market problems of older workers (including unemployment and job-seeking discouragement); how to detect and seek redress for age discrimination; the role that social security and pensions play for older workers; age and work ability; training; and the special employment problems of older women. Part Two is a timely and welcome resource for information specialists, researchers, and older adults looking for work. It provides the most comprehensive guide to resources on and for older workers presently available.

In short, *Older Workers* is a valuable source to what is presently known about the topic. *Older Workers* is also, I believe, a significant contribution toward rethinking retirement—as the labor force faces a shortage of millions of skilled workers.

Elizabeth Vierck
Series Editor
Choices and Challenges

How To Use This Book

Each book in the Choices and Challenges series provides a convenient, easy-access reference tool on a specific topic of interest to older adults and those involved with them, including caregivers, spouses, adult children, and gerontology professionals. The books are designed for ease of use, with a generous typeface, ample use of headings and subheadings, and a detailed index.

Each book consists of two parts, which may be used together or independently:

> A narrative section providing an informative and comprehensive overview of the topic, written for a lay audience. The narrative can be read straight through or consulted on an as-needed basis by using the headings and subheadings and/or the index.

> An annotated resource section that includes a directory of relevant organizations; recommended books, pamphlets, and articles; and software and videos. Where appropriate, the resource section may include additional information relevant to the topic. This section can be used in conjunction with or separately from the narrative to locate sources of additional information, assistance, or support.

A glossary defines important terms and concepts, and the index provides additional access to the material. For easy reference, entries in the resource section are indexed by both topic and title or name.

Acronyms and Abbreviations Used in This Book

AARP	American Association of Retired Persons
ADEA	Age Discrimination in Employment Act
AIME	Average Indexed Monthly Earnings
BFOQ	Bona Fide Occupational Qualification
BLS	Bureau of Labor Statistics
CPS	Current Population Survey
CSCP	Community Service Career Program
DHN	Displaced Homemakers Network
DOL	U.S. Department of Labor
EBRI	Employee Benefit Research Institute
EEOC	Equal Employment Opportunity Commission
EOS	Employment Opportunity Specialist
ERISA	Employee Retirement Income Security Act
FAA	Federal Aviation Administration
GAO	U.S. General Accounting Office
HHS	U.S. Department of Health and Human Services
IRS	Internal Revenue Service
JTPA	Job Training Partnership Act
NCCBA	National Caucus and Center on Black Aged
NCOA	National Council on the Aging
NCSC	National Council of Senior Citizens
NOWIS	National Older Workers Information System
OWL	Older Women's League
RSVP	Retired Senior Volunteer Program

SCSEP   Senior Community Service Employment Program
SCORE   Service Corps of Retired Executives
SSA   Social Security Administration

Older
Workers

Introduction

Medical Detailer. For pharmaceutical house, some academic background in sciences; will call on professionals only. . . . Under 35.

Washington Post and *Times Herald,* January 2, 1955: C6

Executive salesman. . . . Man with proven record in intangible sales. . . . Must be in age range of 25–40.

New York Times, January 3, 1960: W21

Secretary, for maritime and admiralty law office, age to 40.

Washington Post, January 17, 1960: D7

An entire generation has grown up and entered the labor market since employers were permitted to limit their help-wanted ads by age and gender. Want ads courting "young men on the move" and "girl Fridays" might seem quaint today, but they were perfectly legal and not uncommon until the late 1960s. Furthermore, employers could pay "old" workers less than younger ones, and they could force employees of a certain age to retire in order to make room for younger workers, to streamline organizations top heavy with highly paid older employees, to reduce fringe benefit costs, or for a number of other reasons.

With the passage of the Age Discrimination in Employment Act (ADEA) in 1967 (Public Law 90-202, effective June 12, 1968), older workers gained protection against "discrimination in employment on account of age in such matters as hiring, job retention, compensation and other conditions of employment." Employers with 25 or more employees, labor unions with 25 or more members, and employment agencies were forbidden to specify particular ages or age ranges in employment advertisements.

3

Words such as *young, boy,* and *girl*—as well as *old* and *pensioner*—became illegal, and calls for draft-exempt young men or under-30 typists disappeared from the classified ad sections of newspapers, newsletters, and trade journals.

The provisions of the ADEA originally applied to persons between the ages of 40 and 65. Subsequent amendments increased and ultimately eliminated the upper age limit and extended coverage to firms with at least 20 employees. Since January 1987, older persons have, with few exceptions, been *legally entitled* to remain at work for as long as they wish, assuming their performance is adequate.

Fewer Older Adults Are Working

Nevertheless, since 1967 the labor force participation rate of older adults has fallen, and it continues to fall. Discrimination against older workers did not evaporate with the passage of the ADEA; often it just became harder to prove. Companies offer early retirement incentives in subtle and not-so-subtle efforts to persuade their older employees to leave the work force. Health problems force many older workers to retire, while a lack of options such as part-time employment discourages other retirees from even looking for work. Finally, and most important, improvements in the social security program and the spread of private pensions have institutionalized retirement and enhanced the attractiveness of withdrawing from the labor force. More and more workers can afford to retire, and they have been doing so at increasingly early ages. James Schulz (1988b: 2), an economist at Brandeis University, observes that "most older workers want to retire as soon as financially possible" and "once retired, most older persons adapt quickly to their new life situation and indicate a high degree of satisfaction with their lives."

On the other hand, many older Americans say they would like some paid employment, and many employers are increasingly in need of workers. Yet incentives to keep people working longer or to entice them to return to the labor force after retiring have, to date, been relatively few.

Rethinking Retirement

In recent years, both employers and workers have begun to reassess the trend toward early retirement. Several factors have contributed to this reassessment, including (1) concern about the ability of the nation to support a huge cohort of retired baby boomers, (2) the probability that no further substantive improvements will occur in old-age benefits under social security, (3) a slowdown in private pension expansion, (4) a sharp drop in the number of young labor force entrants due to the low fertility rates of the baby bust era, (5) serious skills deficiencies among young workers, and (6) exceptionally low unemployment rates in many parts of the country. Also troubling is the loss of productivity resulting from the retirement of millions of older workers—a productivity that could be contributing to economic growth.

Consequently, some employers are deciding that it makes sense to keep older workers and retrain them in new technologies. Others—especially in the service sector—are eager to attract employees of all ages and have begun to provide incentives such as part-time work with better wages or flexible work schedules. A number of businesses have established job banks of retirees who serve as experienced, knowledgeable temporary labor when the need arises. And others encourage valued employees to remain at work after the age of 65.

This book is predicated on the assumption that there is, indeed, a need to rethink retirement-age policies in the United States, with an eye toward providing opportunities for people to work longer, even well into old age. Prolonged work lives may take the form of postponing retirement, late-life career changes, a reduction in work hours, phased retirement, temporary or occasional work after retirement, labor force reentry, and/or any number of other options.

Such a goal requires educating employers about the potential contributions of older workers, as well as encouraging workers to rethink their work and retirement plans. Some significant obstacles, such as pension plan work restrictions, will need to be eliminated, and a variety of work options for older employees developed. These are long-term objectives—the trend toward early retirement will not be modified overnight. This book is intended for both older adults who want to work and employers who will increasingly need the knowledge, experience, and ability of older workers.

Who Is Old? Who Is Retired?

Middle and Old Age

When does a worker become "old"? Under the provisions of the Age Discrimination in Employment Act, old age technically begins at 40, although many workers—particularly those in or approaching their 40s—would object to being classified as old or even middle-aged during what they consider their prime working years. Anyone 60 and above qualifies as old under the Older Americans Act, while older worker programs funded under the Job Training Partnership Act and the Senior Community Service Employment Program are targeted at workers 55 and over. Age 55 is widely regarded as the age at which employment problems become pronounced. For others, old age begins at 65, the so-called normal retirement age, when full social security benefits become available.

For a number of reasons, including convenience and age cutoffs used in published official statistics, persons aged 65 and older will be considered "old" in this book, and persons 45 (or occasionally 40) to 64 as "middle-aged." These distinctions are not always used by the authors of books or studies on age and employment; when the available data define middle or old age differently, that fact will be noted.

Retirement

Retirement is probably harder to define than old age, although, at first glance, one might think that everyone knows what retirement is. An employee who worked for many years and who has left a job fully and permanently to live on a pension or social security income is clearly retired. But what about the woman who did not work long enough to qualify for a pension or social security benefits in her own right, or whose earnings were too low for decent benefits, and who consequently receives a spouse's social security benefit? Is she retired? Or is she simply "out of the labor force"? And what about the manager who accepts an early retirement incentive well before becoming eligible for social security and takes another job, or "double dips," until turning 62 or 65? Is he or she retired? Is the reentrant—the person who stopped working, began collecting retirement benefits, and then returned to work—still retired even though he or she may now be fully employed? Are pensioners who earn income in the underground economy but who do not report their wages to the IRS properly classified as retired, somewhat retired, somewhat employed, or something else?

Distinctions among different types of workers and retirees are of more than academic interest. For example, the amount of income available from nonwork sources has an impact on the number of workers who might be interested in continuing to work, in working more hours, or in returning to the work force. Unfortunately, it is often possible only to determine whether someone is in or out of the labor force. Labor force participants are persons who are either employed (or away from work for such reasons as vacation, personal leave, or illness) or officially unemployed, which means actively looking for work (an active job seeker is one who has looked for work within the past four weeks). Persons who are out of the labor force—nonparticipants—are neither working nor unemployed. In most instances one can assume that older nonparticipants are retired; older *participants,* however, may have retired from one job and moved on to another, may be partially retired from their career jobs, or may be reentry workers.

Lack of Information Hampers Decision Making

Other limitations hinder the development of programs and policies for older workers. More and better longitudinal data and analyses are needed to determine the relationship between age and, for example, health status, or the relationship between changes in mortality and morbidity. But developing the necessary databases would be costly and results would take many years to gather. In the meantime, new public and private programs and policies for older workers are needed.

When Congress was faced with a decision about raising the retirement age under social security, the decision had to be based, in part, on what the experts knew in 1983. Similarly, employers confronting labor shortages or global competition for markets cannot afford to wait for the definitive longitudinal study on the relationship between age and productivity before they revise their employment and retirement policies or make decisions about implementing alternative work schedules or expanding training programs. And workers themselves must make employment decisions and retirement plans on the basis of educated guesses about distant inflation rates, their own health status, and the ability and willingness of future generations of workers to support them.

What This Book Is About

This volume examines some of the programs and policies—both public and private—that have been implemented to keep older persons at work for a longer period of time. It also attempts to answer some of the practical questions that employers, practitioners in the field of aging, employment specialists, job trainers, workers themselves, and others frequently ask about work and aging. What, for example, are the prevailing employment and retirement trends and how amenable are they to change? How does the law protect older workers? What public and private programs and policies assist or thwart older workers in their efforts to remain in the labor force or to reenter it after retirement? What do recent changes in social security mean for employees and employers?

As the population of the United States ages, particularly as the baby boomers begin to reach middle and old age, these questions are likely to take on a more urgent tone. Congress will increasingly worry about the costs of supporting a growing elderly population. Employers will wonder where to find skilled workers. And workers will worry about the adequacy of their retirement benefits.

Part One, "Working in an Aging America," briefly reviews older worker employment and retirement patterns in the twentieth century. Chapter 1 paints a statistical portrait of the older worker and reviews how that portrait has changed over time. Chapter 2 is an examination of the Age Discrimination in Employment Act. Chapter 3 considers how social security, pension plans, and other financial issues affect work and retirement decisions. Chapter 4 is concerned with the impact of age on ability to work and productivity, while Chapter 5 discusses training for older workers, including both private sector efforts and the two major federal training programs for older workers: the Senior Community Service Employment Program (SCSEP) and Job Training Partnership Act (JTPA) programs. Chapter 6 addresses the special problems and needs of older women, and Chapter 7 examines specific policies and programs that promote older worker employment. Chapter 8 looks at the future directions of employment for older workers.

Part Two provides both older workers and their current or potential employers with information on services, programs, and resources for finding work and developing and implementing programs to increase the employment opportunities of older workers. Chapter 9 is a selective compilation of largely national public and private groups, including organizations, associations, government agencies, and self-help groups, that promote employment opportunities for older workers. A few of the organizations serve mainly as sources of information on older worker issues.

Chapter 10 is an annotated bibliography of key publications intended to assist and inform older workers, job seekers, employers, employment counselors, job trainers, and others. Selection criteria included potential usefulness to older workers, older persons in search of work, employers and their representatives, and/or practitioners seeking to expand older worker employment prospects. A few academic titles are included because they also contain practical information. The references are divided into "Publications for the Older Worker or Job Seeker" and "Publications for the Employer, Practitioner, and Older Worker Adviser." Readers are encouraged to skim through both sections for publications of interest to them.

Chapter 11 is an annotated listing of computer-based information, videos, and films aimed at expanding readers' understanding of older workers and their problems, solutions to those problems, and prospects for employment. The book ends with a glossary of key employment-related terms relevant to older worker employment programs and policies.

Older Workers examines both older workers' employment preferences and employers' responses to those preferences. It is designed to aid employers, workers, employment counselors, job trainers, and others who must make decisions about work, workers, and the economy in the face of numerous uncertainties.

PART
ONE

Working in an
Aging America

Chapter 1

Twentieth-Century Trends in Work and Retirement

Most old people work as long as they can and retire only because they are forced to do so.

Stecker, 1951: 15

Overall, a desire to retire was given more often than any other reason for leaving a last job.

Sherman, 1985: 24

FACTS

- In 1989, fewer than 12 percent of Americans 65 and older were working.

- Since 1950, the total number of persons aged 65 and older has increased from 12.4 million to over 29 million, but the older work force has remained nearly stable at around 3 million.

- Workers are much more likely to begin collecting social security benefits at the minimum age, 62, than to wait until age 65, even though their monthly benefits are lower as a result.

- The availability of income other than earnings is the major factor behind early retirement.

- Two million nonworking older Americans report that they would return to work if they could.

The Retirement Phenomenon

Times have changed, and most older people are not working as long as the 1951 quote at the beginning of the chapter would indicate. As of 1989, only 3.4 million men and women aged 65 or older—less than 12 percent of the total "older" population—were working, and another 91,000 were looking for work. In contrast, some 26 million older Americans were retired, engaged in full-time homemaking, too sick to work, or, in a few cases, enrolled in school. These individuals were, in short, "out of the labor force."

Although a number of social and economic trends characterize the twentieth century, one of the most pronounced is the withdrawal of older workers from the labor force and the widespread agreement that people are entitled to some leisure at the end of their working years. Not only are older Americans less likely to be working today than in the past, they are leaving the labor force sooner. Workers more commonly begin collecting social security benefits at the youngest possible age, 62, rather than wait until the "normal" age of 65.

In the delightfully informative *Growing Old in America,* historian David Hackett Fischer (1978: 44) reports that in the early United States "there was no fixed age at which retirement was formally required or generally expected. Retirement in that sense did not exist"—a statement he could not make about the present. Retirement may not be formally required, and there is no "fixed" retirement age, but it is generally expected that workers will retire and that in many cases they will do so sooner rather than later: the *average* retirement age under social security is now about 63.

Not all early beneficiaries are fully or permanently retired; some continue to work while collecting social security; a few will return to the labor force after a period of withdrawal. Many share their time and expertise as volunteers, while others keep busy with hobbies or other activities. At present, however, paid work engages only one in nine older Americans.

Although the average age at which workers first begin to collect retirement benefits has been dropping, the number of older persons potentially available for work has been rising dramatically. Over the course of the twentieth century, the number of persons 65 and older has grown from 3.1 million in 1900 to 12.4 million in 1950 to over 29 million in 1989—a more than ninefold increase overall! Since mid-century, however, the older labor force has hovered at around 3 million, occasionally inching above that figure and occasionally dipping below, but never deviating very sharply from it.

The Feminization of the Older Work Force: Gender Differences in Work and Retirement

A century ago, older persons, males and females combined, were about three times as likely as they are now to be in the labor force. That figure, however, obscures divergent labor force trends for men and women, as well as the magnitude of the drop in labor force participation among men. In 1900, most older men *had* to work, since earnings were usually their only source of income, and their labor force participation rate of just over 63 percent (see Table 1.1 and Figure 1.1) reflected that fact. Over the last nine

Table 1.1   Labor Force Participation Rates of Men and Women Aged 45–64 and 65 and Over, Selected Years, Actual 1900–1989[a] and Projected 2000 (in percentages)

	MEN				WOMEN			
YEAR	45–64	45–54	55–64	65+	45–64	45–54	55–64	65+
1900	90.3			63.1	13.6			8.3
1920	90.7			55.6	16.5			7.3
1930	91.0			54.0	18.0			7.3
1940	89.4			42.2	20.0			6.0
1944	93.5			50.9	31.2			9.6
1950	91.9	95.8	86.9	45.8	33.1	38.0	27.0	9.5
1960	91.9	95.7	86.8	33.1	44.3	49.8	37.2	10.8
1970	89.3	94.3	83.0	26.8	49.3	54.4	43.0	9.7
1980	82.0	91.2	72.1	19.0	50.7	59.9	41.3	8.1
1989	80.2	91.1	67.2	16.6	58.5	70.5	45.0	8.4
2000	81.8	90.5	68.1	14.7	65.5	76.5	49.0	7.6

Sources: U.S. Bureau of the Census, 1965; U.S. Department of Labor, 1985 and 1990; Fullerton, 1989.
[a]Figures for 1900–1940 are from decennial censuses; figures for 1944–1989 are from current population surveys.

Midlife and Older Women's Attachment to the Labor Force Grows as Men's Weakens

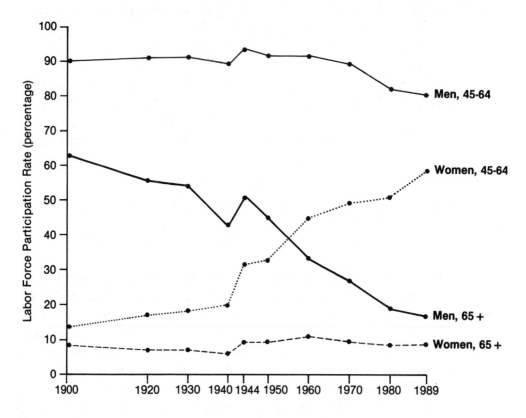

Figure 1.1   Labor Force Participation Rates of Midlife and Older Men and Women, 1900–1989. Sources: U.S. Bureau of the Census, 1965; U.S. Department of Labor, 1985 and January 1990.

decades, however, that rate has plummeted. Except for the first half of the 1940s, when the war effort and labor shortages created a demand for older workers, the 1900s have witnessed a fairly steady long-term decline in the labor force attachment of older men. By 1989, less than 17 percent of these men were either working or looking for work.

Older women's experiences, not surprisingly, bear little resemblance to those of men the same age. Until recently, women have not been expected to work outside the home, and for the most part they have not done so, particularly in their later years. In 1900, the labor force participation rate of older woman stood at 8.3 percent, and while that rate has varied somewhat over the course of the century, also rising slightly during World War II, it has never fluctuated by much. By 1989, 8.4 percent of all older women were in the labor force.

With respect to labor force participation, older never-married women seem to resemble older men more than they do other older women. The participation rate of these women, never as high as that of men but much higher than the rate for married women, has also fallen off sharply. Eligibility for retired worker benefits under social security and private pensions has enabled many of these women to do what older men with long work histories are doing—namely, retire. Barring intervention, these trends may carry over to older married women, as their lifelong participation in the labor force strengthens.

Since the 1950s, more middle-aged men have also been withdrawing from the labor force. Table 1.1 and Figure 1.1 clearly demonstrate a growing tendency toward relatively fewer men working in their early 60s, 50s, and even late 40s, although the withdrawal of men in these age groups has been neither as sharp nor as consistent as it has been among men 65 and older. By contrast, middle-aged women have been marching into, not out of, the labor force over much of the course of this century. As of 1989, 70.5 percent of all women between the ages of 45 and 54 were in the labor force, nearly double the percentage of 1950.

The effect of these trends is that the older labor force—indeed, the labor force as a whole—is increasingly female (see Figure 1.2). At the turn of the century only about one in ten middle-aged and older labor force participants was a woman; today more than two out of five are women, a development that has significant implications for employer personnel policies. At one time, it might have been reasonable to base employment policies on the assumption that all older workers were men, thus overlooking the particular needs and interests of aging female workers and their families. This no longer makes sense, as policymakers in the public and private sectors are increasingly discovering.

Why Retirement?

Concern about society's ability to support a growing population of older nonworkers, as well as impending shortages of skilled workers, is bringing pressure on public and private policymakers to examine the factors responsible for recent retirement trends.

18

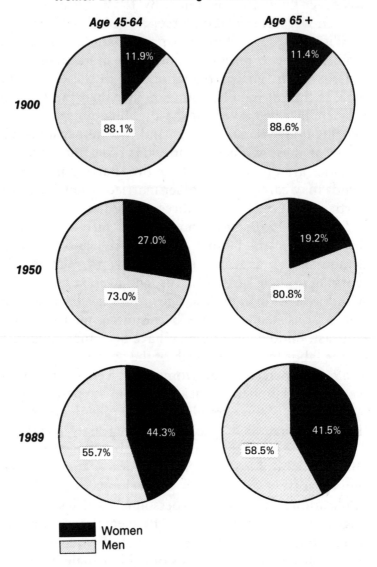

Women Become a Growing Presence in the Labor Force

Age 45-64   Age 65 +

1900

11.9%   11.4%

88.1%   88.6%

1950

27.0%   19.2%

73.0%   80.8%

1989

44.3%   41.5%

55.7%   58.5%

■ Women
☐ Men

Figure 1.2   Women as a Percentage of the Midlife and Older
Labor Force, 1900, 1950, and 1989. Sources: U.S. Bureau of the
Census, 1965; U.S. Department of Labor, January 1990.

Changes in the Economy

As discussed below, social security, which was enacted in 1935 and which paid its first retired worker benefit in 1940, has undoubtedly influenced the work and retirement decisions of older workers. So too have private pensions, perhaps even more than social security in some cases. But men were withdrawing from the labor force in increasing numbers well before the first retired worker drew a social security check, and the private pension system did not begin to expand appreciably until after World War II. Prior to that time, few workers could count on income from private pension funds. (Even today, less than one-fourth of all older retirees receive private pension income.)

The labor force participation rate of older men declined by about as many percentage points in the first four decades of the twentieth century as it did during the second four. As the country shifted from an agrarian to an industrial society, opportunities for older worker employment declined along with the shift (see Treas, 1986). Self-employment opportunities, which gave older workers more control over whether they remained at work and how much they worked, began to shrink. In 1900, more than one-third of all employed workers could be found in the agricultural sector, but by 1988, less than 3 percent were involved in farming. Not only have older workers traditionally been more concentrated in agriculture than younger workers, but farm work is, within limits, an occupation that permits some modification of work schedules, perhaps in response to reduced physical capacity. And both agriculture and self-employment lack employer inducements to retire.

The decline in agricultural employment and the shift to an industrial economy meant fewer opportunities for older workers, who were not believed to be up to the demands of factory work. As Malcolm Morrison (1986: 348) points out:

> The intense speed required for industrial work was thought to increase stress, which, it was assumed, would result in an absolute decline of productive capacity with age. With an increasing immigrant labor supply, union demands for reduced weekly work hours, and the advent of automation, this "wear-and-tear" theory gained wide credence and was used to justify both the dismissal of older workers as well as the imposition of age limitations in hiring.

Employers who might have been worried about the ability of older workers to perform in a fast-paced industrial workplace had an alternative—an adequate supply of desirable (young) workers freed them from concerns about maximizing older worker productivity.

Mandatory Retirement

Many workers have, indeed, been forced out of the workplace by mandatory retirement policies, particularly when the economy was shifting to an industrial base. Nevertheless, it would be wrong to assume that, at least since 1950, such policies have been a significant factor in retirement decisions. For the last ten years, almost all workers have been legally entitled to remain at work until age 70 (and now forever, if they choose), and yet few have done so. The amendments to the Age Discrimination in Employment Act that eliminated mandatory retirement are too recent to have had an appreciable effect on middle-aged and older workers' retirement plans. Still, if mandatory retirement at age 65 were instrumental in forcing workers to retire, then the 1978 raising of the upper age limit from 65 to 70 should be reflected in current labor force statistics. That evidence has not appeared.

According to Schulz (1988a), even in the early 1960s, when workers were not protected by *any* federal age discrimination provision, fewer than 1 in 10 retirees could be said to be physically capable of working but unable to do so because of mandatory retirement rules. By the 1980s, beneficiaries who began collecting social security were even less inclined—1 out of 20—to say that they had been retired against their will (Sherman, 1985).

Although employers cannot require workers to retire at some fixed or arbitrary "old" age, they are also not required to encourage older workers to remain on the job. Employers eager to rid themselves of older workers may structure their pension plans in such a way as to promote early retirement. The U.S. Department of Labor (1989c: 47) reports that as of 1983, nearly four out of five pension plans either had no *minimum* retirement age or provided full pension benefits at or before the age of 62. Moreover, "*37 percent of those plans allowed for full-benefit retirement as early as age 55*" (emphasis added). Over the past decade, early retirement incentive plans have become common in large firms, often, if an American Management Survey is any guide, with the intent of paring down staff (American Association of Retired Persons, 1987b).

Employers cannot force employees to accept early retirement incentives, but they may pressure them to do so. They can also make early retirement attractive by augmenting private pensions until workers are eligible for social security benefits at age 62. Such incentives might prove too tempting to resist, especially if they carry a time limit and workers cannot be sure that they will still be available at a later date. Under such circumstances, the extent to which workers can be said to be retiring voluntarily is questionable. Early retirements, of course, could be minimized by making early labor force withdrawal less attractive financially.

Poor Health

Although health problems do force some people to retire, workers are far less likely to cite poor health as a reason for leaving the labor force today than they were in the past. As recently as 1968, over half of all new social security beneficiaries were contending that they had retired for health reasons, but 15 years later, that figure had dropped to less than 30 percent. The shift to a service economy and workplace changes have allowed some employees with health limitations to remain at work. Moreover, a worker who retires for health reasons may not be completely unable to work. An alternative work schedule or a different job could be all that it takes to keep an older worker productive.

Before retirement became widely accepted as a legitimate social role, a health problem or disability was almost the only valid reason for men to be out of the labor force. Society has become more tolerant about leisure activity, which has made it easier for workers to admit that they have retired for reasons other than health, as the second quote at the beginning of this chapter suggests.

Physical inability to work, therefore, does not appear to explain the growing trend toward early retirement. The U.S. General Accounting Office (1985) has estimated that about two-thirds of male private pension beneficiaries under the age of 62 are receiving regular, rather than disability, benefits from their employers. However, very early retirees are substantially more likely to retire because of health problems or disability. Retirement for health reasons is also much more common among blacks than among whites (Parnes, 1988).

On the other hand, some truly unhealthy workers delay retirement because they lack adequate income alternatives. Older workers who report health problems but who lack income other than earnings are far more likely to remain at work than persons with health problems *and* pension or other income.

Financial Incentives

The availability of income from nonwork sources is the major factor responsible for early retirement (Achenbaum, 1986; Crown et al., 1987; Ruhm, 1989; Schulz, 1988b). In fact, while midlife and older workers have substantially higher incomes than their retired counterparts, the real or perceived advantages of stopping work and the availability of social security or pension income apparently offset lost earnings (see, e.g., Crown et al., 1987: vii). Thus, social security "retirement" rates initially peak at age 62, when retired worker benefits are first available, and then again at 65, when full benefits (described in Chapter 3) become payable.

The Part-Time Alternative

Even though the trend toward early retirement sometimes seems irreversible, permanent and complete labor force withdrawal may not be the preferred option of all individuals nearing the end of their careers. To the contrary, interest in some form of post-retirement employment is revealed in many surveys. For example, even though the majority of workers polled by Louis Harris and Associates in 1978 admitted that they were looking forward to retirement, nearly one-fourth—and almost one-half of the self-employed—said that they would like to continue working part-time as long as they could (U.S. Congress, 1979). Employees in a southern California study by McConnell et al. (1980) were also interested in continued employment on a part-time basis:

45 percent in the same job and 27 percent in a less demanding one. A strong preference for postretirement part-time employment, primarily in the same line of work, was expressed by respondents to a National Council on the Aging (1981) poll, and, as recently as January 1990, the Commonwealth Fund reported on an estimated 2 million nonworking Americans aged 50 to 64 who would return to work if they could (Harris and Associates, undated).

Among the Commonwealth Fund's respondents classified as "ready and able to work," two-thirds said they would be willing to work full-time. This seemingly high figure might be due to the relatively young ages (50–64) of the respondents, as well as to the fact that they were not working at the time of the survey. Even more—83 percent—would opt for part-time work.

Interest in part-time work may be tied to the social security earnings test (discussed in Chapter 3) that limits the amount of money a retired worker beneficiary may earn without losing at least some social security benefits. According to Libassi (1990), 45 percent of the retirees working at the Travelers Companies would put in more hours were it not for the earnings test.

Older people who continue working seem to act on their stated preference for part-time work. Nearly half of all employees 65 and older are working part-time by choice, in contrast to less than 14 percent of the total work force. Still, there are only about 1.3 million older part-time workers out of a total elderly population of more than 29 million.

Labor Market Problems of Older Workers

The alacrity with which older workers who have the means to do so leave the workplace may mask some very real labor market problems. Workers who retire for ostensibly voluntary reasons might indeed have preferred some alternative to full-time retirement, if one were available. As noted above, many older workers maintain that they would like part-time work after they retire, but relatively few older persons are working part-time.

One problem may be that part-time workers typically earn less than full-time workers, even when they are doing equivalent work. While this may seem discriminatory, it should be pointed out that other costs—such as recruitment and training—are not necessarily lower for part-time employees. For instance, if employers need two part-time workers to take the place of one full-time worker, some costs will double. Thus, to recover costs, employers pay part-time workers less (see Sandell, 1988: 213).

Unemployment

Without retirement income, unemployment rates among older workers, which compare favorably to those of younger workers, might be higher. Unemployment in the United States today is largely a problem of teenagers and young labor force entrants. By midlife, the unemployment rate for both men and women is well below average, and the rate remains low even among older persons. As of 1989, less than 3 percent of the 65 and older labor force, but 15 percent of the teenage labor force, could be classified as unemployed. Similar patterns are evident among minority workers, although unemployment is a greater problem for middle-aged and older black men than it is for white men. The same holds true among women.

In a discussion of the unemployment problems of older workers, the U.S. Department of Labor (1989c) contends that the older the job seeker, the less serious the job search, undoubtedly because for many of these older job seekers alternative income sources (social security and/or pensions) lessen the pressure to find work. However, as the Labor Department report makes clear, it would be doing many middle-aged and older workers a disservice to suggest that their job searches are frivolous. Administrators of Job Training Partnership Act (JTPA) programs and employment services offices know only too well how desperate the job hunt can be for many aging workers, particularly those who have not yet become eligible for social security or private pension benefits. For these workers—unless they are fortunate enough to have asset income or employed spouses—work is a necessity.

Job-Seeking Discouragement

Older worker specialists have long been interested in the degree to which older people want to work but are not looking for jobs because they do not think they will be successful. Concern about age discrimination or a lack of appropriate skills, rather than a desire for leisure, might propel some older workers out of the labor force. If job-seeking discouragement characterizes a disproportionate number of older persons—as some observers think it does—then unemployment for this age group is a more serious problem than it appears to be.

However, the available data on this issue are not conclusive (see Table 1.2). The vast majority of the 32 million persons 60 years old and older who are not in the labor force report that they do not want to work because they are retired or have responsibilities at home. According to the Census Bureau's Current Population Survey (CPS), less than 2 percent of older persons report that they would actually like to have jobs. Of those 600,000 who report that they would like to be working but are not seeking employment, only about one-fourth might be considered discouraged in the strictest sense of the word. These 168,000

Table 1.2   Unemployment Experiences of Young, Midlife, and Older Persons, 1989

	UNEMPLOYMENT RATE (percentage)	AVERAGE LENGTH OF UNEMPLOYMENT (weeks)	UNEMPLOYED 15 WEEKS OR MORE (percentage)
Total population, 16+	5.3	11.9	21.1
Teenagers, 16-19	15.0	6.7	9.4
Men, 45-54	3.2	20.7	37.1
Men, 55-64	3.5	20.2	37.4
Men, 65+	2.4	15.3	26.4
Women, 45-54	3.2	12.0	23.2
Women, 55-64	2.8	13.8	24.7
Women, 65+	2.9	12.7	24.4

	DISCOURAGED WORKERS[a] (percentage)	PLAN TO LOOK FOR WORK[b] (percentage)
Total population, 16+	8.6	14.7
Teenagers, young adults	17.8[c]	45.3[d]
Men, 60+	2.2	2.2
Women, 60+	1.7	1.7

Source: U.S. Department of Labor, 1990.
[a]Persons not in the labor force who say they would like to work.
[b]Based on all persons not in the labor force.
[c]Persons aged 16–19.
[d]Persons aged 16–24.

job-seeking discouraged represent less than one-half of 1 percent of all persons 60 and above. Older minorities are only slightly more likely to appear as discouraged workers.

It is possible, however, that the above statistics may underestimate the problem. For example, low rates of expressed interest in employment might reflect perceptions of the availability of desirable job opportunities, particularly in the case of job seekers who moved from unemployment to retirement. Certainly the wealth of job-seeking publications for the older worker—and the presumed market for these publications—indicate that many nonworking older persons do, indeed, want employment. The Department of Labor (1989c: 15) points out that "for many retirees, the types of job offers available to older workers are at such odds with their job market aspirations that they may not even consider employment an option." Nonetheless, job-seeking discouragement figures reinforce the conclusion that incentives for delaying retirement or returning to work will have to improve considerably if older workers are to increase their participation in the labor force.

Involuntary Part-Time Employment

Another indicator of labor market problems is involuntary part-time employment, a situation in which workers would prefer to work full-time but cannot find full-time work. If older persons fare worse than younger ones in securing employment, it would stand to reason that they would be more likely to settle for less than their ideal arrangement, in other words, by taking part-time work. Like a number of other labor market problems, however, involuntary part-time employment appears more characteristic of workers just starting out than of mature workers. Younger workers have considerably higher-than-average rates of involuntary part-time employment; rates are lower than average for middle-aged workers but slightly higher in the case of men 65 and older. Overall, in 1989 few older workers were forced to work part-time because they could not find full-time work. In fact, in view of older persons' interest in part-time employment, it may be that many *full-time* older workers are actually involuntary full-time workers who would prefer to work part-time.

Length of Unemployment

Another measure of labor market problems is duration of unemployment. Given age discrimination, skills obsolescence, salary requirements, and other factors, length of unemployment might be expected to increase with age. Yet, according to the Department of Labor (1989c), the belief that older workers have a tougher time finding employment than do younger workers is not supported empirically. Different data sources provide contradictory information about length of unemployment. On average, middle-aged and older workers are less likely than the total unemployed population to be out of work for fewer than 5 weeks, and more likely to be unemployed for 15 weeks. However, although long-term unemployment—measured here as 15 weeks or more—is most common among the middle-aged, the proportion of long-term unemployed drops in the 65-plus age population. One possible reason for this, of course, is that many of the oldest unemployed may choose to withdraw from the labor force, thus lowering the number who could become long-term unemployed.

When the Department of Labor (1989c) examined successfully completed spells of unemployment (that is, the unemployment of persons who eventually found work), it did find a general rise in duration of unemployment among men up to age 64, after which duration of unemployment fell sharply. Among women, duration of unemployment showed little variation until age 65, after which it rose. The authors of the Labor Department report concluded that, while it does take older job seekers longer to find work, that tends to be the case mainly among men 55 to 64 and women 65 and above.

Length of unemployment says nothing about motivation, which varies among job seekers, as the Labor Department report makes clear. Older workers—particularly minorities and reentry women—might experience greater difficulties in finding work than whites or younger women, but many older workers with access to alternative sources of income have the luxury of prolonging the job search until the right job materializes, a fact that would put a positive light on a longer spell of unemployment.

Job Dislocation

Because many older workers are concentrated in declining industries, older workers may be especially vulnerable to job loss through plant shutdowns or layoffs. In some instances, such as layoffs, seniority provisions would mitigate the effect of age, but they would not help much in the event of plant closings. A special 1984 Department of Labor survey of job displacement found that 11.5 million workers aged 20 and older had lost jobs because of plant closings or employment cutbacks between January 1979 and January 1984 (Flaim and Sehgal, 1985). Workers 55 and older were overrepresented among the displaced.

The data seem to support the contention that older workers experience greater difficulties in becoming reemployed after a job loss. Among the displaced workers, older workers experienced longer bouts of unemployment than younger workers: the median period of joblessness for workers 55 and over was 30 weeks, in contrast to 22 weeks for workers 25 to 34. Reemployment rates also tended to be lower as age rose, ranging from 70 percent for workers aged 20 to 24, to 65 percent for workers 25 to 54, to 41 percent for workers 55 to 64, to only 21 percent for the 65 and older population. By far the majority of the oldest displaced workers were out of the labor force by 1984. It is likely that many of these workers took advantage of retirement benefits to terminate their job searches.

Many of the displaced workers who remained in the labor force ultimately found work, but often at lower wages. Earnings losses were more common among older workers and the less educated. The Labor Department (1989c: 31 and 28) warns that "displacement from a job, and particularly a career, often has very serious long-term effects on workers' economic security" and that "even among the reemployed, the impact of displacement is often severe for older workers." For these displaced workers, retraining would seem to be in order; however, retraining programs for displaced older workers are limited.

While the data do not permit any conclusions on the extent to which older workers might have been shielded from job loss by security provisions, it is significant that nearly three in ten job losers between the ages of 55 and 64 had been in their jobs for at least 20 years. Older workers were also far more likely than younger ones to report that they had lost their jobs as a result of plant closings (Flaim and Sehgal, 1985), a development against which contractual security provisions are unlikely to do any good.

Where Older Adults Work

The country's 34 million middle-aged and older workers can be found in virtually every occupation, although there are some age differences in occupational concentration, as highlighted in Table 1.3. The proportion of older men employed in executive and managerial occupations tends to be reasonably high, reflecting, undoubtedly, age-related gains in experience that make these

Table 1.3   Employed Persons by Occupation, Sex, and Age, 1988 Annual Averages (in percentages)

OCCUPATION	ALL AGES, 16+	45–54	55–59	60–64	65+
Men					
Executive, administrative, managerial	13.6	18.6	17.6	17.4	16.4
Professional specialty	11.9	14.0	13.3	13.1	13.1
Technicians and related	2.9	2.5	1.8	1.4	0.9
Sales	11.1	11.2	11.6	12.4	16.1
Administrative support, including clerical	5.7	4.7	5.3	5.2	5.8
Service	9.6	7.0	7.8	9.9	11.8
Precision production, craft, repair	19.7	20.0	19.6	17.4	10.7
Operatives, fabricators, laborers	20.9	18.2	17.8	16.8	10.9
Farm operators and managers	1.7	1.9	3.1	4.1	10.1
Farm workers, forestry, fishing	2.8	1.8	2.1	2.4	4.2
Total percentage	100.0	100.0	100.0	100.0	100.0
Total number (in thousands)	63,273	10,201	3,954	2,638	1,911
Women					
Executive, administrative, managerial	10.8	12.5	10.7	10.3	8.6
Professional specialty	14.4	15.6	13.8	10.2	10.6
Technicians and related	3.3	2.8	2.3	1.5	1.2
Sales	13.0	10.6	11.8	13.2	14.5
Administrative support, including clerical	28.3	28.6	27.5	29.6	24.6
Service	17.9	16.1	19.8	20.6	27.6
Precision production, craft, repair	2.3	2.7	2.4	2.6	2.9
Operatives, fabricators, laborers	8.8	9.9	10.1	10.3	7.2
Farm operators and managers	0.4	0.6	0.9	0.8	1.8
Farm workers, forestry, fishing	0.7	0.6	0.7	0.8	1.0
Total percentage	100.0	100.0	100.0	100.0	100.0
Total number (in thousands)	51,696	8,246	2,938	1,904	1,286

Source: U.S. Department of Labor, Bureau of Labor Statistics, unpublished data.

men attractive as managers and executives. The proportion of workers employed in what might be considered more physically arduous occupations, such as operatives and laborers, shows a not surprising drop with age, although almost as many middle-aged men can be found in this occupational category as among executives and managers. The oldest male workers are somewhat more likely than other workers to be in farm occupations, which—while perhaps permitting some flexibility of scheduling under certain conditions—would by no means be considered "light" work. Sales and service employment also claim a somewhat higher proportion of the oldest male workers and precision, production, craft, and repair work a substantially lower proportion.

Table 1.4   Employed Persons by Industry, Sex, and Age, 1988 Annual Averages (in percentages)[a]

INDUSTRY	ALL AGES, 16+	45–54	55–59	60–64	65+
Men					
Mining	1.0	1.2	1.1	0.8	0.5
Construction	11.4	10.0	10.7	8.8	6.9
Durable manufacturing	15.2	17.9	16.8	15.8	7.8
Nondurable manufacturing	8.4	9.2	9.1	8.9	5.3
Transportation, public utilities	9.7	11.0	11.2	8.9	4.8
Wholesale trade	5.4	5.5	5.4	5.4	6.4
Retail trade	15.1	9.6	9.9	11.5	16.1
Finance, insurance, real estate	5.3	5.6	6.2	6.8	11.1
Miscellaneous services	23.4	23.3	24.3	27.7	36.0
Public administration	5.1	6.7	5.2	5.4	4.9
Total percentage	100.0	100.0	100.0	100.0	100.0
Total number (in thousands)	60,617	9,852	3,762	2,476	1,648
Women					
Mining	0.2	0.2	0.2	0.1	0.2
Construction	1.4	1.4	1.5	1.3	1.1
Durable manufacturing	6.8	7.6	7.1	6.7	4.5
Nondurable manufacturing	7.2	7.7	7.8	8.4	6.4
Transportation, public utilities	4.4	4.5	3.4	3.6	1.9
Wholesale trade	2.6	2.3	2.0	2.5	2.5
Retail trade	19.9	15.1	16.6	18.6	21.8
Finance, insurance, real estate	9.4	8.5	8.6	9.0	7.6
Miscellaneous services	43.4	47.1	46.9	44.1	48.8
Public administration	4.6	5.4	5.7	5.8	5.2
Total percentage	100.0	100.0	100.0	100.0	100.0
Total number (in thousands)	50,019	7,983	2,801	1,795	1,133

Source: U.S. Department of Labor, Bureau of Labor Statistics, unpublished data.
[a]Excludes agriculture and private household.

Age differences in occupational distribution are somewhat less pronounced among women, who, regardless of age, show a clear tendency toward concentration in a very few occupations, most notably those classified as service or administrative, which includes clerical work.

Employment by industry reveals a striking concentration of workers of both sexes and all ages in the service sector, as Table 1.4 shows. One-fourth or more of all men and nearly one-half of all women are employed in service industries. Retail trade is another significant source of jobs, particularly for midlife and older women, while durable manufacturing remains an important source of employment for aging men.

These figures say nothing about employment opportunities or preferences, although the relatively higher concentration of older workers in the service occupations and industries certainly reflects growth of the service sector, while part-time opportunities in sales might explain some of the oldest workers' representation in sales jobs. The key point to be made from the distribution of workers in the occupations and industries in Tables 1.3 and 1.4 is that the numbers of older workers in each of the broad occupational and industry categories would seem to be sufficiently large to test the ability of older workers to perform, a subject that will be addressed in a subsequent chapter.

Chapter 2

Age Discrimination in Employment

I didn't look my age and knew I'd never be hired if I told the truth when I began working for my current employer at age 63. I'm retiring soon at age 77.

"Ask Mary Jane," *Saving Social Security,* May 1989: 26

Ten years ago I was 55 years old and I had a hard time finding a job, so I lied about my age. I will be 65 in two months and I want to continue work. . . . I don't want my bosses to know my age because they insist that all employees leave or retire at 65.

Letter to Ann Landers, *Washington Post,* April 6, 1989
Ann Landers, Creators / Los Angeles Times Syndicates

FACTS

- Charges of age discrimination filed with the federal government rose from about 1,000 in 1969 to more than 17,000 in 1986.
- In one survey, 6 percent of workers 40 and older reported that they had been victims of age discrimination in employment, and 9 percent of workers 63 and older said they had been discriminated against.
- In 1989, the U.S. Supreme Court ruled that fringe benefits are not necessarily covered under the Age Discrimination in Employment Act (ADEA).
- In age discrimination suits, the large majority of plaintiffs are men.

Age Discrimination Is a Painful Reality

"Age discrimination . . . plays a pernicious role in blocking employment opportunities for older workers," contends the Special Committee on Aging of the U.S. Senate (U.S. Congress, 1987: 120). Despite the Age Discrimination in Employment Act, older workers and would-be workers are undoubtedly often victims of age discrimination, although valid figures on who is discriminated against, by whom, and under what conditions are all but impossible to find. Workers and job seekers cannot always tell whether it is their age, as opposed to some legitimate work-related deficiency or other factor, that conspires against them. Nor will employers, for obvious reasons, willingly volunteer the information that they discriminate in favor of younger workers, even when they do. Many employers do, however, tend to think that age discrimination in employment is pervasive (see, for example, U.S. Congress, 1979; Mercer, Inc., 1981).

Formal age discrimination complaints are on the rise. Since the Age Discrimination in Employment Act was passed in 1967, charges filed with the administrative agency having jurisdiction (initially the Department of Labor and now the Equal Employment Opportunity Commission) rose from about 1,000 in 1969 to more than 5,000 in 1976, to about 11,000 in fiscal year 1982, to more than 17,000 in fiscal year 1986 (Friedman, 1984: 22–23; U.S. Congress, 1988: 113).

These numbers do not necessarily prove that age discrimination itself is on the rise. Rather, they might reflect an increase in knowledge of the law and its provisions or a growing awareness of successful suits, which in turn encourage people to risk the time and money needed to file charges of discrimination and see their cases through to conclusion.

Protection under the ADEA

Who Is Covered?

The 1967 Age Discrimination in Employment Act covered workers between the ages of 40 and 65 who worked in firms with 25 or more employees. Amendments in subsequent years raised the upper age limit and ultimately eliminated mandatory retirement, as well as expanded coverage to workers in firms with 20 or more workers. In addition, the law prohibits discrimination by federal, state, and local governments, employment agencies, and labor unions with 25 or more members. Unions cannot refuse membership to older workers, nor can employment agencies legally refuse to make job referrals to older workers. With few exceptions, the provisions of the ADEA apply to workers 40 and older.

Who Is Not Covered?

Workers in businesses with fewer than 20 employees (less than one-fourth of the private sector work force) do not enjoy protection under the ADEA. (State laws, however, may protect workers in smaller firms.) In addition, certain executives or high policy-making employees with sizable pension benefits can be required to retire at 65.

As of 1989, airline pilots could be forced to retire at age 60. The Federal Aviation Administration (FAA) denied a petition to allow them to continue to fly beyond the age of 60, on the grounds that older pilots are more likely to be involved in accidents than younger ones. The FAA did agree, however, to fund a study of the relationship between pilot age and accidents that, depending on the results, could lead to certification of the right to fly on a case-by-case basis.

The elimination of mandatory retirement does not apply to tenured university faculty through the end of 1993. Also through 1993, age-based hiring and retirement decisions may be made by state and local governments for fire fighters and police officers if a particular age limitation was already in effect as of March 3, 1983, and "the action [is] taken pursuant to a *bona fide* hiring or retirement plan that is not a subterfuge to evade the purposes of the Act."

What Is Covered?

Basically, employers cannot discriminate on the basis of age in hiring, job retention, compensation (i.e., wages), and other terms and "conditions of employment." Before 1982, employers could force older workers to shift from company health insurance plans once the employees became eligible for Medicare. This changed when Congress, for budgetary cost-cutting reasons rather than out of concern over the law's discriminatory nature, decided to require employers to offer employees aged 65 and older (and their spouses) the same group health coverage offered younger employees. Thus, for older workers, Medicare has become the secondary rather than the primary payer of health insurance benefits.

In firms with pension plans, pension accruals and contributions must also continue for workers who have passed the plan's normal retirement age. While it might appear that anything less is clearly discriminatory, until recently employers had been allowed to stop older worker pension accruals and contributions in an effort not to discourage them from hiring or retaining older workers. Companies can no longer deny pension coverage to workers hired within five years of a plan's normal retirement age, although they can require employees to work for five years before becoming eligible for benefits in a defined benefit plan.

What Is Not Covered?

Older workers can be terminated when their performance is unacceptable (i.e., "for cause"), and employers can refuse to hire unqualified older workers. Management must, however, apply the same firing and hiring standards to all workers, regardless of age. Bona fide occupational qualifications (BFOQs) can also be used to deny a job to an older worker, although severe restrictions govern the use of age requirements, and employers should be prepared to prove why only a younger worker will do (a legitimate example would be a call for a child actor to play the role of a child in a movie).

Apprenticeships, generally regarded as youth training programs, are excluded from the protection of the ADEA, according to an interpretation by the Equal Employment Opportunity Commission (EEOC). In 1984, the commission unanimously voted to rescind the exemption, but in July 1987 the EEOC reversed itself, the chairman arguing that any decision about eligibility for apprenticeships rested with Congress.

The Department of Labor and later the Equal Employment Opportunity Commission have interpreted the ADEA as prohibiting discrimination in providing fringe benefits. However, because certain benefits are more costly for older workers, employers have been allowed to operate under what is known as the equal benefit or equal cost rule. This has meant that (1) the benefit had to be identical for all workers (e.g., six days of sick leave per year for everyone) or (2) the amount paid for a benefit had to be the same for all workers. In the latter case, the same dollar amount might purchase less of a benefit for older workers. For example, the face value of a life insurance policy would be lower because $100 will buy less life insurance for an older worker than for a younger one. Such differences have been perfectly legal.

In June 1989, the U.S. Supreme Court ruled 7–2 that fringe benefits were not specifically covered under the ADEA and that benefit plans that offered different benefits to different age groups could be challenged only "if they were being used by an employer intent on denying employment to older workers or reducing their wages." The Court had been asked to rule in the case of a disabled public employee in Ohio who had been forced to retire under the state's public retirement system rather than under its more generous disability program. The Court's decision contradicted the federal government's interpretation of the ADEA's fringe benefit provisions. Unless Congress reverses this decision by passing a new law, older workers' fringe benefits are threatened.

Companies that offer early retirement incentives may require departing employees to verify in writing that the decision to leave was entirely voluntary. By so doing, employees waive their right to sue their employers under the ADEA at some later date. There is disagreement over whether these waivers should be curtailed. Opponents argue that the law intended that waivers be strictly limited and used only in situations supervised by the EEOC. Waiver proponents (employers who want the protection of the waivers and the flexibility of early retirement incentives) contend that no one is forced to sign a waiver, although the pressure to do so may be considerable. Bills pending in Congress would strengthen workers' protection against unsupervised waivers.

Who Files Discrimination Charges?

Because age discrimination can be subtle, there are no reliable statistics on how many middle-aged and older workers experience age discrimination and under what circumstances. In a 1986 survey conducted for the American Association of Retired Persons (AARP), only 6 percent of the representative sample of workers 40 and older contended that they had been victims of age discrimination in employment, a figure that rose to 9 percent among workers 63 and older. Relatively few persons, however, responded by taking legal action against their employers (AARP, 1986).

In 1985 and 1986, more than 17,000 age discrimination cases were filed with the Equal Employment Opportunity Commission. Although the issues included in ADEA charges are not necessarily an accurate reflection of existing discrimination, EEOC data indicate that workers are more aware of, troubled by, or willing to fight over certain forms of discrimination than others: perceived unlawful discharge was mentioned in 58 percent of the age charges filed at the EEOC in 1985; 35 percent of the charges involved hiring and/or terms and conditions of employment; and 14 percent dealt with layoffs.

The EEOC charges differ substantially from those mentioned in the national AARP survey cited above, most of which involved denial of promotion or a chance to get ahead. Promotion denials may be more common than outright dismissal (retirement may serve as a suitable substitute for dismissal); however, denial of promotion based on age is undoubtedly harder to prove than illegal dismissal. The charges that ultimately make it to the EEOC are probably those for which there is more solid evidence.

Many charges are terminated by the EEOC because the evidence does not seem to support the allegation of discrimination. Some cases do, however, make it to court. The overwhelming majority of plaintiffs in age discrimination suits are men (81 percent, according to a study by Schuster and Miller, 1984). A majority of suits seem to be brought by professional/managerial workers, followed by blue-collar workers, a fact that led Schuster and Miller (1984: 68) to speculate that the Age Discrimination in Employment Act may be the "only recourse for most senior white male professionals and managers" who feel that they have been discriminated against. Consistent with the charge data from the EEOC, the greatest number of cases concern termination of employment (67 percent)—overt and drastic acts that may be harder to tolerate (Schuster and Miller, 1984: 70) and easier to prove than other forms of age discrimination.

Employees tended to lose their cases in court, perhaps because employers settle the less defensible cases out of court and carry through only on those they are reasonably sure of winning. Interestingly, women were significantly more likely than men to win their cases (64 percent versus 29 percent), although so few women filed that any conclusions about their success or failure should be made with caution.

Signs of Discrimination

While it is not always easy to tell if age has been a factor in employment decisions, workers, job seekers, and job changers should be alert to signs that companies are using age in their decisions about whom to hire, fire, lay off, provide benefits to, promote, or train. These include the following:

1. Older workers being passed over in favor of younger workers with similar or fewer qualifications

2. Older workers being told that no openings exist when it is known that they do

3. Older workers being discouraged from pursuing job leads by interviewers who use "too much experience" as a proxy for age

4. Older workers being replaced by younger workers with the same or fewer skills

5. Older workers being denied opportunities to participate in company-sponsored training programs

6. Older workers being considered not "promotable"

7. Older workers coming up for salary reviews and receiving raises less frequently than younger counterparts

8. Older workers being laid off before younger ones

9. Older workers being paid less than younger workers for the same work

10. Older workers being demoted without just cause

11. Older workers' assignments being transferred to other, younger workers

It may be difficult to obtain the information needed to determine whether or not age discrimination has occurred. Job applicants are unlikely to be told why they were passed over. Information about the compensation of other workers is usually confidential. It may not be clear that assignments given to older workers are less desirable than those given to younger workers. Also, identifying age discrimination is generally harder when a single employee is involved and easier when large numbers of workers are affected, for example, when senior workers are laid off before junior ones.

Seeking Redress

Pursuing a grievance under the ADEA can be a costly, time-consuming, and emotionally debilitating experience, and the potential costs and benefits should be weighed carefully before action is taken. From the worker's perspective, successful resolution of a case may include job reinstatement, back pay and benefits (including social security and pension contributions), interest, court costs, and attorneys' fees, but it does not include damages for pain and suffering. In cases of willful age discrimination, double back pay may be awarded. The lack of damage awards under the ADEA may discourage those with limited resources from suing; an award of back pay, benefits, and lawyers' fees may not be worth the effort. And in the case of unlawful discharge, workers must decide whether or not they would be comfortable working again for an employer they had taken to court.

Efforts to resolve a job-related problem should begin with the employer. If that fails, remedying the problem generally involves three steps, according to Francine Weiss (1984), a specialist in age discrimination law: (1) filing a charge under the company and/or union grievance procedure, (2) filing a charge with a government agency, and (3) filing a lawsuit in court. Before a case is taken to court, the law requires that an effort be made to achieve voluntary compliance.

Should a worker decide to file charges against a company, the company is barred by law from retaliating. The employer need not, however, make the employee feel that the charge is welcome. Employees who do file charges should be prepared to find that the workplace has become even less hospitable than it was before.

Documentation of the alleged discriminatory action is critical, and written records of any discriminatory action should be kept. Sometimes the evidence is obvious, as when only older workers are discharged. In other cases, it may take time to establish a pattern of discrimination.

The law requires that certain steps be taken in filing a charge and in pursuing a case based on age discrimination. Workers who believe that they have been victims of discrimination based on age must exhaust certain remedies *before* taking a case to court (Weiss, 1989). The proper steps, which should be fully understood and followed to the letter, are discussed in very general terms in this section. The EEOC distributes several informative and free brochures on age discrimination charges and litigation, but, like many other legal matters, age discrimination litigation is a complicated business. Soliciting the aid of a lawyer should be considered as soon as an individual decides to proceed.

Filing a Charge

A worker, former worker, or job seeker who thinks that he or she has been discriminated against and who decides to seek redress formally can file an age discrimination charge with the EEOC at the federal level or with a state antidiscrimination agency if one exists. (The first state to pass an age discrimination law was Colorado, which did so in 1903 [Friedman, 1984].) Filing a charge is generally necessary before suing, and such filing may result in a satisfactory settlement without going to court. Strict time limits exist on the filing of charges with the EEOC; according to Weiss (1984), one of the most common mistakes is late filing.

Filing with the EEOC

An age discrimination charge must generally be filed with the EEOC within 180 days of the time that the discriminatory act occurred or notice of the discriminatory action was received, whichever comes first. In states with age discrimination laws (known as deferral states), the charge is filed with the state agency that has jurisdiction over the law. In these states, the filing period is 300 days after the alleged violation (or 30 days after being notified that the state has terminated processing the charge, whichever is earlier); AARP (1987a) recommends filing within 180 days to be on the safe side.

The courts have ruled that discrimination occurs when an employee is *notified* of discharge, not when that employee actually stops working (which is typically after the notification). Moreover, this time limit is not extended while a grievance procedure is being pursued, which leads Weiss (1984) to recommend filing a charge with the government agency while simultaneously pursuing a company grievance procedure.

Under the ADEA, if the charging party decides to sue, the suit must be filed within two years of the alleged discriminatory action, unless the action is willful, in which case the limit is three years. A suit can be filed no earlier than 60 days after the complaint is brought to the EEOC; this restriction is intended to give the EEOC time to try to settle the complaint through conciliation.

A charging party cannot remain anonymous. When filing a charge of discrimination, which must be in writing, the name of the charging party (or person discriminated against) *as well as the person alleged to have discriminated* must be included in the charge. Workers who wish to remain anonymous can file a complaint with the EEOC, but complaints are given lower priority than charges (AARP, 1987a).

If the EEOC determines that its filing rules (threshold requirements) have been met—the charge is signed, and the date and description of the act are noted, along with the name of the company or union allegedly committing the act—the charge is assigned to an equal opportunity specialist (EOS) for an independent investigation. (See Kalet, 1986, for further discussion.) The role of the EOS is to solicit evidence, determine if the charging party was treated differently, interview witnesses, and verify the accuracy and completeness of information gathered during the process.

As a result of its efforts, the EEOC may determine that discrimination has occurred and attempt to remedy the situation through conciliation. If this process is successful, a settlement agreement will be prepared. If conciliation cannot be achieved, the EEOC may file a suit, although it does so in relatively few cases. Charging parties may file suit on their own only if the EEOC declines to, or if the EEOC issues a "no cause" determination, that is, concludes that there appears to be no evidence of discrimination.

Unfortunately, although workers who decide to seek redress under the ADEA must begin with the EEOC or state age discrimination agency, they cannot rely on the agency to solve their problems. The U.S. General Accounting Office (GAO, 1988b) has questioned the thoroughness of the investigatory efforts of the EEOC. Large numbers of cases have not been fully investigated, apparently so that processing can be expedited. The GAO notes that in fiscal year 1987, the EEOC found evidence of discrimination in less than 3 percent of the charges it closed. Out-of-court settlements provided some relief to charging parties in another 13 percent of the closed cases, but in these cases there was no actual ruling that discrimination had occurred (GAO, 1988b: 2).

The GAO has suggested that the EEOC might be more interested in reducing its work load than in the charges themselves. It has also pointed to less-than-adequate monitoring of investigations by state agencies. While the EEOC has voiced objections to the GAO report, GAO's findings are hardly encouraging to age discrimination victims who are hoping for help from the EEOC.

Reducing the Chances of Being Sued

Employers should be aware that age discrimination suits have been on the increase, that victims win some of these cases, and that some voluntary agreements and court awards have involved sizable sums of money. The aging of the work force means more potential victims and a corresponding increase in an employer's odds of being sued.

"Age-neutral" employment policies and practices can reduce those odds considerably. Companies can familiarize supervisors, personnel administrators, and others in positions to make decisions about hiring, firing, compensation, and the like with the terms of the ADEA and make it clear that neither discrimination against nor harassment of older workers will be tolerated.

Age Audits

Grumman Corporation, which has a history of accommodating older workers, recommends age audits of the work force as a way of pinpointing and eliminating potential trouble spots before they get turned into lawsuits (Knowles, 1988a). In an age audit, a company compares the age distribution of its work force with that of the total (or perhaps regional or local) work force to identify any discrepancies. The percentage of employees of a certain age should equal the percentage of workers of the same age in the larger work force. Large discrepancies should be cause for investigation: If older workers are underrepresented in the company, what might be the reason? Is it because of something the employer is doing or not doing that discourages the hiring or retention of older workers? Or is the business in an industry typically unattractive to older workers? If that is the case, would changes in the conditions of work make a difference?

Similar age audits can also be conducted for specific job categories (e.g., managers, technical workers, and clerical workers). Do any of the categories have a dearth or an excess of older workers? Again, if the answer is yes, why might that be? Are, for example, older workers excluded from certain technical jobs because they lack up-to-date skills? If so, are they given an equal chance or encouraged to participate in company-sponsored training programs? What reasons might there be for overrepresentation of older workers in certain occupations? Is there a tendency to hire older workers only for certain jobs, or to promote them only to certain positions?

A concentration of workers of a certain age in certain occupations is not necessarily evidence of discrimination or any other type of problem. Certain workers may be over- or underrepresented in certain job categories for legitimate reasons. Age audits will, however, highlight any need for action and help prevent problems before they occur. Grumman recommends periodic examination of all employment programs, policies, and procedures to ensure equal treatment of all workers under all circumstances.

An Age Discrimination Suit?

Factors To Consider before Taking Action

Employees who feel that they are victims of age discrimination should:

1. Marshall evidence by keeping detailed records of the alleged discriminatory action(s): Who did or said what, and under what circumstances? Obtaining sufficient evidence can be difficult, as in the case of a hiring decision. It may be possible to elicit assistance and corroboration from other employees, although those employees may be reluctant to get involved.

2. Attempt, if at all possible, to work out a solution with the employer.

3. File charges with the EEOC only after carefully weighing the pros and cons of such action.

4. Find out exactly what has to be done in filing a suit and adhere to the requirements. To protect one's right to file a private lawsuit, one must file a charge with the EEOC within 180 days of the alleged discriminatory act, unless the act has occurred in a state where a state or local deferral agency has authority to deal with age discrimination in employment. In that case, an individual has up to 300 days to file, unless the charging party has been notified that the state has terminated processing the charge. If that has happened, the charging party has 30 days to file a charge. (The EEOC and the deferral agency have a work-sharing arrangement, and there

should be cross-filing. Only one agency—generally the one in which the charge was filed—will investigate the charge.)

5. An EEOC officer will be assigned to examine the charge, and if there appears to be "reasonable" cause to believe that discrimination has occurred, the EEOC will attempt to settle the case.

6. If no voluntary settlement can be reached, the EEOC may file a court case on behalf of the plaintiff, although this happens in relatively few cases.

7. An individual may sue his or her employer. If the decision to sue is made, the case must be filed within two years of the alleged discriminatory act (three years in the case of willful discrimination), but no sooner than 60 days after the charge has been filed with the EEOC. If the EEOC has decided to take legal action, a private suit may *not* be filed.

Chapter 3

Money Matters and the Work/Retirement Decision

> Before the Social Security Act was passed, there was no typical retirement age in the United States. Most people worked until they (or their employer) decided they could work no longer. . . . The architects of Social Security arbitrarily selected 65 as the age of benefit entitlement. . . . Sixty-five has become ingrained in people's expectations.
>
> National Commission on Social Security, 1981: 120

FACTS

- For approximately six out of ten older Americans, social security amounts to at least half of their income, and for about one in seven, it is the only source of income.

- Fewer than 30 percent of older adults receive private pension income.

- Most experts agree that it takes about 65 to 70 percent of preretirement income to maintain a comparable standard of living in retirement.

- A General Accounting Office survey of employees covered by pension plans found that more than 70 percent were wrong about when they would be eligible for normal retirement benefits.

- Employers can legally reduce employees' private pension benefits by a portion of their social security benefits.

Social Security: The Largest
Source of Retirement Income

While the right to keep working regardless of age evolves from the Age Discrimination in Employment Act (ADEA), the willingness to remain at work is influenced by social security and pension income. Monthly social security benefits go to all but a handful of the elderly, who receive benefits primarily as retired workers or as spouses or widows of retired workers.

As of 1990, the average retired worker could expect a monthly social security check of $566, for a total of slightly under $7,000 a year. The elderly depend heavily on social security: for approximately six out of ten older Americans, social security amounts to at least half of their income, and for about one in seven, it is the only source of income (U.S. Department of Health and Human Services, 1988: Table 40).

By contrast, fewer than 30 percent of older adults receive private pension income, and those who do typically get far less from their pensions than they do from social security. Fortunately, future retirees will fare better when it comes to private pensions, because pension coverage has expanded and the length of time workers have participated in pension plans has increased. Consequently, both the number of private pension recipients and the size of the average benefit are expected to rise. It is unlikely, however, that the proportion of private pension recipients will ever equal that of social security recipients.

For most Americans, social security will remain the most dependable and prominent source of retirement support through the end of this century and into the next. If he or she lives long enough, virtually every working American will become a social security beneficiary. Thus, decisions about work and retirement should be based, at least in part, on a knowledge of what is required and what is permitted under social security.

What Is Social Security?

Social security is a federal income transfer program enacted in 1935 to protect people against loss of income from certain events over which they were believed to have little control—retirement, disability, or death of the family breadwinner. Although social security "insures" more than retired workers, the discussion in this chapter will focus on social security and decisions about whether to continue working or to retire. For the middle-aged or older worker, when and how to stop working may be as important as securing or maintaining employment or advancing on the job. Although savings, private pension eligibility, a spouse's income, and a host of other variables enter into the work/retirement decision, as workers approach age 62, social security plays an increasingly important role. Social security may also affect post-retirement work decisions.

In addition to the approximately 38 million Americans who receive benefits as retired workers, disabled workers, dependents of retired workers, divorced spouses of eligible workers, and survivors of deceased workers, more than 128 million employees support the recipients through social security payroll taxes. As of 1990, individual earnings up to a maximum were taxed at a rate of 7.65 percent. Employers contributed another 7.65 percent on behalf of all of their full- and part-time employees. For tax purposes, the self-employed are considered to be both employer and employee and so must pay both the employer's and the employee's share of the payroll tax. (The law allows self-employed workers to deduct half of the tax as a business expense.)

In the early years of social security, retired worker benefits were paid to a small portion of the older population; initial provisions of the law covered only workers in commerce and industry. Over the next five decades, the program expanded substantially, and with the 1983 amendments to the Social Security Act, coverage became almost universal. Aside from a few state and local employees and federal workers hired before 1984, all workers—full- and part-time, self-employed or wage and salary, in profit-making or nonprofit institutions—have been brought under social security. They pay taxes and can, assuming they work long enough, count on receiving retired worker benefits when they retire.

It is largely because of social security that the poverty rate among older Americans has dropped sharply over the past several decades. Today, the poverty rate among the elderly who do not receive social security is more than twice as high as it is among those who do (U.S. Department of Health and Human Services, 1988: Table 54).

Who Can Collect Social Security?

Social security retired worker benefits are paid to people who meet certain criteria. Benefits are based on a worker's "covered earnings," which are simply the earnings on which social security taxes are paid. (Earnings above a maximum—$51,300 in 1990, an amount that increases annually—are not subject to the social security payroll tax. Nor are the earnings of government employees who are not part of the social security system, although these workers might, at some point in their lives, work in covered employment and so become eligible for social security.)

Quarters of Coverage

Although there are some exceptions, workers generally need what is known as 40 quarters of coverage to qualify for social security benefits upon reaching retirement age. A quarter of coverage is defined in terms of a dollar amount, rather than a fixed number of weeks or months of work. In 1990, $520 counted as one quarter of coverage. Workers can earn a maximum of four quarters of coverage in a calendar year. Thus, earnings of $2,080 (4 × $520) and $50,000 were the same as far as quarters of coverage are concerned. However, these sums were not equal when it comes to the ultimate benefit, which is based on lifetime covered earnings, so the higher the earnings, up to the maximum earnings on which taxes are paid, the larger the benefit.

Anyone born in 1929 or later (i.e., workers who will begin reaching age 62 in 1991) must have 40 quarters of coverage to be insured fully and eligible for retired worker benefits at age 62. Workers born before 1929 need fewer quarters, the exact number of which can be obtained by calling the Social Security Administration (SSA) number listed in the telephone book. Workers employed for 10 consecutive years will generally accrue the 40 hours of coverage required to qualify for social security benefits, but work quarters need not be consecutive. Most men and, increasingly, most women will have no trouble accumulating the necessary quarters of coverage to qualify for social security benefits in their own right, although, for a number of reasons, many married women will continue to do better by claiming benefits based on the earnings records of their husbands.

Benefit Levels under Social Security

Wage Replacement

Social security does not replace earnings dollar for dollar. Instead, it replaces a portion of earnings, and that portion (known as the wage-replacement rate) varies among workers. Most experts agree that it takes about 65 to 70 percent of pre-retirement income to maintain a standard of living in retirement comparable to one's preretirement standard of living. That simply means that anticipated income from social security, private or other public pensions, investments, and savings should equal about two-thirds of earnings at the time of retirement.

The wage replacement rate is not the same for all workers. Social security benefits will replace *roughly* (1) 60 percent of earnings for workers who have been minimum-wage earners all of their lives, (2) 40 percent for "average" wage earners, and (3) 27 percent for workers who have earned the maximum on which social security taxes were paid.

The apparent inequities in wage-replacement rates evolve from the assumption on the part of social security's architects that the lower the earnings, the greater the proportion of earnings that would have to be replaced for social security to ensure a modestly adequate benefit in retirement. Workers were expected to supplement their social security benefits with income from savings and private pensions, but it was recognized that this would be more difficult for low-income workers to accomplish than for more affluent ones.

Calculation of Benefits

In order to calculate a worker's social security benefit, the Social Security Administration reviews earnings between 1951 and the year of retirement and deletes the five lowest years of earnings before computing what is known as average indexed monthly earnings (AIME). This deletion serves to raise average earnings over the working life. The remaining earnings are also adjusted to account for general wage increases.

For workers who have been out of the labor force prior to retirement, up to five years of no earnings are considered the years of lowest earnings and are deducted from the AIME computation. Workers who had more than five years out of the labor force, which includes many of today's midlife and older women, will have any additional years of zero earnings averaged into their AIME calculation. Because of the deletion of five years of zero earnings, their actual five years of lowest earnings will also be included in the benefit calculation.

Benefits and Retirement Age

Retirement at 65 or Earlier?

Full retirement age, sometimes referred to as normal retirement age, is 65. That is when workers with enough quarters of coverage can begin collecting full social security benefits, or 100 percent of the amount to which they are entitled based on their quarters of coverage, work histories, and earnings records. Assuming they have enough quarters of coverage, workers can begin collecting social security as early as age 62. Opting for benefits any time before age 65, however, results in a benefit reduction that takes into account the fact that social security benefits must be paid to early retirees over more years than is the case when workers retire at 65.

The benefit payable between ages 62 and 64 is what is known as actuarially reduced. At age 62, the benefit is 20 percent lower than it would be if first awarded at 65, but workers who retire at age 62 will receive about the same total lifetime benefits that they would get if they waited until age 65 to begin collecting. Workers who begin to collect benefits somewhat later but still before 65 will also see their benefits actuarially reduced; however, the size of the reduction will depend on the exact age at which they apply for benefits. The reduction amounts to five-ninths (or 0.5556) of 1 percent for each month prior to age 65 that the benefit is paid (0.5556×36 months = 20 percent).

Because of the benefit reduction, later retirement means a higher monthly benefit, additional earnings, more time to set aside savings for retirement, and perhaps added accruals in a private pension fund. Nonetheless, despite the apparent advantages of waiting, a growing proportion of workers has been opting for reduced benefits since they were first made available to women in 1956 and to men in 1961.

Social Security and Private Pensions

Although eligibility for social security is not related to private pension eligibility, workers need to be aware of such factors as pension eligibility, anticipated pension income amount, and post-retirement work restrictions (some pension plans prohibit paying a salary and a pension to a worker at the same time) before making any irrevocable retirement decisions. Private pension plans may also require actuarial reductions in benefits for early retirement, but, as noted elsewhere in this book, many private plans either do not reduce the benefit at all for early retirement or do not require a full actuarial reduction. Eligibility ages for private pensions bear no relationship to social security benefits and eligibility.

However, workers should be aware of a process known as *integration*, which enables employers to reduce some of an employee's private pension benefit by a portion of the social security benefit. In so-called integrated plans, the pension benefit is calculated and a percentage of the social security benefit subtracted from that benefit. By law, the private pension cannot be reduced by more than 50 percent (and bills have been introduced in Congress to eliminate this reduction entirely), but any reduction obviously means a lower private pension benefit than would otherwise be available. Employees should check with their benefit plan administrators at work to determine if there is an offset of this type and, if so, its size.

Delayed Retirement

Employees who delay retirement beyond age 65 get somewhat more from social security. Retirement benefits for workers between the ages of 65 and 70 increase by a certain amount for each additional year of work. An additional year of work resulted in a 3.5 percent increase in benefits in 1990. This was not, however, a full actuarial increase. Thus, over the expected life of a social security recipient, the late retiree would actually receive somewhat less in total benefits than a comparable worker who retired at 65.

In an effort to encourage people to work longer, Congress approved amendments to the Social Security Act that gradually phase in a higher delayed-retirement credit. For example, benefits will increase by 4 percent a year for workers delaying retirement beyond age 65 in 1992. The delayed-retirement credit will rise to its maximum of 8 percent in the year 2008. This increase will be a full actuarial increase, which means that delayed retirement should not result in lower lifetime benefits. In other words, the social security gains from working longer should offset any losses from collecting benefits for fewer years.

Changes in Retirement Age

To restore long-range solvency to the social security trust fund, in 1983 Congress introduced retirement disincentives as well. Social security's full retirement age—now set at 65—will begin to rise by two months per year for workers reaching age 62 between 2000 and 2004. Eligibility for full social security benefits will reach age 66 in 2005 and remain there until 2016. It will then increase by another two months per year for workers turning age 62 between 2017 and 2021. Assuming no further modifications, workers planning to collect social security benefits in 2022 and after will have to wait until they are 67 to collect their full—or unreduced—benefits. They will still be able to collect social security benefits at age 62, but the reduction for such early receipt will be far greater than it is today: the current reduction of 20 percent will increase to 30 percent.

Given the importance of social security as a source of retirement income, one might expect that the retirement-age increase, coupled with relative benefit reductions for early retirement, will keep people working longer. Not many experts seem to think that will happen, however. Fields and Mitchell (1987), for example, estimate that an increase in the full or normal retirement age to 68 would increase the average retirement age by less than two months. Others express similar reservations about the impact of a higher social security retirement age. Undoubtedly, employees' ability to set aside additional savings, as well as their access to private pensions, spouses' earnings, employers' decisions about augmenting social security, and a number of other factors will continue to have a significant impact on workers' retirement-age decisions.

Postretirement Employment

Most people who receive social security retired worker benefits consider themselves retired and most are, in the sense that retirement involves the cessation of work. Some, however, continue in some form of employment (and continue to pay social security taxes) while collecting social security benefits. These workers have their social security benefits adjusted upward to reflect added contributions from postretirement work. But social security beneficiaries are "penalized" if they work too much; they cannot have unlimited earnings (income from other sources, such as investments, is ignored) and still collect all of their social security benefits.

Social security was enacted to *replace,* not to supplement, wages. Less well known, perhaps, is the fact that social security was intended to allow older workers to leave the labor force, thus creating job openings for younger workers whose opportunities were indeed limited during the Great Depression. Continued employment of an older social security recipient would have undermined that objective.

To ensure that social security was utilized as intended, a limit was placed on the amount a beneficiary could earn and still collect social security benefits. The 1935 law precluded "regular employment," a rather vague concept that was changed to "earnings of less than $15 per month" in 1939. That simply meant that social security beneficiaries could not earn more than $15 without forfeiting some of their benefits. By today's wage and salary standards, $15 per month might not seem like much, but it was 16 percent of the median monthly wages of white full-time workers of the time (Achenbaum, 1986: 209).

A social security recipient between the ages of 62 and 64 in 1990 could earn up to $6,840 per year (or $570 per month) and continue to receive all of his or her social security benefits. Earnings above that amount were reduced by $1 for each $2 in earnings. Workers between the ages of 65 and 70 could earn up to $9,360 per year ($780 a month); earnings above that amount resulted in a social security benefit reduction of $1 for each $3 in earnings.

The earnings ceiling is increased annually, and, after the age of 70, workers are entitled to earn any amount without loss of benefits. As this is being written, both the Senate Finance and the House Ways and Means Committees have approved legislation that would liberalize but not eliminate this earnings test.

There have been periodic proposals in Congress to eliminate the earnings limitation on the grounds that it is an excessive tax and that it discourages older persons from working. This latter point, however, is debatable, since most older persons do not work at all and are thus unaffected by the current earnings restriction. However, the limitation on earnings may affect the number of work hours. Iams (1987), for example, found that employed male social security recipients under age 65 had median earnings of $3,600 in 1982, below the $4,440 in allowable earnings. Recipients between the ages of 65 and 70 could earn up to $6,000, but had, in the case of men, median earnings of $5,460, again below the exempt amount but close enough to suggest that the earnings limitation has some impact among those who work.

While it is risky to predict what Congress will do, it seems likely that public sentiment will move in the direction of eliminating the earnings test. Whether elimination would have a significant effect on the employment behavior of older workers is, however, questionable, if the experiences of today's older workers are any guide. On the one hand, some recipients might return to work and others might be induced to work more hours. On the other hand, Labor Department economists warn that the consequences of eliminating the earnings test might not be as favorable as some proponents anticipate, if it enables part-timers who currently earn more than the exempt amount while receiving reduced benefits to work less without the benefit loss (Herz and Rones, 1989).

The Employee Retirement Income Security Act

The Employee Retirement Income Security Act (ERISA) of 1974, as amended, is a complicated piece of legislation enacted to ensure that workers will actually receive the private pensions on which they are planning. ERISA's provisions, which protect some 70 million workers, deal with such matters as the rights of spouses to survivor benefits, minimum standards for pension plans, and pension plan funding. This section deals only with those provisions that are most relevant to work and retirement decisions.

Unlike payroll contributions to social security, which are required by law of all companies in the private sector, employers are not required to offer their employees anything in the way of private pensions. If they do, however, ERISA mandates that those plans adhere to certain standards. ERISA does not insist that all workers in a firm be covered by a pension plan, but there are rules about who can be excluded; discrimination against older workers is no longer permitted.

Employer-Sponsored Pension Plans

Beyond knowing whether they are covered and the age at which they are eligible to receive benefits, workers need to understand their company pension plan's policies on vesting and portability.

Vesting means the irrevocable right to accrued pension benefits at retirement age. Some plans are 100 percent vested from the outset, which means that every dollar invested in a plan by an employer "belongs" to the employee, who is entitled to receive that dollar and any earnings from its investment when he or she retires.

The law does not require immediate 100 percent vesting. Companies may insist that workers participate in a plan for a period of time before vesting. Under current law, two vesting schedules are permitted for plan years starting in 1990. Under the more common of the two, employees must be 100 percent vested after five years of plan participation. Workers who change jobs before the fifth year are not vested and have accrued no right to future benefits. Decisions about changing jobs or retiring will seldom be based solely on vesting, although it should be an important consideration before making a move.

Portability refers to the right of employees to take their employers' pension contributions with them when they move to a new job and to "invest" those contributions in a new pension plan. Most private pensions are not portable, even for vested workers. Thus, vested workers who change jobs and retain pension accounts with their former employers will eventually receive pension benefits, but the benefits will not be as large as they would be if workers were able to roll over the contributions into the plans of their subsequent employers.

The law requires employers to provide employees with information on their rights and entitlements under their pension plans, and workers should request and read this information. Many workers do not make the effort to find out something as simple as when they can begin collecting benefits. When the U.S. General Accounting Office (GAO) looked into workers' knowledge of their pensions plans, it discovered that millions of workers were unfamiliar with such basic information as eligibility for early or normal retirement benefits. More than 70 percent of the employed pension plan participants were *wrong* about when they would be eligible for normal retirement benefits, leading the GAO (1987b: 1) to conclude that "unless workers obtain, or employers provide, accurate pension plan information before workers make decisions affecting their careers, they may make work and retirement decisions they later regret."

Pension Plans and the ADEA

When the Age Discrimination in Employment Act was passed in 1967, there was some concern that requiring employers to provide pension coverage to new workers nearing retirement age or to continue accruals or contributions for those who kept working beyond retirement age might actually discourage employers from hiring or retaining older workers. Ironically, therefore, the anti-age-discrimination law permitted a form of age discrimination. Companies with defined benefit pension plans (which use a formula, such as one based on a combination of age and years of service, to calculate pension benefits) were allowed to exclude from their pension plans new workers who were within five years of a plan's normal retirement age. Employers could also stop contributing to the plans for workers who had reached normal retirement age.

Neither of these exclusions is permitted any longer; however, companies are allowed to have certain age and service eligibility requirements for plan participation. Employers can, for example, exclude workers under the age of 21 or with less than one year of service from plan participation. They can also—and this is important for older employees who may want part-time work—refuse coverage to anyone who works fewer than 1,000 hours per year. Employers need not provide pension coverage to part-time workers, even if they cover full-time workers.

Pension plans may also put restrictions on employment after pension receipt. In some cases, companies are not allowed to rehire their retirees, or they may restrict the amount of work that rehired retirees may do while receiving pension benefits.

Other Financial Matters

Health insurance coverage is a primary concern for aging Americans. Eligibility for Medicare begins at age 65; however, it bears repeating that individuals who remain at work beyond age 65 must be offered the same health insurance protection that is offered younger workers. Many employers offer supplemental health insurance to their retirees, which is a very costly and valuable benefit.

In recent years laws have been passed that guarantee surviving wives or husbands shares of their deceased spouses' private pensions, provide some health insurance protection to job losers or the surviving spouses of deceased workers, lower the age of eligibility for pension plan participation, and ensure that survivors of vested pension plan participants collect benefits. Because the provisions of these laws, as important as they are, are less relevant than others to the employment and retirement issues discussed in this book, they are not covered here. Information on many of the provisions, should, however, be part of a well-rounded preretirement planning program.

Retirement Planning

Increasingly, many companies, particularly large ones, offer preretirement preparation programs for their older workers. Such programs might cover retirement employment opportunities, volunteering, health problems in later life, housing needs, legal matters, and financial planning. Financial planning, which includes information on pensions and insurance, is more common than some of the other types of planning that might be offered (Morrison, 1985).

Preretirement planning programs must be offered early in an employee's working life so that he or she can make choices. Workers who discover at age 55, for example, that their pensions are integrated with social security, are not indexed to keep pace with inflation, or will replace only about 20 percent of pre-retirement earnings have relatively little time (and perhaps few opportunities) to add to their anticipated retirement income.

Another potential problem involves how specific preretirement planning programs are about future income needs and retirees' ability to meet those needs. In the first place, many programs are only a few hours in length, and there is a great deal of often complicated information to impart. In the second place, employers are often eager to get their pension-age workers to retire, and a program that paints too bleak a retirement picture may have the unintended effect of discouraging retirement. It may therefore be left to workers themselves to ask hard questions, such as the following:

What exactly does integration do to my pension?

What would be the impact on my pension if inflation averages 3 percent, 7 percent, or 10 percent over the next ten years?

If I find that I cannot live on my retirement income, what are my chances of reentering the labor force and finding a job?

Midlife workers should be aware of the importance of preretirement planning and should enroll in a company's program at the earliest possible age, perhaps asking their employers to lower the age at which workers can participate. If they are employed in companies that lack preretirement programs, they should urge their employers to develop preretirement planning programs, hire consultants to offer programs, or purchase one of the many preretirement programs available for sale. Alternatively, workers may enroll in preretirement programs offered at many of the nation's community colleges.

Chapter 4

Age and Work Ability

I have two fixed ideas. . . . The first is the comparative uselessness of men above forty years of age. . . . My second fixed idea is the uselessness of men above sixty years of age, and the incalculable benefit it would be in commercial, political, and in professional life if, as a matter of course, men stopped work at this age.

Dr. William Osler, 1905 Retirement Address, Johns Hopkins University

The question "Can older workers remain competitive?" is not the real issue facing the United States today. Rather, it is: "How do you convince corporate America that older workers are and can remain competitive?"

Knowles, 1988b: 16

FACTS

- Men who have reached what is considered normal retirement age can expect to live almost 15 more years, in contrast to the 12 years expected when social security was enacted. Women at age 65 now have nearly 19 years ahead of them, up from about 13 in 1935.

- Research demonstrates that although there may be some performance decline with age, many aging workers continue to operate at peak efficiency.

- Older workers are seen by employers as loyal, dedicated, stable, committed to quality, able to get along with co-workers, prompt, and dependable. However, executives also express reservations about older workers' comfort with new technologies, quality of educational background, flexibility, and desire to get ahead.

• Although work disabilities are more than twice as common among persons 55 and older as among persons in their mid-40s to mid-50s, most older adults do not have disabilities that interfere with work.

Age and Job Performance

Fortunately, most modern employers would not agree with the theories of Dr. Osler expressed above, at least when it comes to people in their 40s. Nonetheless, many employers have negative stereotypes of older workers that must be reversed before they will provide those workers with incentives to remain at work.

Studies of the relationship between age and productivity demonstrate that although there may be some performance decline with age, *many aging workers continue to operate at peak efficiency.* Moreover, there is often more variation *within* age groups than among them. After reviewing the available research, the U.S. Senate Special Committee on Aging concluded that "no pattern of higher or lower productivity [characterizes] any particular age group" (U.S. Congress, 1984: 61). Indeed, when age-related differences in productivity occur, they seem to be minor, and many older workers actually do better on many jobs than younger ones. These observations confirm earlier findings published by Meier and Kerr (1976).

However, in a more recent evaluation of the available literature on age and job performance, Stagner (1985) contends that the results on age differences are ambiguous. Several studies, for example, show that performance does improve with age but also that it peaks relatively early. The performance of skilled and semiskilled industrial workers, for example, was shown to improve until it peaked somewhere in the 30s and 40s, generally declining thereafter (Davies and Sparrow, 1985). Even so, age-associated declines were relatively small, and, significantly, *the performance of workers in their 50s was always superior to that of the youngest workers.*

That productivity increases and then peaks was also noted in what has become a classic study of the footwear and household furniture industries (U.S. Department of Labor, 1957). Output per person-hour improved up to the age of 35, after which performance began to decline. But, as was the case with the workers above, the decline was not pronounced, and the performance of workers in their 60s was only 14 percent to 17 percent below peak. Clerical workers, 6,000 of whom were also studied by the Department of Labor, did not, however, seem to show comparable age-related variations in output; older workers in this study were just as productive as younger ones (Kutscher and Walker, 1960).

Research on more than 1,300 workers between the ages of 21 and 63 who serviced machines at four different skill levels suggests that training may offset performance decline (Davies and Sparrow, 1985). Efficiency, defined as speed of work, was found to be unrelated to age at any of the skill levels. However, when it came to quality—a ratio of the number of operations the machine completed successfully after servicing, compared with a national average—performance peaked in the 30s for the most complicated skill level (one of the machines was described as "extremely sophisticated") and somewhat earlier for the least complicated one. A slow decline occurred thereafter, which, interestingly, was sharper in the case of the simpler skill. By ages 51 to 55, quality performance was 14 percent below peak at skill level 1 and 9 percent lower at skill level 4. The smaller decline for the more complicated machine, suggest Davies and Sparrow, "was mediated by training experience—that is, the amount and kind of training received and how recently the training was given. Older engineers have more training experience and such experience appears to benefit to a greater extent the quality of performance on more complex, as opposed to less complex, machines" (pp. 3–4).

The Need for More and Better Productivity Research

Research on age and job performance suffers from a number of weaknesses, including (1) a lack of rigorously controlled studies that move beyond narrow and specialized groups, limiting any generalizability to the total population or to other occupational groups; (2) sample sizes that are too small to control for factors other than age that might explain productivity differences among workers; and (3) frequent reliance on the ratings of supervisors who may themselves be biased. Finally, some of the major studies are two or three decades old and may not be applicable to work in high-tech or service sector jobs.

Employers' Attitudes about Older Workers

According to public opinion polls, employers generally hold positive attitudes about older workers, although it is not always clear exactly who they think of as "older" workers: Do they mean persons in their 60s or 70s or, more likely, men and women approaching a firm's early retirement age? Older workers, however defined, are seen by employers as loyal, dedicated, stable, committed to quality, able to get along with co-workers, prompt, and dependable (American Association of Retired Persons [AARP], 1989). Older workers also compare favorably to younger workers on a number of measurable attributes. They have fewer on-the-job injuries; however, the severity of the injuries they do suffer tends to be greater than that of younger workers' injuries; avoidable work absences decrease with age, especially among men, although absences tend to be longer (Davies and Sparrow, 1985); job turnover rates are lower; and job stability after training is typically greater.

Companies generally give older workers high marks when it comes to experience and applaud the performance records of these workers (AARP, 1989). Some employers, at least those interviewed by William Mercer, Inc., in 1981, even argue that older workers "perform as well on the job as younger workers" and are more likely than younger workers to be dedicated company employees.

With such favorable attitudes about older workers, why are there so many early retirement incentive programs and a lack of interest in hiring older workers? Two serious problems appear to be older worker "plateauing" and "obsolescence," which are seen to constitute a "moderate, great or very great human resources management problem" in many organizations, according to the Commerce Clearing House (1988). (Plateaued workers are those who have essentially stopped advancing on the job; their career progression has leveled off. Career obsolescence in this study was described as a falling behind in the "ability to use new techniques or master new skills in present jobs.")

The negative consequences associated with plateauing and obsolescence mentioned by about half or more of the personnel administrators studied included clogged channels of promotion, lower morale among other workers, and—perhaps most critical as far as opportunities for older workers are concerned—lower overall productivity of the department or unit.

Executives in positions to hire older workers also express reservations about characteristics regarded as crucial in an economy in flux, namely, comfort with new technologies, quality of educational background, flexibility, and a desire to get ahead. These attributes are viewed by employers as critical to success in today's business world (AARP, 1989). In sum, as important as loyalty, commitment, dedication, and other positives are, they will not assure older workers a continued place in the corporate hierarchy. Employers clearly see bottom-line implications in a lack of technical skills, for example, while it is more difficult to assign a dollar value to company loyalty or co-worker compatibility.

Health Status of Older Workers

Many people experience physiological impairments such as decreased vision and hearing, an increase in chronic health problems, less energy, and a slowing of performance as they age. Yet these deficiencies are neither uniform within individuals (that is, all systems do not weaken at the same time or at the same rate) nor uniform across individuals (some persons "age" at a more rapid rate than others). Chronological age alone is usually a poor measure of functional age, or ability to perform.

Most older people are probably physically and mentally capable of working, on average, far longer than they do today. Americans in general are living longer (see Table 4.1); since 1900, life expectancy at birth has increased by 25 to 30 years and at age 65 by 3.3 years among men and by 6.7 years among women. Men who have reached what is considered normal retirement age can expect to live almost 15 more years, in contrast to the 12 years expected when social security was enacted. Women at age 65 now have nearly 19 years ahead of them, up from about 13 in 1935. Further life-expectancy improvements are anticipated beyond the turn of the century.

Table 4.1   Improvements in Life Expectancy at Birth and at Age 65, by Sex, Actual 1900, 1935, and 1986 and Projected 2000 and 2025

| | LIFE EXPECTANCY (in years) | | | |
| | AT BIRTH | | AT AGE 65 | |
YEAR	Males	Females	Males	Females
1900	46.4	49.0	11.3	12.0
1935	59.4	63.3	11.9	13.2
1986	71.4	78.5	14.6	18.7
2000[a]	73.9	80.8	15.6	20.1
2025[a]	75.4	82.3	16.5	21.2

Source: Wade, 1988.
[a]Intermediate life expectancy projections.

While life expectancy has improved dramatically in this century, it is not clear whether this has resulted in improved health (National Research Council, 1988). The exact relationship between longer life expectancy and health status is important, because a presumed positive relationship has been used to justify raising the retirement age. The 1983 proposal to raise the age for full benefits under social security was not without its vociferous opponents. At issue was not only the promise to workers that they could retire at age 65 but also concern over the burden that a higher retirement age would impose on older workers, many of whom were perceived to be unable to work.

For the purposes of discussion here, the most relevant question is the extent to which health limitations affect work ability. Obviously, the answer depends on what the limitations are and on what jobs are involved.

Work Disabilities among Older Workers

Physical limitations increase sharply with age, as does the severity of the limitations, which may be the more relevant measure as far as work capacity is concerned. Workers aged 65 to 69 are three times as likely as workers 45 to 54 and six times as likely as those 35 to 44 to report severe functional limitations (Berkowitz, 1988). These limitations include impairments in seeing, hearing, speaking, lifting or carrying, walking, using stairs, and getting

Table 4.2　　Persons with Work Disability, by Age, 1988 (in percentages)

AGE	WITH WORK DISABILITY	NOT SEVERE	SEVERE
16–24	3.8	2.1	1.7
25–34	5.6	2.9	2.7
35–44	7.1	3.4	3.6
45–54	10.3	4.3	6.0
55–64	22.3	8.3	14.0
65–69	25.4	NA	NA
70–74	26.8	NA	NA

Source:　U.S. Bureau of the Census, 1989: Tables 2, 10.

around outside as well as inside, and can obviously affect work performance.

More specific information on *work* disabilities is available from a 1988 population survey by the U.S. Census Bureau (1989), which shows a steady increase in both the presence and severity of work disability with age (see Table 4.2). A work disability—defined as "a health problem or disability which prevents [someone in the household] from working or which limits the kind or amount of work [he or she] can do"—is more than twice as common among persons 55 and older as among persons in their mid-40s to mid-50s. (Differences by sex are minor.) *Nonetheless, it is worth noting that most of the respondents reported no disability that might interfere with work, and that substantially fewer had severe disabilities. These findings confirm conclusions that physical limitations do not prevent most older persons from continued employment.*

Still, there is a relationship between reported work disability and employment rates, as is evident in Table 4.3. At all ages, men and women with work limitations are far less likely to be employed than are those without limitations, but after about age 55—and especially after age 65—the apparent impact of disability on employment becomes less pronounced. With or without disabilities, persons 65 and older tend not to be employed.

It is probably true that most workers maintain a reservoir of ability that can accommodate age-related physical decrements. Although health and job performance are undoubtedly related, many variables come into play; Berkowitz (1988: 90) contends, for example, that while health and functioning may not improve

Table 4.3   Percent Employed by Work Disability
Status, Age, and Sex, 1988

	MALES		FEMALES	
AGE	With Work Disability	Without Disability	With Work Disability	Without Disability
16–24	31.3	60.6	31.6	55.8
25–34	41.6	90.3	36.1	70.7
35–44	37.6	93.7	34.9	74.6
45–54	33.8	93.9	19.9	71.4
55–64	18.8	77.2	12.6	50.0
65–69	9.4	30.8	4.4	17.8
70–74	6.5	18.2	2.4	8.9

Source: U.S. Bureau of the Census, 1989: Tables 4, 10.

with age, people "may improve in knowledge and wisdom." Those attributes that appear to improve with age, such as wisdom and experience, might well offset some of the physiological changes (e.g., reduced speed) that affect performance. Finally, the late ergonomist Ross McFarland (1973: 11) reminded us that "most of us are unsuited in some ways, either physically or psychologically, for most jobs. . . . But essentially, all persons are at the same time suited for some activities while unsuited or unfit for others." *Moreover, what appears to be an age-related performance decline may actually be the result of a mismatch between the job and the worker, which suggests that better matching of workers and jobs could result in a more productive work force.*

The Costs of Employing Older Workers

Concerns about older worker productivity must also be examined within the context of what it costs to hire or retain one employee over another. Contributing to concerns about business competitiveness are employee compensation costs (U.S. Congress, 1984). Wages and salaries, for example, tend to increase up until age 50 or so and then level off, which means that older workers will typically earn more than younger ones. Companies may therefore yield to the temptation to retire older workers and replace them with younger, presumably cheaper ones. During mergers and periods of corporate downsizing, the potential dollars saved by reducing the number of highly paid older workers have considerable appeal, at least over the short run.

In addition, despite the fact that most older workers are probably healthy enough to keep working longer than they do, at any given time older workers are, on average, less healthy than younger ones (Berkowitz, 1988), and health expenditures and other compensation costs are greater for older workers than for younger ones (U.S. Congress, 1984, 1985b). However, under the Age Discrimination in Employment Act, employers can control some costs under the equal benefit or equal cost provision, which allows companies to provide less in the way of benefits to older workers as long as what they pay for those benefits is the same for younger and older workers.

Those who argue in favor of divesting their work forces of older employees may be overlooking the costs of recruiting and training new workers. These costs may be minimal if unskilled workers are needed and available, but they can be substantial when highly experienced workers are necessary. In addition, employers may incur the costs of relocating new workers, assisting spouses in finding work, and "down time" as workers adjust to their new work environment. It may even be necessary to recruit several workers to replace one retiring employee. The Senate report cited above found that in the case of a life insurance agent, for example, such replacement costs could amount to several hundred thousand dollars (U.S. Congress, 1984: 6). More appropriate and cost-effective strategies might include changes in job placement and accommodation in the form of office or workplace redesign, better lighting, and task modification. Such strategies may well be a future necessity, as the pool of younger workers shrinks.

Chapter 5

Training Older Workers

If the U.S. is to remain competitive in world markets, the Nation must provide for a skilled, productive, adaptable workforce, one that makes use of the talents and contributions of all available human resources.

U.S. Department of Labor, 1988: 8

Learning . . . is a lifelong process.

Executive Office of the President, 1990: 104

FACTS

- In 1984, employers spent an estimated $12 billion to $30 billion on formal worker training programs, and many billions more on informal training.

- Of that amount, more than two-thirds was spent on training workers between the ages of 25 and 44.

- Three in ten companies have adopted skill training for older workers.

- Many experts believe adults learn best by doing, rather than through classroom lectures.

- In a recent AARP survey, about two-thirds of workers 40 and older reported that they had received some job training over the previous three years.

Employers Spend Billions on Training

According to the Department of Labor's Commission on Work-force Quality and Labor Market Efficiency, 10 percent of 17-year-olds in the United States are functionally illiterate, while fully one-half of all 18-year-olds have yet to master even *basic* language, mathematics, and analytic skills. In many parts of the country and sectors of the economy, employers already face a shortage of skilled workers. Increasingly, they are also unable to find entry-level employees with the basic skills necessary to benefit from employer training programs (U.S. Department of Labor, 1989b). As the shortage of skilled workers spreads and as the costs of recruiting and training new workers rise, employers may begin to reevaluate their retirement policies and calculate the savings that might be realized from retraining and retaining their existing workers.

At present, most worker training occurs in the private sector and is supported by private funds. In 1984, employers spent an estimated $12 billion to $30 billion on formal worker training programs, and many billions more on informal training (Mangum, undated). Although "prime-age employees," workers between the ages of 25 and 44, made up only about half of the labor force, they received more than two-thirds of the money spent on formal training (Mangum, undated). The American Association of Retired Persons (AARP, 1989) recently reported that only about three in ten companies have adopted skill training for older workers, a figure almost identical to that found by the Commerce Clearing House (1988). This statistic has not changed since 1985, even though executives seem more receptive to the idea that training would be effective in increasing the utilization of older workers (AARP, 1989).

By law, older workers cannot be denied training if it is offered to other workers, except in the case of legitimate apprenticeship programs. This does not mean, however, that employers have to encourage older workers to participate in training programs, and most of them probably do not. Thus, older workers themselves may need to take the initiative.

Older Workers Are Good Candidates for Training

The ability to learn continues well into old age. In fact, one evaluation concluded that training outcomes were better for older than for younger workers (Doering et al., 1983).

Learning Time May Be Longer

Older workers may not be as quick at learning new tasks as younger workers or as they themselves were when they were young (Poon, 1987; Sterns and Doverspike, 1988). However, it is not clear how much of the difference in learning speed is due to age, per se, as opposed to health status, educational attainment, motivation, familiarity with the learning materials, or anxiety.

A quarter of a century ago, Birren (1964: 152) stated that "with the gradual rise in years of educational attainment, more adults reach their older years with a positive attitude toward abstract learning, as well as toward learning of new operational skills." This observation is even more appropriate today, given continued improvements in educational attainment among older workers.

Companies and human resource executives seem to feel that certain techniques, such as self-paced learning, experiential training, on-the-job coaching, or pragmatic training are more effective in teaching older workers (Commerce Clearing House, 1988). Practical hands-on learning by doing, as opposed to abstract theoretical classroom teaching, is often thought to be best for teaching new skills to adults. There is some evidence to indicate that the longer the training (i.e., the more practice time allowed), at least up to a limit, the better older workers do (Newsham, 1969). However, a recent review of the training literature for the Commission on Workforce Quality and Labor Market Efficiency led to the conclusion that *"not a lot [is] known about how to best train workers for specific technologies"* (Kearsley, undated: 2; emphasis added).

Though it may not be clear what techniques work best in teaching various types of workers—whether old, young, minority, or female—*the important point is that older workers can be effectively retrained.* Moreover, not only can older workers be trained, but even those with serious labor market impediments, such as low levels of education and histories of employment in unskilled jobs, can be trained to utilize new technology. In one study, unskilled freight and baggage handlers were successfully trained to do complex tasks, some linked to a computer and requiring a high degree of accuracy (Stewart, 1969). A now classic study of older forklift operators at Aer Lingus also demonstrated that older operatives could be successfully retrained in more complex, technologically new, and demanding work (Mullan and Gorman, 1972).

More recent studies show that older individuals can also master new computer technology, although, again, it may take them somewhat longer to become proficient than it does younger workers. In one case, older trainees (between the ages of 55 and 67) did less well than younger trainees in a word-processing study, possibly because some of the procedures were relatively far removed from ones they probably knew well as typists (Elias et al., 1987). Nonetheless, as in the freight handler study, *regardless of age, the subjects made few overall errors and all of them were capable of learning the basics.* In view of impending shortages of skilled labor, the fact that there may be few totally untrainable workers is perhaps more important than whether younger trainees are faster or somewhat more efficient learners than their relatively older counterparts.

Are Older Workers More Costly To Train?

Few companies have apparently systematically analyzed the costs and benefits of training older workers (Commerce Clearing House, 1988). However, the limited research suggests that any added costs of training older workers may be offset by savings elsewhere. For example, Treat et al. (1981) observed that while younger people were more effective learners, some age-related learning differences narrowed with practice over subsequent weeks. In another study, younger trainees were more likely to survive a training program, but the differences that favored them reversed over time: two years after training, older trainees (35 and above) were substantially more likely still to be with the company. In addition, the costs of retraining rather than retiring older workers should be balanced against replacement costs, which, with recruitment, relocation, and training of new workers, can amount to one to two times a year's salary (Knowles, 1988b).

Assisting the Older Learner

Getting help may be a critical aspect of success for older persons learning new technologies. In one experiment that involved learning word-processing skills, older trainees (65–75) seemed to acquire information at the same rate as younger ones (18–30) when they were assisted, although it took them longer to select and carry out correct procedures. In a second study, help was severely restricted, and older adults were not as successful (Hartley et al., 1984).

Prior Experience

Conventional wisdom argues that older workers bring experience and expertise to a learning environment that may be relevant to their training. However, when learning a new skill requires unlearning or shedding old habits, experience and expertise can interfere with the training process. Sterns and Doverspike (forthcoming) raise the somewhat disturbing possibility that "expertise gain over years of experience can be no longer valued with a change to new computer controlled production approaches. . . . new technologies demand new kinds of expertise." In other words, prior experience might not have the mediating effect in training that it has had in the past, although it is also likely that as individuals become more familiar and comfortable with new technologies, they will once again bring relevant expertise to other "high-tech" training situations.

Employers' Attitudes about Training Older Workers

Despite the evidence cited above, many employers continue to be biased against training older workers. Personnel administrators surveyed by the American Society of Personnel Administration and the Commerce Clearing House tended to place the blame on workers themselves, contending that "older employees experience difficulty in mastering new concepts, ideas and approaches." They also cited "moderate to great resistance to training" by older employees. In contrast, midlife and older workers themselves overwhelmingly say they would be interested in training programs, primarily to improve their employment opportunities (AARP, 1986).

As noted before, human resource executives recognize the many positive attributes of older workers, such as loyalty, dependability, and a strong work ethic, but they remain skeptical about older workers' comfort with new technology. And executives who make decisions about older worker training are apt to regard comfort with new technologies as a crucial employee attribute. Over the second half of the 1980s, despite some encouraging developments in attitudes about older workers, the gap between executives' concern about the importance of technologies and their beliefs about older workers' technological resistance widened. Nearly three-fourths of the executives in the 1989 AARP study agreed that "our younger employees represent the future of the industry and we should focus our training and development efforts on them" (AARP, 1989: 14).

Few would deny the importance of educating and training younger workers. The country's competitiveness, to say nothing of the well-being of future elderly people, depends on the productivity of these young workers. Nevertheless, older workers, especially if retrained, can also contribute to productive growth and, as a result, reduce some of their anticipated burden on retirement income systems.

Older Workers' Attitudes toward Training

For various reasons, older workers may be reluctant to ask for or to take advantage of training programs. However, even though older employees tend to agree with employers who say that younger workers are more comfortable with new technologies, this does not mean that they are uninterested in learning about them.

Although there are no data on how well represented older workers are in company training programs, many older workers do, apparently, take advantage of whatever opportunities exist. About half of the corporate executives who reported training programs to the Conference Board said that older workers were as likely as others to participate in training (Rhine, 1984). About two-thirds of the respondents in AARP's survey of workers 40 and older reported that they had received some job training over the previous three years. Unfortunately, details on what the training involved—and whether it was in formal training programs or something more informal—were not provided. The survey did note, however, that it was generally on-the-job training designed to upgrade skills (AARP, 1986).

Tuition Assistance Programs

Tuition assistance seems to be common among firms that have worker training policies (Commerce Clearing House, 1988; Rhine, 1984). Taking advantage of such assistance might be a way for employees to "prove" to employers (1) that they are not resistant to training and (2) that they can succeed in training programs. Job-related courses can be found at local trade schools, community colleges, four-year colleges, and universities, more and more of which are tailoring both programs and schedules to the demands of older students who may want evening or weekend classes. Adult education courses, which technically include "all courses and organized activities taken part-time and identified as adult education by respondents" (U.S. Department of Education, undated: 1), are popular in the United States, but participation in these courses drops with age, from just under 20 percent of persons aged 25–34 to less than 5 percent of the 65-plus population.

Most adult education students are enrolled for job-related reasons, whether to get new jobs, advance in current jobs, or start their own businesses. Interestingly, employers actually tend to provide or pay for more of the adult education courses taken by men between the ages of 45 and 54 than by any other group. Courses taken by women are less likely to be subsidized by employers, but even so, employers provided or subsidized more than half of all adult education courses taken by middle-aged women.

Private Sector Training Programs for Older Workers

Few good examples of training programs for older workers exist in the published literature. Even the National Older Worker Information System (NOWIS) of AARP offers little in the way of training information. What information on company training programs for older workers does exist tends to be dated, anecdotal, and lacking in specifics on costs and benefits. Nonetheless, several available examples still illustrate the value and success of such programs.

Observing that the skills of retirees out of the labor force can quickly become rusty, the Travelers Companies trains returning retirees in keyboard skills and changing office technologies. Travelers uses self-paced computerized training programs with a high degree of success and, at the request of the older workers themselves, trains workers of all ages in the program.

Training in office skills is also the focus of Southwestern Life Insurance Company, which has actively sought out older workers in need of training. The fast-growing temporary help industry has found that reentry workers, many of whom are older, must be updated in new office skills, and several agencies have developed successful programs. Older workers are also being trained in the skills needed to perform adequately in the fast-food industry, where jobs are on the increase.

Worker retraining is a key component of corporate policy at AT&T, which is not surprising, given the rapid changes in the communications field. A number of training programs provide employees with the opportunity to upgrade their jobs or to move to new positions within the company. Although not intended solely for older workers, a corporate education program offering courses in the sciences and engineering or in business skills during and after business hours has particular appeal to older workers whose skills need updating.

Control Data Corporation has offered a number of training programs to its employees, one of which was designed to encourage professional employees between the ages of 30 and 55 to consider new employment opportunities within Control Data, instead of leaving the company.

General Electric has been widely cited for its efforts in the late 1970s to train workers in the new skills required by the shift from analog to digital technologies in electronics. The average worker in these successful training programs was middle-aged. Opportunities to continue to stay up to date have been provided through GE's Continuing Engineering Education Program.

Grumman Corporation, known for the age audits discussed in Chapter 2, offers career development programs that have special appeal to midlife and older workers. These involve midcareer training programs and management and professional development courses. Women in particular benefit from several programs that train reentry workers and assist current workers in developing new skills.

Pitney Bowes has offered tuition reimbursement to encourage its employees to move on to new careers after retirement, while Crouse-Hinds Electric provides training to workers of all ages, including long-term employees, in an effort to update worker skills in another rapidly changing field, that of electrical products manufacturing.

The National Caucus and Center on Black Aged, Inc., a non-profit agency rather than a business, sponsors a 26-week training course in housing management that prepares older persons, especially minorities, for new careers as housing managers. The program is important because of its appeal to older minority group members, for whom training opportunities are especially rare.

One of the problems with the above anecdotes is that they provide almost no information on the number or characteristics of the trainees, the proportionate representation of older workers, the training successes and failures, and what happens to the workers after training. It is doubtful, for example, that many of the trainees are "old"—that is, 65 or above—in part because so few people that age remain in the labor force to be trained. It is also unlikely that many of them are—except perhaps in the fast-food industry—55 or older. How older trainees fare compared with younger ones is not known, but it can be assumed that in those companies that continued their training programs and kept enrolling older workers, the programs were a success. What is important about these programs, as well as about other programs and policies for older workers, is that employers implement them not out of any sense of civic responsibility or altruistic feelings for older workers, but because the programs contribute to the bottom line.

Federal Training Programs for Older Workers

The federal government's role in training older workers rests primarily with the Senior Community Service Employment Program (SCSEP) and the Job Training Partnership Act (JTPA), although few observers would argue that either the SCSEP or the JTPA meets the needs of many of the people it is supposed to help. Both programs have eligibility requirements that severely restrict the type of person who may participate; as a result, relatively few midlife and older persons are involved.

The Senior Community Service Employment Program

SCSEP (Title V of the Older Americans Act) was established to promote useful part-time opportunities in community service for low-income persons. In fiscal year 1974 there were fewer than 4,000 enrollees in the program, but by 1988 their numbers had grown to nearly 65,000 (U.S. Congress, 1988).

SCSEP participants must be at least 55 years old and have incomes that do not exceed 125 percent of the poverty level. The program is administered by the Department of Labor's Division of Older Worker Programs in the Office of Special Targeted Programs in the Employment and Training Administration.

SCSEP is primarily a job creation program, not a job training program, and individuals who seek training that will enhance their employment opportunities in the private sector will generally be disappointed. For the most part, SCSEP participants are placed in public service jobs requiring little in the way of technical skills. These jobs include positions in day-care centers, schools, hospitals, and senior centers. Although the secretary of labor has ordered that a certain proportion of SCSEP participants must be placed in private sector employment, SCSEP has traditionally focused on minimum-wage public service jobs. And while SCSEP participants may receive on-the-job training after placement, preplacement training is rare. Training in some of the newer technologies is even rarer, in part because of program administrators' reservations about the abilities of program participants (Centaur Associates, Inc., 1986).

SCSEP employment provides some much-needed money to the low-income participants, as well as needed public services to communities. However, it does not enhance the private sector marketability of the participants, in part because of the lack of training.

SCSEP gives grants to national nonprofit sponsoring organizations, such as the National Council on the Aging or the National Council of Senior Citizens, and state agencies that receive federal funds to manage the employment programs. The states may administer programs directly or they may enter into contractual arrangements with national sponsors. For 1990, congressional appropriations of $338 million were estimated to fund approximately 56,000 slots. States, however, do not always charge all of their administrative costs to the program, and they may also receive supplemental funding, which enables them to expand some services. This, plus program turnover, means that additional participants can be accommodated during the year. Even so, a doubling of SCSEP participants would serve but a fraction of the income-eligible older population.

Obviously, income eligibility alone is not an indicator of demand for employment services; many older persons with limited financial resources are retired and, despite struggling financially, have little interest in returning to work. A rather substantial portion of the 55-plus population is 75 or above and probably not—for eminently understandable reasons—very eager to work.

Even though it does not serve a large number of people, SCSEP is an important program because it is aimed at persons who face employment barriers that are often insurmountable in the private sector: SCSEP participants are disproportionately female (almost 70 percent), minority (37 percent), poorly educated (nearly half with less than a high school education), and older (more than half are over 65). Some 80 percent have incomes below the poverty level.

To find out about opportunities and to confirm eligibility for participation in SCSEP, contact one of the prime sponsors listed in Chapter 9 of this volume.

The Job Training Partnership Act

The largest government-sponsored training program is the Job Training Partnership Act, enacted in 1982 as a replacement to CETA, the much-maligned Comprehensive Employment and Training Act. While JTPA is primarily a program for youth, older workers, at least as of 1990, may be served under JTPA's Title II-A block grant to the states and through a 3 percent Title II-A set-aside specifically targeted at persons 55 and older. A total of 90 percent of the Title II-A funds must be used on the economically disadvantaged. The other 10 percent can be spent on trainees who are not economically disadvantaged but who face certain employment barriers; the law specifically mentions older workers and displaced homemakers in this section.

The goal of the Job Training Partnership Act is "to afford job training to those economically disadvantaged individuals and other individuals facing serious barriers to employment who are in special need of such training to obtain productive employment." The income criterion for JTPA participation means that a large number of middle-aged and older workers who could benefit from skills updating are not qualified.

Under Title II-A, local governments and private sector planning agencies jointly administer training programs for disadvantaged youths and adults. Programs may involve classroom training, job search assistance, on-the-job training, and what is classified as "other" assistance. In 1988, the Senate Special Committee on Aging concluded that "the impact of JTPA on mature and older workers is probably minimal" (U.S. Congress, 1988: 121)—an observation supported by statistics published by the Department of Labor and by research done by the National Commission for Employment Policy (NCEP). Older workers are underrepresented in JTPA programs, probably because many of them have the choice of leaving the labor force rather than becoming unemployed (Sandell and Rupp, 1988). Studies of CETA participants showed similar underrepresentation (Rupp et al., 1983).

Some potential JTPA participants may be discouraged from enrolling by the jobs for which they would be trained and in which they would be placed. Although age breakdowns are unavailable, only about one-fifth of the male graduates and about one-tenth of the female terminees are placed in "higher skill" occupations (U.S. General Accounting Office, 1989). A call for innovative and/or successful training programs under the 3-percent set-aside yielded such suggestions as training in weaving, woodworking and landscaping, sales and clerical work, and geriatric nursing assistance (Alegria and Figueroa, 1986), jobs of questionable interest to most older workers. While some of the jobs for which older workers are trained under the set-aside do, as the law specifies, seem to be in growth industries, there is less evidence that states have "given consideration to assisting programs involving training for jobs . . . reflecting the use of new technological skills" (Section 124(c) of the JTPA).

The 3-percent set-aside will probably be eliminated as a result of JTPA amendments being considered by Congress in 1990. Under the proposed changes, however, older workers would still be served with targeted funds.

The Carl D. Perkins Vocational Education Act

Under the Carl D. Perkins Vocational Education Act of 1984, money is available for training, research, demonstration programs, and supportive services for adults, single parents, displaced homemakers, and women attempting to secure nontraditional jobs. The act mandates, among other things, a set-aside of 8.5 percent targeted to programs for single parents and displaced homemakers. Homemakers are defined as persons who work "primarily without remuneration to care for the home and family and for that reason have diminished marketable skills." Displaced homemakers—primarily middle-aged and older women—are individuals who have lost, generally through divorce or widowhood, the financial support they had while caring for a family.

In 1990, the act was up for reauthorization. Both the House and Senate bills would retain set-asides for single parents and displaced homemakers, although funding levels may be lower than under current law. Nonetheless, programs funded under this act will remain an important source of training for midlife women.

To date, much of the interest in promoting older worker employment and training opportunities has been restricted to advocacy organizations for the elderly, a small number of businesses confronted with highly specialized skills shortages, and industries that have traditionally drawn their employees from the now shrinking pool of younger workers. Soon all employers may need to entice more people into the labor market, and older workers may become a much more valuable resource, a development that would lead to a continuing expansion of training programs in both the public and private sectors.

Chapter 6

Older Women, Work, and Economic Security

For older women, age discrimination commonly acts to compound a lifetime of sex discrimination in the labor market.

Roundtable on Older Women in the Work Force, undated: 11

By the year 2020, poverty among elderly Americans will be confined primarily to women living alone.

Commonwealth Fund Commission on Elderly People Living Alone, 1987: OR-2

FACTS

- In 1988, women accounted for 72 percent of the aged poor, up from 67 percent in 1970.

- Of all middle-aged women in 1979 who had ever worked, over three-fourths had at least one work interruption of six months or longer. About nine out of ten of these women had stopped working for "family reasons."

- In contrast, less than one-third of the men in the same age group had experienced such lengthy work interruptions, and only about 5 percent did so for family reasons.

- The average time women spent out of the work force for family reasons was 9.5 years.

- Nearly half of women currently working full-time are not covered by pension plans.

85

- In 1985, the Office of Technology Assessment estimated that there were 2.2 million women aged 35–64 who were widowed, separated, divorced or had husbands incapable of working.

Older Women Are Economically Vulnerable

Growing old accentuates the economic vulnerability of women in the United States. Some 2.5 million women aged 65 and older are impoverished, and many more have incomes not far above the official poverty level. For a variety of reasons, women predominate among the elderly poor, and their concentration in this unenviable population is on the rise: as of 1988, women were 72 percent of the aged poor, up from 67 percent in 1970. Gender, particularly when combined with living arrangements, is a potent predictor of poverty: of all aged poor in America, over half are what are technically referred to as female "unrelated individuals," the majority of whom are women who live alone.

Women's Employment Histories

There are many reasons aged women find themselves so precariously situated: widowhood and the expenses of long-term care for a spouse are two of the more common ones. However, a major factor is employment history. Many of today's older women have had little work experience and/or have been in and out of the labor force, work patterns that result in few benefits in later years. Even women with lifelong attachment to the labor force have been concentrated largely in low-wage, nonunionized, and smaller firms where private pension coverage is uncommon. Thus, many older women today depend on their husbands' benefits—either as spouses or as widows—for economic support in old age.

Despite continued concern about the well-being of older women, serious legislative initiatives to raise income levels under public retirement income systems (such as social security) are lacking in the United States. Rather, legislative efforts have focused on *lessening* dependence on public pension systems. For most people, this requires more paid work.[1]

Retirement benefits in the United States are tied to work experience. Time out of the labor force to meet the demands of a family is not specifically acknowledged as "work" for social security purposes. As noted in Chapter 3, the social security benefit computation excludes a worker's five years of lowest earnings, which for women may well be years of no earnings. Moreover, women (and men) may lose accumulated private pension credits if they leave the labor force to care for families, further undermining their future economic security.

Factors Enhancing Women's Employment Opportunities

Increasingly, women are expected to enter the paid labor force, and that is what middle-aged and younger women have been doing. Women's employment prospects have been enhanced by laws and by U.S. Supreme Court decisions striking down barriers to their advancement. Obstacles that confronted women in the past are now illegal, largely as a result of the passage of Title VII of the Civil Rights Act, which eliminates employment discrimination on the basis of, among other things, sex. Earlier restrictions on when and where women could work and what they could do have been eliminated.

By virtue of being gender neutral, employment laws in the United States promote equality, and even though discrimination against women persists, the working woman of the 1990s is very different from her counterpart of the 1960s. However, true equality in the labor force—even if guaranteed and even when achieved—will not necessarily ensure income sufficiency in old age.

Impediments to Continuous Employment

The problem is that the typical female employee does not resemble the typical male employee, particularly in regard to continuity of labor force attachment. Women continue to assume primary responsibility for the care of home and children, and the caregiving role either requires or encourages women to move in and out of the labor force. Even when children become independent, a woman's caregiving role is by no means over: mortality advances ensuring that more people will live to very old age place new caregiving burdens on the middle-aged children—generally daughters or daughters-in-law—of aging relatives.

Of all middle-aged women in 1979 who had ever worked, over three-fourths had at least one work interruption of six months or longer; about nine out of ten of these had stopped working for "family reasons" (U.S. Bureau of the Census, 1984). In contrast, less than one-third of the men in the same age group had experienced such lengthy work interruptions, and only about 5 percent did so for family reasons. Men have been far more successful than women in avoiding the double burden of work and caregiving responsibilities, although they are somewhat more likely today to engage in full-time family care than they were in the 1970s. Of the 20.9 million men who were out of the labor force in 1989, 2.1 percent said they were keeping house, up from 1.5 percent in 1975!

Absences for family reasons, as opposed to those for illness or unemployment, are frequently long—an average of more than 9 years among women in the Census Bureau survey. While future generations of middle-aged women will undoubtedly have more continuous work histories than these respondents (currently over half of women return to the labor force within a year of giving birth), a high percentage of young women will still drop out of the labor force to care for their families, sometimes for extended periods. Many young women in the Census Bureau survey had also had at least one work absence of six months or longer, generally for family reasons, and nearly one in five of these young women had already spent at least one-fourth of their potential work years away from work (U.S. Bureau of the Census, 1984).

In its 1989 Mother's Day report, the Older Women's League (OWL) contends that women will spend an average of 17 years caring for children and 18 caring for older parents. Not all elder care is the equivalent of a full-time job, but much of it is when the older person is impaired. The Commonwealth Fund Commission reports that some 9 percent of the caregivers of impaired elderly—most of whom are women—have had to quit work;

many more have been forced to juggle work schedules, reduce work hours, or take time off from work to handle their caregiving responsibilities (Rowland, 1989).

Women's work patterns (especially when combined with other factors, such as employment in jobs that do not have private pension coverage) quite clearly result in more women who reach retirement age without social security supplements.

Women and Private Pensions

More future retirees of both sexes are accruing private pension benefits. Still, many women not now working in jobs covered by private pension plans (nearly half of all full-time working women) will never draw pension benefits. Firms not offering private pension protection tend to be small, nonunionized, and in the service sector—where substantial numbers of women are employed and where there is less coverage than in large, unionized, and/or manufacturing establishments. The costs of setting up and maintaining pension plans may be beyond the reach of many of these smaller businesses, and Congress is unlikely to mandate the provision of such benefits, at least in the foreseeable future. In addition, when pensions are based on highest years of earnings, stable, long-term workers—among whom women do not predominate—are the winners.

The modest provisions of the 1984 Retirement Equity Act, which apply to private pensions, implicitly recognize some of the problems of women, although this law is also couched in gender-neutral terms and applies as well to men who may fall into certain categories. The act lowered the minimum vesting age, as well as the age at which a worker must be enrolled in a firm's pension plan. It also barred plans from treating a one-year maternity or paternity leave as a break in service and allowed workers to leave and return to their jobs without loss of pension benefits if the break does not exceed a certain length of time.[2]

Another major advance occurred with the passage of the Tax Reform Act of 1986, which lowered the number of years it takes a worker to vest in a pension plan (see Chapter 3). A shorter period of vesting assists *all* mobile workers and those who, for whatever reason, move in and out of the labor force, but it is especially important to women.

There has, however, been no fundamental reexamination of the philosophical underpinnings of social security, which remains a system based on the standard of a single-earner household with, if there is one, a dependent spouse. A radical rethinking of social security that acknowledges the changing nature of the family might involve what is known as "earnings sharing," which would treat work in the home as legitimate employment for social security benefit purposes.

Characteristics of Midlife and Older Women Workers

Today's midlife and older women constitute a heterogeneous population. Women who are now 65 and above often confronted policies against the employment of married women; during the Depression, many states actually proposed legislation to bar married women from employment (Shaw, 1988). The middle-aged and older female population includes women who never had much expectation, if any, of working outside the home, as well as some who expected to engage in paid employment for a large portion of their lives. Women now reaching middle age were young adults when the major piece of anti-sex-discrimination legislation—Title VII of the Civil Rights Act—was passed. "The contrast," says Shaw, "for women who are now 40 years old could hardly be greater" (p. 56).

Reentry

Not surprisingly, given their employment histories, midlife and older women are much more likely than men to be labor force reentrants. According to the U.S. Department of Labor (1989c), more than one-third of all female job seekers aged 45 or older in 1987 were labor force entrants, generally reentrants, a proportion double that of unemployed men. Each week, roughly 180,000 women aged 45 and above are unemployed entrants.

Reentry women are not necessarily consigned to a period of unemployment. Many apparently find work immediately, return to former jobs, or are offered work before returning to the labor force. What is disturbing, however, is that the women with the fewest financial resources to conduct long job searches are those reentry women who are unemployed longest (U.S. Department of Labor, 1989c). These are typically displaced homemakers, women who—generally through death of a spouse or divorce— have lost their primary source of support and need to secure employment quickly.

Reentry women are clearly at a different stage of work life than men of the same age (Shaw, 1988). Further, their lack of work experience results in limited opportunities and lower earnings. Skills obsolescence, however, may not have the effect of lowering the wages of reentry women, who seem to catch up quickly with their counterparts who have continuous work experience (Shaw, 1985). Unfortunately, this "improvement" may result from women's concentration in low-wage, relatively unskilled jobs, where "catching up" is easy.

Occupational Segregation

Table 1.3 (in Chapter 1) revealed the occupational distribution of employed midlife and older women, some 60 percent of whom work in retail sales, administrative support, and services (Herz, 1988)—traditional female occupations for which the average wages are often far below those of the total work force.

It is this concentration in low-wage, female-dominated jobs that troubles women's advocates and others worried about the economic status of women. While there have been dramatic increases in the proportion of women in such nontraditional fields as law, medicine, and veterinary medicine, the gains have, quite understandably, not been equal across the life span. And, overall, most jobs remain highly segregated by sex. Time should work out many of these problems, although it will be many years before occupational and earnings equity yield retirement income equity as well.

The extent to which women select jobs that enable them to move into and out of the labor force with relative ease is a matter of considerable debate. Anticipating a long employment break could lower an individual's incentive to improve work skills (Kahne, 1985). Women may also be reluctant to enter nontraditional jobs, or employers may hesitate to hire women in such positions (Shaw, 1988), despite the fact that the so-called nontraditional jobs for women often pay much better than traditionally female occupations. Proponents of pay equity, also known as comparable worth, argue that the devaluation of "women's" jobs rather than any intrinsic differences between the sexes accounts for wage differences, and that more objective evaluations of merit would equalize wages. Other factors that may account for wage differences include training, course of study, and educational attainment—many midlife and older women have not finished high school and, with age, the probability of their being college graduates decreases sharply.

Part-Time versus Full-Time Work

Another reason that women of all ages earn less than men is that they are more likely than men to be part-time workers. Part-time employment is especially common among the oldest female labor force participants. This type of employment often involves entry-level, dead-end jobs paying very low wages. Part-time workers, for example, make up less than one-sixth of the total labor force but two-thirds of the workers earning minimum and sub-minimum wages (Conway, 1990).

Displaced Homemakers

The executive director of the Displaced Homemakers Network (DHN) has put the number of displaced homemakers at 11 million, with 5 million under age 65 (Miller, 1989). In 1985, the Office of Technology Assessment estimated that there were 2.2 million women 35–64 who were widowed, separated, divorced, or had husbands incapable of working (U.S. Congress, 1985a).

Although estimates of the exact number of displaced homemakers vary widely, there is general agreement that many—indeed millions of—women who lose the support of a spouse are in desperate need of employment. Divorced women, many of whom have minor children to care for, are especially likely to need to find work quickly. Alimony awards are rare today, and child support—while easier to collect than in the past—is often inadequate. Following a divorce, the income of women drops by an estimated 30 percent (Duncan and Hoffman, 1985) to more than 70 percent (Weitzman, 1985).

Widows also qualify as displaced homemakers, but for them, employment does not appear to be a "highly desirably alternative" (Morgan, 1984). Younger widows and widows who experience declines in their standard of living are more likely than other widows to seek employment. In contrast, older widows seem disinclined to look for work, in part because access to social security and perhaps private pension income lessens the pressure to seek employment.

Displaced job-seeking homemakers are women who, because of age and lack of work experience and updated skills, face multiple barriers upon labor force reentry. Such women need training, advice on how to find jobs, other supportive services, and income. One of the prime sources of support and information for displaced homemakers is the Displaced Homemakers Network. Local programs, aided by a national umbrella organization, work to improve the employment and training opportunities of this special population. According to the organization's director, as of 1987 the DHN was serving nearly 1,000 local programs with technical assistance, resources, and information (Miller, 1989).

Most DHN programs are small and poorly funded and are thus unable to provide all of the services that displaced homemakers need. Although states also fund displaced homemaker programs, the amounts appropriated tend to be relatively low— between $200,000 and $800,000 in 1987 (Miller, 1989). Despite these low levels of funding, however, local DHN programs have been instrumental in enhancing the employment opportunities of displaced homemakers.

Displaced homemakers are also eligible for participation in Job Training Partnership Act (JTPA) programs if they are economically disadvantaged. In addition, the JTPA singles out displaced homemakers as a group facing special employment barriers. As noted in Chapter 5, up to 10 percent of JTPA's Title II-A funds may be used to assist such individuals, even if they are not economically disadvantaged. Nonetheless, the DHN found a number of disincentives to serving displaced homemakers in JTPA programs, including the mandated private-public partnership that encourages a "bottom-line" approach to service provision. Relatively little money is available for supportive services, the provision of which would increase the cost of placement. Displaced homemakers, however, are often in need of supportive services and other specialized assistance, such as skills assessment, counseling, and intensive training.

JTPA performance standards are based on such measures as the rate of entered employment, costs, and average wage at placement. This may, according to the DHN, result in "creaming" of those most likely to secure employment, which would not include displaced homemakers. Displaced homemakers who do get training through JTPA are typically trained for clerical or health field jobs, employment that is not especially lucrative.

Displaced homemakers are also served under the Vocational Education Act of 1963, as amended. This law stipulates that vocational education funds can be used specifically for "persons who had solely been homemakers but who now, because of dissolution of marriage, must seek employment." Amendments in 1976 included sex equity provisions for vocational education.

The Carl D. Perkins Vocational Education Act of 1984 went even further, requiring (1) that 8.5 percent of the state grants be targeted to single parents and homemakers and (2) that special consideration be given to displaced homemakers. The set-aside was apparently responsible for the increase from just over 400 displaced homemaker programs to more than 900 two years later (Miller, 1989). In addition to training, supportive services such as child care and transportation may be provided under the act.

The Displaced Homemakers Network is probably the best source of assistance for women who are displaced. Local programs can refer homemakers to appropriate job training programs funded by the JTPA or the Carl D. Perkins Vocational Education Act. If a local program is unavailable, the national office can often help.

Programs and Policies To Aid Older Women Workers and Job Seekers

Many older women face serious employment obstacles. Age and gender conspire against them, as do their discontinuous work histories and lack of technological skills. Among those who have work, low-wage, female-dominated jobs provide limited opportunity for training and advancement.

Few employment and other programs are specifically targeted at older workers in general; programs for older women are also limited. As reported in Chapter 5, the two most important federal employment programs for older workers are restricted to the economically disadvantaged. One study of experimental Senior Community Service Employment Program (SCSEP) projects noted that divorced or widowed women not yet eligible for social security were among the most desirable participants; these women could be counted on to complete the program successfully, for they were motivated and eager to learn (Centaur Associates, Inc., 1986).

A large number of midlife and older women who need to work resemble displaced homemakers in all respects save that of losing a spouse. For some, the pressure to secure employment may be less pronounced, but others confront the same barriers to employment as displaced homemakers. Unless they are economically disadvantaged or dislocated workers, older women in search of training or employment are not eligible for the main government training programs.

Midlife and older women who are not displaced homemakers obviously do not have access to the very important services offered by displaced homemaker programs. These women must rely on their own informal networks or on the community organizations, women's groups, and local educational institutions that offer counseling, training, and job-seeking assistance to reentry women.

The U.S. Employment Service provides job referrals, counseling, testing, and training referrals to workers, including midlife and older women. While it is often used as a last resort by workers who have exhausted other job-seeking methods, it should not be dismissed out of hand. One study of the Employment Service found that job referrals made by the service resulted in a significant increase in the earnings of older women, mainly because they helped women find work (Johnson et al., 1983).

Skills Enhancement

Adult education programs can provide midlife and older women with some of the skills they need to reenter the labor force or advance on the job. Such women are, however, less likely than men in the same age groups to enroll in vocational education programs for job-related reasons. They are also less likely to be enrolled in courses paid for or provided by employers. Midlife and older women employed in companies that offer or pay for training should insist that they be allowed to take advantage of the offers. They should also be encouraged to weigh the compensation advantages of nontraditional employment and to consider training programs that might help them get jobs in those higher-paying occupations.

Volunteer work can enhance job skills and lead to paid employment, sometimes in the volunteer agency and sometimes elsewhere. Career counselors can advise women on how to translate their volunteer experiences into language appropriate for inclusion in a resumé.

Notes

1. Shifting some of the support burden to future retirees was the goal of the 1983 amendment to the Social Security Act that increased full retirement age. By eliminating mandatory retirement with the 1986 amendments to the Age Discrimination in Employment Act, Congress sought to make it easier for older workers who want to prolong their work lives to do so.
2. The Retirement Equity Act includes two other provisions of considerable importance to women but less directly related to their own work histories. Workers can no longer unilaterally choose not to elect survivor benefits in private pension plans. Also, in the event of the death of a vested worker, the surviving spouse no longer need fear losing eligibility for retirement benefits.

Chapter 7

Employment Opportunities for Older Workers

Expanding employment opportunities [for older workers] is a win, win, win situation.

Peter Libassi, Senior Vice President, The Travelers Companies, 1990

FACTS

- According to a 1984 survey, only 4 percent of more than 350 firms made any effort to discourage retirement before age 65, and those companies did so only for workers with scarce skills or high performance records.

- Many older retirees would prefer part-time work, or "partial retirement," in the same field to total retirement.

- In 1988, three-fifths of all full-time workers but less than one-fifth of part-time workers were covered by pension plans.

- About one in eight full-time workers was on a flexible work schedule in 1985, with older workers having a higher rate of flexible scheduling than all but 35- to 44-year-old workers.

- Contingent workers, including part-time workers, represent between 25 and 35 percent of the work force. Most of these are women and younger workers.

Valuing Older Workers

The Travelers Companies understands the value of older workers. Ever since the early 1970s, this financial services corporation, known primarily for its insurance, has been rehiring its retirees; more recently, it established a job bank of eager-to-work retirees from the Travelers and other insurance companies in the Hartford, Connecticut, area. In Peter Libassi's words, it is "good old American self-interest" that accounts for his company's promotion of older workers—their older workers produce.

Unfortunately, the Travelers older worker program is one of relatively few corporate efforts to take advantage of the skills and talents of America's older adults. In 1984, the Conference Board reported that only 4 percent of the more than 350 firms it surveyed made any effort to discourage retirement before age 65, and those companies did so only for workers with scarce skills or high performance records (Rhine, 1984). Studies by the Commerce Clearing House (1988) and the Conference Board (Axel, 1989) found little evidence that substantial numbers of employers were developing formal programs or policies that would utilize older workers.

Although the true extent of older worker involvement is unknown, there are enough examples of programs and policies to hire, retain, train, and/or retrain older workers to indicate that, at least under certain circumstances, such programs and policies make good business sense. The American Association of Retired Persons' National Older Workers Information System (NOWIS), apparently the only national database of older worker programs (Jessup and Greenberg, 1989), lists about 100 programs nationwide that might serve as models for employers. The resources in Part Two of this volume also highlight older worker model programs and policies that have been tried and found viable. Neither of these lists represents a systematic survey of America's business establishments. Undoubtedly, many policies and programs, especially in small firms, remain hidden.

A clue to why more elderly are not working, when survey responses suggest that some of them want to, may lie in a marked preference for part-time employment *in the same line of work* (see McConnell et al., 1980; National Council on the Aging, 1981). Few employers, however, offer their retirement-age employees the option of moving to part-time work, and while it may be theoretically possible for an older worker to find comparable work in another company, barriers to older worker employment limit the potential for success.

The number of part-time jobs increased at least as rapidly as full-time jobs during the 1980s. Nonetheless, although there are notable exceptions, the overall quality of part-time work in the United States leaves a great deal to be desired. Part-time jobs are frequently low-status jobs that pay less than equivalent full-time work. Fringe benefits may be few or nonexistent. For example, as of 1988, about three-fifths of all full-time workers but less than one-fifth of part-time workers were covered by pension plans (Levitan and Conway, 1988), and many part-time workers lack any health insurance coverage. Opportunities for training or advancement are often nonexistent.

Alternative Work Options

Economist Hilda Kahne (1985) makes a persuasive case for what she calls "new concept" part-time work, which involves increasing not only the number but also the diversity of part-time jobs and enhancing part-time work with better wages, prorated fringe benefits, and opportunities for advancement. As a result, many of the advantages of full-time work would accrue to part-time workers as well. Greater availability of "good" part-time jobs might substantially increase the number of older workers.

If the 40-hour, five-day workweek is the standard work schedule, typical of about two-thirds of all full-time workers (Smith, 1986), then part-time work can be considered an "alternative" option. Kahne's "new concept" part-time work would definitely be an improved alternative. There are, however, other possible options for dividing the workweek, or even the work year or work life, that might appeal to older workers. Although such alternatives are currently available to, or feasible for, a minority of the work force, their numbers are expected to increase.

Alternative Work Schedules

Variations on the standard 9 A.M. to 5 P.M. workday or five-day workweek are known as alternative work schedules, one of the most common of which is flextime or flexitime. Employees on flextime are typically allowed some leeway in their arrival and departure times but are required to be on-site during a core period—for example, between 10 A.M. and 3 P.M. daily. Under this type of arrangement, employees might work from 7 A.M. to 3 P.M. or from 10 A.M. to 6 P.M.; such workers are, if they work 35 or more hours during the week, considered full-time workers, but flexible hours can also apply to part-time work.

Flextime may be more or less flexible, depending on the needs and desires of the business. Employees might be granted the right to set arrival and departure times but required to adhere to whatever alternative schedule they select. Or employees might be allowed to vary arrival and departure times as they choose, as long as they work the contracted number of hours during a pay period. The added flexibility of this latter arrangement has obvious advantages over a more rigid alternative schedule, in that workers can handle unforeseen emergencies. Overall, only about one in eight full-time workers was on a flexible work schedule in 1985, with older workers having a higher rate of flexible scheduling than all but 35- to 44-year-old workers. Somewhat surprisingly, flexible schedules are more common among men than among women (Mellor, 1986).

Companies with flexible work schedules may benefit from decreased tardiness and absenteeism on the part of their workers, more efficient scheduling of work, and added hours of service to the public; however, flexible work schedules can also increase time-keeping demands, require greater supervision, and increase certain costs associated with longer hours of operation (Mellor, 1986).

Another alternative work schedule is the compressed work-week, which allows workers to compress their required hours of work into a shorter period, perhaps by working four 10-hour days. As is the case for those on flextime, workers on compressed schedules have a block of nonwork hours—perhaps an extra day per week—that can be used for personal or family business, going to school, doing volunteer work, or engaging in other activities.

Although there is some evidence of compressed part-time schedules (Smith, 1986), it is typically the full-time job that gets compressed. Therefore, it is doubtful that compressed schedules, even if widely available, would appeal to large numbers of older workers, given their expressed interest in part-time work. Even older workers who want to work full-time might find compressed workweeks too demanding. Such schedules could, however, provide middle-aged workers with a concentrated period of time to test new employment or retirement opportunities or to obtain training for new careers.

For some employees who work fewer than 40 hours per week, the workweek has been expanding (Smith, 1986); that is, part-time work is being spread over more days per week. Older workers may have been affected by this development if they work in retail establishments.

Job Sharing

In job sharing, two (or possibly more) workers split one job, dividing the work equally or along some other lines. Decisions about how to assign responsibilities and complete tasks are typically left to the job sharers themselves; each partner might, for example, work 2.5 days per week, two weeks per month, or half the year. Academics have been known to share a single teaching load, with one partner working one semester and then switching with the other partner.

Workers clearly gain from job-sharing arrangements. Such arrangements can be a boon to women who want to retain job skills and recency of employment while devoting time to their families or other pursuits. Young workers stand to benefit from the transfer of the skills and knowledge of more experienced partners. In many instances, job sharing can meet older workers' desire for part-time but similar work.

Job-sharing advantages accrue to employers as well. When job sharers bring different skills and abilities to their jobs, employers increase the available expertise and abilities of their work forces. Job-sharing arrangements might make it easier for employers to retain valued employees, such as highly skilled older workers or young mothers who want to work less but still maintain some attachment to the work force. Older job sharers who transfer skills and workplace knowledge to new employees help the employer as well as the new worker. Finally, job sharers can also efficiently fill in for their partners when necessary, thus minimizing disruptions due to illness, family problems, vacations, or other absences.

Creating new approaches to employment might reveal to companies a surprisingly wide range of jobs that can be split or shared in some way; in many instances, however, it is the employees themselves who convince their employers to give job sharing a try.

Work Sharing

Although it qualifies as an alternative work option, work sharing is generally not an option that workers would chose if other alternatives—namely, continued full-time work—were available. To avoid layoffs during recessions and slack periods when there are simply too many employees for the available work, work may be spread over the available work force. All employees might end up working fewer hours than they normally do (e.g., 32 hours per week rather than 40).

Because older workers are overrepresented in industries vulnerable to layoffs, they could find themselves in work-sharing situations. Work sharing is not, however, particularly common; nor, all other things being equal, is work sharing likely to be attractive to many employees.

Flexplace or Alternative Work Sites

Technological advances have made it easier to shift work away from a centralized location to alternative sites. Computer terminals may be set up in satellite offices in the same town, in other cities, or even in lower-wage countries. The home can also serve as an alternative work site, and home-based employment, which has its staunch advocates and equally vocal opponents, is nothing new. Using Bureau of Labor Statistics data, Horvath (1986) estimated that as of 1985, about 8.4 million people regularly worked at home for at least eight hours per week as part of their primary job.

Definitions of who qualifies as a home-based worker vary and can be imprecise; the home-based worker can include anyone from a woman who babysits a few hours a week to someone who operates a full-time consulting business. Work done at home may range from knitting winter clothing to filing insurance claims to writing newspaper columns. While much work is anything but "high tech," the drop in prices for personal computers and communications equipment is certainly a contributing factor in the continuing expansion of home-based work.

Advantages of Home-Based Work

Just as home-based work has been promoted as a solution to child-care problems of parents of young children, middle-aged and other adults may find it easier to combine paid work in the home with caregiving responsibilities to parents, spouses, or other relatives. Home-based work can also be attractive to the elderly and to handicapped workers who might have difficulties commuting to an on-site job.

Home workers set their own hours and generally decide when and how much to work. Assuming they can afford to pass up some projects, they can refuse unappealing or inconvenient assignments. Home-based workers have fewer commuting problems than their office-based peers, and many work-related expenses, such as transportation, clothing, and meals away from home, are eliminated or reduced. Workers who are relatively immobile may find working at home the only feasible work alternative.

Persons whose skills are especially marketable may be in a position to negotiate compensation packages comparable to what they would receive as wage and salary employees. Some older workers may not have to worry as much about the disadvantages of home-based work—for them, the convenience of working at home may outweigh any disadvantages. They may, for example, have adequate income and benefits from other sources and not need health insurance, fringe benefits, promotion opportunities, or on-the-job social contacts.

Disadvantages of Home-Based Work

It is important to distinguish between the home-based worker who is voluntarily self-employed and the one who is treated as self-employed but who works at home exclusively for one employer. Home-based workers who are, or who are treated as, independent contractors are not on anyone's payroll and are ineligible for the statutory and fringe benefits provided to regular workers. As contract workers, for example, they are not eligible for workers' compensation or unemployment insurance (Christensen and Murphree, 1988).

It is clear that this work arrangement saves employers money, and the arrangement may be fine for some home-based workers, particularly professionals. But home-based workers must "buy" their own fringe benefits if they are to have them, and they must also pay both the employer's and the employee's portion of the social security payroll tax, which amounts to a hefty deduction from earnings. The lack of pension coverage is especially troublesome, although some home-based workers might be able to afford individual retirement or Keough accounts on their own.

Home workers are generally paid only for completed products, such as the paper that has been typed or the data that have been entered into a computer. This may seem fair on the surface, but it becomes inequitable when home-based workers are compared with their office counterparts. Much office work encompasses "down time" (time spent on the telephone, talking with co-workers, waiting for a job assignment) for which office employees are paid. Whether down time should be compensated is debatable, but, in any case, the fact that home workers do not get paid for it is one of home work's disadvantages.

Moreover, the home-based worker is excluded from the important social network of the office and may miss out on learning about or being considered for promotions and training opportunities. One possible solution to this problem is to require home-based workers to come to a central office periodically for meetings, conferences, or updates.

Labor unions worry about the exploitation of home workers, whose work contracts and working conditions cannot be monitored adequately. Pointing to the unsafe, unhealthy work environments of so many of the immigrant home workers earlier in this century, they argue that such work should not be permitted. Others worry that home-based workers can easily be taken advantage of, especially if their English-speaking abilities and knowledge of the law are limited. Enforcement of health and safety standards, for example, with regard to heat, lighting, ventilation, and the like, would be virtually impossible, if, indeed, government were considered to have a role in such enforcement.

Proponents of home-based employment, however, contend that this type of work offers a reasonable alternative for persons who, for whatever reasons, cannot, do not want to, or will not work in a plant or office.

Contingent Work

Contingent work, which is viewed as "marginal" employment, commonly means anything other than full-time, permanent wage or salary employment. It typically includes part-time employment, moonlighting, self-employment, temporary work, and employee leasing (leased employees are persons who work for an agency that leases them out to other businesses). However, even though part-time work generally provides less in terms of wages and benefits than full-time work, many part-time workers have long-term, stable relationships with their employers. Similarly, many self-employed workers, such as doctors, accountants, or financial advisers, are anything but "marginally" attached to the labor force.

The term *contingent* may therefore be more appropriate to employment where a lack of job security and a variation in hours worked are the chief characteristics (Polivka and Nardone, 1989). While contingent workers tend to have short-term assignments, contingent work does not necessarily mean short-term employment. Contingent workers may be hired for long-term renewable assignments, but there is no guarantee of continued employment. Polivka and Nardone contend that contingent workers can be viewed as "on demand," essentially at the mercy of the varying needs of employers.

Contingent workers represent a minority of the work force—perhaps 25 to 35 percent when part-timers are included and far fewer when they are not (Belous, 1989). On any one day, an estimated 900,000 workers are employed by temporary agencies (Conway, 1990). Certain companies, particularly in manufacturing and low-wage service industries, hire a disproportionate share of contingent workers. More than half of agency temporaries are in administrative support, while another 25 percent work as operators, fabricators, and laborers (Conway, 1990). However, the list of temporaries is expanding and now includes such diverse occupations as health care specialists, computer scientists, and engineers. Firms may hire retired executives as temporary consultants (Polivka and Nardone, 1989), and a growing number of companies seem to be hiring their own retirees on a temporary basis. These workers are considered contingent workers.

Women and younger workers predominate among the contingent work force, where wages are low and benefits often are nonexistent. Temporaries, for example, earned an average of only $6.42 per hour in 1987; however, earnings variations are wide. Professionals do quite well. At $24.74 per hour, engineers had the highest earnings among contingent workers in 1987, followed by computer systems analysts/scientists at $18.17. General office clerks earned $5.11; word processors, $9.46; and construction workers, $3.72 (Williams, 1989), barely above the minimum wage. Less than one-fourth of temporaries work in firms with health benefits (Polivka and Nardone, 1989).

Workers who choose contingent work do so for a variety of reasons: they have other responsibilities that preclude full-time or even permanent part-time work, they want only occasional or temporary work, or they like the diversity of placements. Contingent work makes it easier for employers to remain flexible in the face of economic uncertainties, to respond to unanticipated or special orders, to meet anticipated peak or seasonal demands, and to avoid layoffs when there is too little work to go around. Contingent workers can also save companies a great deal of money, especially when employers pay contingent workers less than they pay their permanent workers and/or provide few or no fringe benefits.

Although growth of the contingent work force is not necessarily expected to be explosive (Plewes, 1988), a number of trends point to its expansion. These include the growth of the service sector, which is amenable to such work, continued work force automation (Axel, 1988b), and efforts to accommodate women workers with children and possibly older workers. Global competition, threatened mergers, and takeovers may also make employers reluctant to add to their permanent staffs unless absolutely necessary. And while contingent work has some disadvantages for employers, the lack of benefit expenses enhances its attractiveness.

The advantages of part-time and contingent work may be greater for older workers who have less need of certain benefits. It also allows workers to set their work hours below the social security earnings ceiling or below pension restrictions. Workers can refuse to accept assignments that they do not like or are too busy to handle. Contingent work may also be attractive to older workers with specialized skills who command higher wages, to persons wanting less than full-time regular work, and to reentry women who need to brush up on job skills and gain some recent work experience. Older workers may also find fewer employment barriers because contingent work requires only a short-term commitment from employers.

Job Transfer and Job Redesign

Other alternative work options include *job transfer* (a shift to a less arduous or stressful job) and *job redesign* (which may involve a change in the work environment, e.g., better lighting). These options enable employers both to retain older workers who might otherwise leave the labor force and to accommodate handicapped workers. Changes in the conditions that make continued work difficult or unappealing can help keep workers productive longer.

How many employers accommodate workers through job redesign or transfer is not known, but the numbers are probably low. Root and Zarrugh (U.S. Congress, 1985c) found that redesigning the environment was rare; when it occurred, it tended not to be the result of a company- or systemwide reexamination of job structures but a response to the needs of particular individuals. In fact, most job transfer and work environment changes probably result from workers who "select" themselves out of jobs they are no longer capable of performing. McConnell et al. (1980) found relatively little interest in job transfer or redesign, particularly if it were to involve a cut in pay.

Phased Retirement

A reduction in work hours that allows workers to ease into retirement while receiving pension income and earnings is known as phased or partial retirement. This form of retirement may be in the form of sabbaticals, longer vacations, reduced workweeks, or spreading less work over more time.

Estimates on the number of formal phased retirement policies in the United States vary widely—from about 3 percent (Rhine, 1984) to 25 percent of companies (Paul, 1987), although the lower figure is probably more accurate. Root and Zarrugh (U.S. Congress, 1985c) found that transitions to retirement often involve a form of part-time employment, often with a new firm, but this does not occur as a result of formal phased retirement policies.

Perhaps the most extensive and well-known system of partial retirement is in Sweden, which introduced a national partial retirement option in 1976. Workers between the ages of 60 and 65 may reduce their work hours and continue to earn income while receiving a portion of their pensions. The wage replacement level is currently set at 65 percent (Berglind, 1989). To qualify, workers must have a certain amount of recent work experience. Under the partial pension scheme, employees are allowed to reduce work hours by at least 5 hours per week, but must work a minimum of 17 hours per week. Sweden's partial retirement program has been extremely popular.

Transitional Employment

While phased or partial retirement programs may be uncommon in the United States, a transitional period between work and retirement is not as unusual as some observers believe. In fact, many workers seem to have experienced partial retirement before full retirement. For example, Quinn (1981) observed that 12 percent of the self-employed white men in the first wave of the Retirement History Survey and 5 percent of the wage and salary workers called themselves partially retired, proportions that probably rose over time. Sum et al. (1988: 5) found that "about one third of all career jobs end by age 55 and almost half by age 60, yet less than one in nine workers has retired by the latter age."

Clearly, substantial numbers of workers are moving on to transitional or bridge employment for a number of years before permanently leaving the labor force. On the positive side, this shows that older workers can find employment, but on the negative side, most of the transitional work seems to involve changes in occupation and industry and lower wages.

Self-Employment

Although most of the discussion in this section has focused on wage and salary workers, the growth in home-based and contingent work suggests that self-employment may become increasingly common. Silvestri and Lukasiewicz (1989) project that self-employment will increase by some 10 percent by the turn of the century. The largest share of this growth is expected to be among executive and managerial workers, followed by service workers and those in professional specialty occupations. If these projections stand up, there should be an increase in older self-employed workers as well.

Some workers retire from wage and salary employment and move into self-employment, perhaps capitalizing on a hobby or side business interest. Most older self-employed individuals, however, seem to have aged as self-employed workers. For example, in an analysis of new social security beneficiaries, Iams (1987) found that more older men switched to self-employment from wage and salary work than vice versa, but the net increase in self-employment was very small. Most older self-employed social security recipients had been self-employed before they began collecting benefits.

Starting a business in retirement is very different from continuing to work as an entrepreneur. An older worker on a pension may be in a position to become self-employed, but investing in one's own business is a risky venture. Few older persons have the liquid assets that many new businesses demand; those who do must be able to afford to lose them. Several books listed in Part Two of this volume advise readers on the pros and cons of starting businesses.

Volunteer Work

Volunteer activity is really an alternative to work, rather than an alternative work option. It does, however, provide almost limitless opportunities to utilize one's talents and abilities while contributing substantially to the community. Volunteers can generally dictate what they will do, when they will do it, and for how long. As such, they are free of many of the strictures of paid workers.

Nonprofit organizations, social service agencies, schools, and churches are among the institutions that use volunteers. Some states have offices of volunteer service and may even, as Maryland does, publish directories of volunteer opportunities. Local newspapers and public libraries can also direct willing volunteers to places in need of assistance.

ACTION is the federal government's domestic volunteer agency. Almost 30 years old, ACTION oversees a number of full- and part-time volunteer programs, some specifically designed for low-income elderly people and some that pay stipends. In one ACTION program, VISTA volunteers, who must be at least 18 years of age, work in locally sponsored projects around the country on a full-time, full-year basis for one to two years to alleviate poverty in the United States. They may deal with illiteracy, drug abuse prevention, child abuse, and neighborhood revitalization. Under the Retired Senior Volunteer Program (RSVP), which operates through grants to local public and private nonprofit organizations, retired older persons volunteer in a wide range of community service projects, aiding youth or operating runaway shelters, for example. Low-income persons 60 and over are eligible to become "Senior Companions" to other adults with special needs in an effort to help them remain independent. Persons 60 and older may also be eligible to join the Foster Grandparent Program, where they work with children who may be retarded, disabled, institutionalized, disturbed, or abused, or who suffer from other problems. Low-income grandparents receive a stipend. (For ACTION addresses, see Chapter 9.)

Established in 1964 and funded largely through the U.S. Small Business Administration, the Service Corps of Retired Executives (SCORE) is a volunteer organization that provides American businesspeople with free business counseling and training. More than 13,000 SCORE volunteers, the vast majority of whom are retired, offer their business and managerial expertise to small businesses at no charge in about 750 counseling locations around the country. Volunteers are unpaid, although they are reimbursed for travel. Persons starting small businesses can tap into this network of information and practical advice on virtually every aspect of running a business.

Although most volunteers are not seeking to be paid, many do apply for paid employment when positions become available in the agencies for which they are volunteering. Volunteer activities can also serve as a means of developing skills, learning new work force technology, and obtaining training that will lead to paid employment elsewhere.

According to Riley and Riley (1986), only a minority of elderly engage in unpaid volunteer work, although there are many examples of successful older volunteers. For instance, in Brookline, Massachusetts, which has a high proportion of elderly people and a high proportion of minority schoolchildren, older persons "were recruited as volunteers for tutoring, for teaching English as a second language, and for the sharing of life experiences" (Moody, 1986: 202). Moody cites "striking success" in recruiting the elderly as school volunteers across the country. Certainly, older volunteers can perform much-needed functions in fiscally strapped and deteriorating school systems.

In *Older Americans: An Untapped Resource,* the National Committee on Careers for Older Americans (1979) identifies numerous ways older persons can serve their communities, either as paid workers or as volunteers. These include, but are by no means limited to, the following: tutoring the functionally illiterate, preparing young persons for the world of work, serving as health outreach workers and assisting discharged patients, aiding the deinstitutionalized, working as paralegals or home health aides, doing home repairs for the elderly, and serving as surrogate parents for unwed mothers. In 1979, the committee recommended that public and private organizations work to achieve "the opening up of broader opportunities for the productive involvement of older persons . . . simultaneously in three areas: (1) paid employment, (2) self-employment, and (3) volunteer services" (p. 57). That recommendation is as valid today as when it was made.

Organizations can make an effort to recruit older volunteers through targeted publicity campaigns and by making these workers feel a true part of the volunteer association. Recruitment efforts might involve training where appropriate, transportation and/or financial assistance with transportation if necessary, and reimbursement for out-of-pocket expenses.

What Employers Are Doing

Businesses turn to older workers for a number of reasons: they are faced with a shortage of qualified workers, they believe older employees have something to offer, they seek to enhance their corporate images, and/or they hope to avoid age-discrimination lawsuits. Programs or policies that foster the employment of older workers may be introduced, as Jessup and Greenberg (1989) suggest, to stabilize a young and mobile work force, as a "pretest" or preparation for the older work force of the future, or to develop a work force that deals well with customers.

Financial disincentives to continued employment may be strong and, when coupled with health problems, boredom, job dissatisfaction, or some other retirement push, can undermine efforts to encourage workers to stay on the job. Employers have been taking a second look at some of these disincentives. Although the numbers may still be few, corporate examples of virtually every alternative work option can be cited. A number of these follow.

Older Workers in the Fast-Food Industry

Explosive growth in the fast-food industry, combined with a shortage of the young workers on whom the industry has traditionally depended, has motivated establishments like Kentucky Fried Chicken and McDonald's to look at new sources of labor, including the elderly. McDonald's, in particular, has mounted a campaign to attract older workers by offering part-time and flexible schedules, higher wages, and more attractive fringe benefit packages.

McDonald's works in partnership with contracting state government agencies, with both McDonald's and the contracting agency contributing money for administrative and operating expenses. The McMasters Program trains workers 55 and older for four weeks under a special coach. In addition, a workshop trains managers in effective ways of dealing with older workers and dispels myths about such workers. A video of the workshop is available for viewing by supervisors around the country.

The potential for employment at McDonald's and similar establishments should be considerable; food preparation work is among the occupations whose numbers are increasing the most. However, it seems doubtful that fast-food establishments will be first choice for large numbers of older people looking for employment. On a part-time basis, the work is perhaps less stressful than it is on a full-time basis, but it is still arduous work. And any preference for postretirement employment that is similar, if not identical, to preretirement work would seem to rule out this line of work for many potential older workers. Nonetheless, McDonald's and Kentucky Fried Chicken are pointing toward the future for many service establishments, and how well they succeed in attracting and keeping older workers—and under what conditions—should be of great interest to other businesses.

Corporate-Community Partnerships

IBM's Community Service Career Program (CSCP), begun in 1988, offers retirees the opportunity to apply highly honed skills in new and perhaps stimulating ways. Qualified IBM employees who are eligible for retirement can consider "second careers" in nonprofit community-based organizations. IBM's stated objective for this program is to help meet community needs while providing selected employees a postretirement alternative.

Under CSCP, IBM employees and nonprofit agencies enter into a contractual agreement that guarantees full-time employment for at least two years at not less than $10,000 per year. IBM, which must approve the contract, pays retirement benefits and a percentage of base salary for two years. IBM candidates bring expertise to a wide range of community issues: AIDS, affirmative action, literacy, substance abuse, and employment preparation. IBM's CSCP workers must agree not to go to work for a competitor for at least two years, by which time it might be assumed that technology will have so changed that the knowledge of IBM a former employee would bring to a competitor will be outdated.

Temporary Service Agencies

Businesses have long hired workers through temporary service agencies on a short-term basis. They may do so through many companies, such as Kelly Services, a temporary employment agency that has made hiring of older workers, particularly women, a management priority. Older workers have been targeted because of their interest in the type of work Kelly offers—temporary and part-time. Kelly not only recruits but trains its workers in using new office machinery.

Retiree Job Banks

Despite the appeal of temporary employees, some companies are not satisfied with the sometimes uneven quality of these workers and prefer to hire retired workers on their own. A case in point is F. W. Dodge Company, a data-gathering firm based in Kansas with employees around the country. Dissatisfaction with the use of temporaries led the company to redesign some positions as part-time jobs and to recruit retirees to fill them. Of the redesigned jobs in 120 cities, 90 percent were filled by retirees in their 60s (American Association of Retired Persons, 1988).

Some companies have set up job banks of their own and other retirees. Job banks are essentially rosters of individuals, often but not always company retirees, who are available for short-term and frequently short-notice assignments. Retiree banks have become numerous enough to warrant a study by the Conference Board (Axel, 1989). The Conference Board observes that job banks "appear to be prevalent in labor intensive firms (such as banks and insurance companies) and in some manufacturing settings where particular skills are sought for technical production jobs" (Axel, 1989: viii). The jobs available to rehired retirees tend to be clerical, data-entry, or word-processing jobs, which use skills that, once learned, are easily transferable. Some firms, however, rehire their retired professionals on a short-term or temporary basis.

Job banks make more sense in large corporations with an adequate supply of retirees that can justify the costs of maintaining such banks. Smaller firms can get by with more informal approaches to rehiring retirees, can rely on temporary agencies, or can even consider developing a job bank of retirees from several related businesses.

Some businesses may have restrictions on how many hours, if any, former retirees may work without forfeiting pension benefits and so may need to modify their pension plans to permit retirees to work. An alternative is to contract with an outside agency that handles the payroll for retired workers.

One of the best-known job banks is that of the Travelers Companies, mentioned at the beginning of this chapter. Travelers maintains a roster of several hundred of its retirees. Travelers retirees may work 960 hours in any 12-month period without losing pension benefits. At the present time, there are about 750 registrants in the bank, and perhaps 250 retirees are working in any one week.

Travelers retirees are paid in the middle of a job's salary range and are thus probably better paid than they would be if they worked for a temporary agency. They are eligible for fringe benefits, work in a familiar environment, and usually engage in work with which they are at least somewhat familiar. Because retirees out of work for as short a time as two years are often not technologically current, Travelers also opened its training program to them. According to Travelers Vice President Libassi, the job bank saves the company $1.5 million per year in temporary agency fees. In fact, the bank has been so successful that it has been opened up to retirees of other companies in the Hartford area.

Although administrative support jobs seem most common among retired temporary workers, some jobs are highly technical. For example, Aerospace, a nonprofit firm engaged in national security research and development projects, brings retirees, including many engineers, back to the work force as "casual" employees who can work fewer than 20 hours a week and still receive full pension benefits.

Flextime and Flexplace

Control Data Corporation, which manufactures and services large computers in plants around the world, offers flextime schedules and flexplace opportunities (computer work at home). It, too, rehires retirees for special projects and maintains a pool of temporary part-timers and its own job bank. Training and retraining opportunities are available, as are unpaid leaves of absence with benefits for up to 12 months to pursue special interests. These programs are not restricted to older workers but may be of particular interest to them.

Bankers Life also maintains a retiree employment pool that promotes older worker employment. As of 1984, about 30 percent of the workers in its home office were 65 or older (U.S. Congress, 1985c).

Older "independent contractors" are common at Texas Refinery Corporation, a Fort Worth business with sales forces around the world. The company has an age-neutral hiring policy, so older workers are common. Those workers, who are highly regarded by management, may work either part- or full-time.

Phased Retirement

Polaroid's policy of "rehearsal retirement" allows unpaid leaves of absence for up to six months to workers 55 and older. Neither pay nor benefits are available to workers in this program, which probably limits its appeal, although workers may purchase their own benefits. Through tapered or phased retirement, Polaroid workers who meet certain requirements can reduce the hours they work by the day, week, or month over a period of years. Wages are reduced to compensate for reduced hours and pension credits are prorated; however, full medical benefits are paid.

For more than a decade, Varian, a high-tech firm, has offered a phased retirement program whereby workers within two years of retirement can, as long as they work 20 hours per week, reduce their workweeks to four days in the first year and three days in the second. Salaries and fringe benefits are prorated, but only a handful of the company's employees take advantage of the program in any one year. The prorated salary and corresponding lower pension benefit might be contributing factors, but, according to Kahne (1985), workers can make voluntary contributions to the pension plan to offset any drop.

John Deere formerly had a long-standing phased retirement program, but gave it up because of declining business demand. Other phased retirement plans have been provided by Towle, a small silver firm, which let workers with 30 years of service take off an extra 40 days during the four months prior to retirement. Participants received one extra day a week during the first month, two during the second month, and so on (Kahne, 1985). New England Mutual Life has also offered extra paid vacation to workers between the ages of 62 and 64. In all cases, some restrictions as to age and years of service have applied.

Combining Programs

No highlighting of older worker programs and policies should fail to mention the Grumman Corporation, which has long promoted the employment of older workers. Grumman hires its retirees as full- or part-time workers, maintains and encourages participation in a company skills bank, hires temporary retirees through temporary agencies, and, perhaps most important, conducts regular age audits of its work force to identify places of over- or underrepresentation of older workers.

Pioneer Programs

Part-time and temporary work, alternative work schedules, flexplace, and phased retirement programs are among the ways employers have responded to the needs and preferences of their employees. The work force of the 1990s and beyond will be increasingly diverse, and employers who hope to compete for the best workers will have to rethink their approach to the traditional workweek. In addition, many midlife and older workers will continue to want good, full-time work, and others will require training and retraining to remain marketable.

A number of companies in the rapidly growing service and information industries, as well as in manufacturing, have begun to revise their employment policies with recent and projected work force changes in mind.

Who are the some of the pioneers?

Aerospace, for hiring its own retirees and allowing them to work for up to 999 hours per year without forfeiting pension benefits.

Control Data Corporation, for its midlife worker training and retraining programs, one of which was designed to encourage the retention of those workers in new jobs within the corporation; for its job bank; and for its flextime and flexplace work options.

Crouse-Hinds ECM, for its policy of retaining valued employees, including older ones, and for retraining them through several major training programs that have a variety of objectives, such as learning new technologies, earning a two-year college degree, and continued learning through postretirement college courses.

F.W. Dodge Company, for the recruitment of retirees for permanent, part-time positions.

General Dynamics, for assessing the physical abilities of employees to ensure optimum performance through the appropriate matching of abilities and job requirements.

Grumman Corporation, for aggressively pursuing anti-age-discrimination policies; for promoting the use of age audits in the work force; for actively recruiting its retirees to return to work (and for rehiring those retirees on a full- or part-time basis, with variable or flexible work schedules); for its midlife career development programs; and for its efforts to hire and provide training to older women.

Kelly Services, Inc., for special recruitment efforts targeted at older temporary workers.

Minnesota Title, for its job-sharing program.

Mutual of Omaha, for eliminating age restrictions in hiring new workers before such restrictions were eliminated by Age Discrimination in Employment Act amendments.

Polaroid, for a variety of retirement options, including phased retirement and rehearsal retirement.

Teledyne Wisconsin Motor, for a transitional retirement program that includes added vacation time, additional life insurance, and an increase in pension benefits for participants in the program.

Texas Refinery Corporation, for an age-neutral recruitment policy resulting in a sales force with a high proportion of workers aged 60 and older.

The Travelers Companies, for developing and promoting a job bank of retirees; for expanding the job bank roster to retirees from other companies; for revising its pension system so as not to penalize part-year retired workers; for retraining retired workers returning to temporary work; and for staying attuned to the needs and preferences of its older workers.

Varian Associates, for a retirement transition program that allows employees to begin reducing their workweeks up to three years before they plan to retire.

The Future of Older Worker Programs

Programs such as those cited above are rarely created for altruistic reasons. Much of the interest in contingent workers, for example, is the result of economic uncertainties and corporate downsizing. Corporate downsizing also results in early retirement incentive programs, which may induce workers to retire when they would prefer to remain at work. The recent Conference Board study on job banks reports that "since early 1986, a total of 15,000 people at IBM were persuaded to retire, and 80 percent of them held jobs that were eliminated." Early retirement at another firm led to a drop from 42 to 38 in the average age of the work force (Axel, 1989: 2).

The number of older worker programs in the NOWIS database today is below what it was in the early 1980s when NOWIS was housed at the University of Michigan. As a result of budgetary cutbacks, mergers, and other factors, a number of programs no longer existed at the end of the decade. For some of the same reasons, some of the firms mentioned in this chapter are curtailing their older worker programs.

Over the short run, older worker programs and policies will probably expand slowly. Many more employers need to be educated about the advantages of employing older workers, and financial and other disincentives to continued employment will need to be addressed. Nonetheless, although hard data on the costs and benefits of older worker programs and policies are lacking, many of the ones discussed in this chapter have been and continue to be successful. With the expected decrease in the number of younger workers in the coming years, more programs and policies will be developed to hire, retain, and retrain older workers.

Chapter 8

Directions for
the Future

We are witnessing the end of yesterday's retirement.

Dychtwald and Flower, 1989: 207

Due to slower economic growth, fewer new job opportunities, and a changing economy—older workers will be continually pressured to leave work prior to the termination of their productive years.

Schuster, Kaspin, and Miller, Syracuse University, 1987: i

FACTS

- Midlife and older labor force participants, most of them middle-aged, will account for more than 70 percent of the projected labor force growth between 1988 and 2000.

- Over the same period, the number of workers between the ages of 20 and 34 will decline by nearly 4.7 million.

- Overall, the 20 fastest growing occupations will account for less than 9 percent of the projected occupational growth between 1988 and 2000.

- Employer-provided or -supported training can be expected to increase in the future as businesses respond to the limitations of younger labor force entrants.

Midlife Workers Will Account for Most Labor Force Growth

The Bureau of Labor Statistics (BLS) projects that through the end of the century, the labor force participation rate of older men and women will continue to drop—slightly in the case of women but by almost two percentage points in the case of men (Fullerton, 1989). Middle-aged women, however, are expected to show further increases in labor force participation (from 69 percent to 76.5 percent for women 45 to 54, and from 43.5 percent to 49 percent for women 55 to 64). The rate for middle-aged men is also projected to rise, mainly as a result of a 1.1 percentage point increase in the participation rate of the 55 to 64 age group.

BLS projections translate into an increase of more than 14 million more midlife and older labor force participants, most of them middle-aged, who will account for more than 70 percent of the projected labor force growth between 1988 and 2000. Over the same period, the labor force composed of persons between the ages of 20 and 34 will, if projections hold up, decline by nearly 4.7 million. Coupled with these changes is a projected growth of some 18 million in the number of new jobs over the 1990s (Silvestri and Lukasiewicz, 1989).

Despite this growth and a dwindling supply of younger workers, employers may look to other sources of labor besides older workers: if women of childbearing age had participated in the labor force at the same rate as men (76.4 percent instead of 57.4 percent) in 1989, the labor force would have been larger by nearly 19 million workers and job seekers. Millions of women work less than full-time and might be encouraged to increase their work hours, thus adding to the supply. Incentives such as job-guaranteed parental leave, employer-provided day care, and flexible work schedules might increase women's labor force participation or work experience rates well above current projections.

Most of the new job opportunities will be in the service sector. Conventional wisdom says that service sector employment should be especially appropriate for older workers because jobs in that sector are assumed not to be especially physically demanding. While that may be true, it should be stressed that many service sector jobs (e.g., nursing, food-counter work) can be both arduous and stressful. Also, some research suggests that, like anything else, successful employment in the service sector is less a function of age than it is of training and prior experience in similar work (Shilkoff, 1978).

Where the Jobs Will Be

There are at least two ways of evaluating occupational growth. One is to look at the "fastest-growing" occupations, the top 20 of which can be seen in Table 8.1. *Fastest-growing* refers to percentage increases; the table shows, for example, that the number of paralegals will increase by 75 percent by the year 2000, while the number of medical assistants will grow by 70 percent. These seem like substantial increases, but because there were only 83,000 paralegals nationwide in 1988, a 75 percent increase will add only 62,000 jobs to the economy by the end of the 1990s. Similarly, only 104,000 more medical assistants are projected, despite the 70 percent increase. Overall, the 20 fastest-growing occupations will account for less than 9 percent of the projected occupational growth between 1988 and 2000.

In contrast, *largest projected job growth* refers to numbers of jobs, and the 20 occupations with the largest projected job growth will account for almost 40 percent of occupational growth. Table 8.2 reveals, for example, that the number of retail salespersons will increase by some three-quarters of a million, a sizable number of new jobs that represents only a 19 percent increase.

Thus, job growth alone will not provide older workers with better-paying lines of work unless they are employed in those jobs already. Furthermore, the 20 occupations that will produce the most jobs, as demonstrated in Table 8.2, are not among the more desirable, at least as of 1988. Many of them (e.g., janitor, waiter, cashier, truck driver, food counter worker, and general office clerk) would probably rank near the bottom of a job seeker's list of priority positions, if given the choice. That probably holds for both young and old, but as Schulz (1988b: 2) has

Table 8.1   Fastest Growing Occupations, 1988–2000[a]
(in thousands)

| OCCUPATION | EMPLOYMENT | | CHANGE IN EMPLOYMENT 1988–2000 | |
	1988	Projected, 2000	Number	Percentage
Paralegals	83	145	62	75.3
Medical assistants	149	253	104	70.0
Home health aides	236	397	160	67.9
Radiologic technologists and technicians	132	218	87	66.0
Data processing equipment repairers	71	115	44	61.2
Medical records technicians	47	75	28	59.9
Medical secretaries	207	327	120	58.0
Physical therapists	68	107	39	57.0
Surgical technologists	35	55	20	56.4
Operations research analysts	55	85	30	55.4
Securities and financial services sales workers	200	309	109	54.8
Travel agents	142	219	77	54.1
Computer systems analysts	403	617	214	53.3
Physical and corrective therapy assistants	39	60	21	52.5
Social welfare service aides	91	138	47	51.5
Occupational therapists	33	48	16	48.8
Computer programmers	519	769	250	48.1
Human services workers	118	171	53	44.9
Respiratory therapists	56	79	23	41.3
Correction officers and jailers	186	262	76	40.8

Source: Silvestri and Lukasiewicz, 1989: Table 5.
[a]Moderate growth alternative.

said, as we age, "most of us become very choosy about the work we do." Older workers with retirement income prospects can afford to be choosy about the jobs in Table 8.2.

Not only are many of the "new" jobs in Table 8.2 intrinsically unrewarding, they are poorly paid as well. The median earnings of full-time workers in about two-thirds of them were less than the median earnings of all full-time workers in 1988—that is, less than $20,000 per year.

Table 8.2   Occupations with Largest Projected Job Growth, 1988–2000[a]
(in thousands)

| | EMPLOYMENT | | CHANGE IN EMPLOYMENT 1988–2000 | |
| | | | | |
OCCUPATION	1988	Projected, 2000	Number	Percentage
Salespersons, retail	3,834	4,564	730	19.0
Registered nurses	1,577	2,190	613	38.8
Janitors and cleaners, including maids and housekeeping cleaners	2,895	3,450	556	19.2
Waiters and waitresses	1,786	2,337	551	30.9
General managers and top executives	3,030	3,509	479	15.8
General office clerks	2,519	2,974	455	18.1
Secretaries, except medical and legal	2,903	3,288	385	13.2
Nursing aides, orderlies, and attendants	1,184	1,562	378	31.9
Truck drivers, light and heavy	2,399	2,768	369	15.4
Receptionists and information clerks	833	1,164	331	39.8
Cashiers	2,310	2,614	304	13.2
Guards	795	1,050	256	32.2
Computer programmers	519	769	250	48.1
Food counter, fountain, and related	1,626	1,866	240	14.7
Food preparation workers	1,027	1,260	234	22.8
Licensed practical nurses	626	855	229	36.6
Teachers, secondary school	1,164	1,388	224	19.2
Computer systems analysts	403	617	214	53.3
Accountants and auditors	963	1,174	211	22.0
Teachers, kindergarten and elementary school	1,359	1,567	208	15.3

Source: Silvestri and Lukasiewicz, 1989: Table 6.
[a]Moderate growth alternative.

On the positive side, relatively few of the jobs in Table 8.2 can be exported; they are labor intensive and must be performed on-site. And while technology may change or improve the nature of those jobs, it is unlikely to eliminate them.

The majority of the occupations in Table 8.2 are female dominated. Consequently, new job opportunities for women should be reasonably good over the 1990s. In fact, if the gender percentages for the occupations in Table 8.2 hold steady, women will end up with about 65 percent of the 7.2 million new jobs in those 20 occupations by the year 2000.

Opportunities for Older Workers

As the older worker recruitment program used by McDonald's demonstrates, when employers cannot find alternative workers, they provide older adults with incentives to work. Employers have not yet identified a similar need for older workers in jobs that require advanced education or highly sophisticated skills, making any substantial change in retirement patterns unlikely in the near future. Current employer and employee attitudes about older worker capabilities and interest in employment are probably too entrenched. Nonetheless, even if few employers eagerly seek out aging workers during the next decade or so, work force and workplace changes should open up opportunities for older workers, including the following.

An increase in less traditional work options. Employers who offer these options will probably not be targeting older workers; rather, they will be responding to the needs and demands of working mothers who require flexibility in their work schedules. Even so, to the extent that employers begin to make such options available, older workers can respond to them.

Increased wages and benefits. In the face of labor shortages, employees can demand more, and employers must comply if they are to attract workers who might have alternative options. Older workers may not yet have the bargaining power that other workers have, but they can benefit from the improved compensation packages introduced for other workers.

A need for increased flexibility on the part of businesses. To remain competitive, businesses must be able to respond quickly to changed market imperatives. Contingent workers can often provide employers with needed flexibility. Although contingent work is not without its negative aspects (see Chapter 7), it can be the perfect work option for some older workers, particularly those with scarce skills who can negotiate high fees and other desirable terms of employment.

Technological advances. These will continue to change the nature of the workplace and to affect the growth of alternative work sites. Working at home will become more common. Despite some disadvantages, home-based work can be appealing to older persons who cannot or will not travel to an office.

Workplace accessibility. Efforts to make workplaces more accessible to disabled persons will also benefit aging workers with physical limitations. Such efforts might make employers more receptive to other workplace modifications such as job redesign or job transfers.

Employer-provided or -supported training can be expected to increase over the next years as businesses cope with the limitations of labor force entrants. The chief concern is with the work readiness and technological capability of younger workers; however, employers who provide or support training programs are legally barred from discriminating against older workers who want to participate.

Changing attitudes about women in the work force should extend to midlife and older women, making the workplace more hospitable to these workers than in the past. The expansion of jobs that have traditionally employed midlife and older women will increase opportunities for aging women, although the persistence of gender segregation in the work force will continue to have a depressing effect on their wages.

Slower growth, increased competition, corporate mergers, and downsizing could serve to counter some of these positive developments, however. Older employees who wish to continue to work may have to resign themselves to the need to resist pressures for early retirement.

Other institutional impediments to continued employment remain, such as the social security earnings test and the lack of a full actuarial increase in social security benefits for delayed retirement. Pension plan restrictions may prohibit or limit the number of hours retirees may be employed by their former firms. Personnel practices often thwart the introduction of alternative work options, as do employer concerns over the added costs associated with part-time work. The higher social security retirement age and the increase in the delayed retirement credit may cause some workers to reevaluate their retirement plans, although it is doubtful that many will elect to keep working in the absence of other incentives.

Employers still need to be convinced that older workers—whom they value in many respects—are flexible, can become technologically proficient, and will remain productive if they delay retirement. They also worry about the potential costs of older workers. Over the short run, at least, it will be up to older workers to prove themselves to their employers, and the evidence seems to be on their side. Older employees do make good workers, they can continue to learn, their skills can be updated, and they can become technologically proficient.

PART
TWO

Resources

Chapter 9

Directory of Organizations

Numerous organizations, associations, government agencies, and self-help groups exist to aid midlife and older workers and would-be workers deal with almost every conceivable issue or problem, such as finding jobs, locating training opportunities, fighting age discrimination, and becoming volunteers. Other organizations and associations can provide employers and employment practitioners with information on the aging work force and strategies that will enable them to take advantage of that changing work force. Some of the most well-known and well-established organizations are highlighted in the listing below.

Readers interested in older worker programs around the country are urged not to stop with this directory: local, state, and regional resources are available to help them. They can contact their State Employment Service for information on employment openings, job-seeking services, or training programs for older workers; their state's department or agency on aging or an Area Agency on Aging might have a directory of state and local older worker programs; their local senior centers may be able to point them in the direction of jobs or training programs; they can find listings for local displaced homemakers' organizations in the telephone book; they might also want to investigate local "Over Sixty" clubs or like-sounding groups.

Similarly, employers, employment counselors, or older worker advocates can capitalize on many resources in their localities, for example, university research institutes for regional employment and economic data or special studies on older workers, senior community service employment programs for potential employees, or state employment offices for posting job announcements.

Every effort has been made to ensure that the following names, addresses, and telephone numbers are correct, but by the time this book goes to print, some of the names or addresses will have changed, and some of the organizations may even have closed their doors. The author regrets any inconvenience that this, or any inadvertent errors, may cause.

ACTION
1100 Vermont Avenue, NW
Washington, DC 20525
(202) 634-9108

ACTION's programs generally involve volunteer rather than paid employment, although some volunteers receive stipends, in-service meals, and transportation. Programs specifically for the aged include (1) the Foster Grandparent Program, in which low-income persons 60 and older provide companionship to children with problems; (2) RSVP (Retired Senior Volunteer Program), in which older persons engage in critical community service projects; and (3) the Senior Companion Program, under which low-income persons 60 and older help other adults remain as independent as possible. Older persons may also work to alleviate poverty as VISTA (Volunteers in Service to America) volunteers. ACTION regional offices are listed below.

Region I (Connecticut, Maine, Massachusetts, New Hampshire, Rhode Island, Vermont)
10 Causeway Street, Room 473
Boston, MA 02222-1039
(617) 565-7000

Region II (New Jersey, New York, Puerto Rico, Virgin Islands)
6 World Trade Center, Room 758
New York, NY 10048-0206
(212) 466-3481

Region III (Delaware, District of Columbia, Kentucky, Maryland, Ohio, Pennsylvania, Virginia, West Virginia)
U.S. Customs House, Room 108
2nd and Chestnut Streets
Philadelphia, PA 19106-2912
(215) 597-9972

Region IV (Alabama, Florida, Georgia, Mississippi, North Carolina, South Carolina, Tennessee)
101 Marietta Street, NW, Suite 1003
Atlanta, GA 30323-2301
(404) 331-2859

Region V (Illinois, Indiana, Iowa, Michigan, Minnesota, Wisconsin)
10 West Jackson Boulevard, 6th Floor
Chicago, IL 60604-3964
(312) 353-5107

Region VI (Arkansas, Kansas, Louisiana, Missouri, New Mexico, Oklahoma, Texas)
1100 Commerce Street, Room 6B11
Dallas, TX 75242-0696
(214) 767-9494

Region VIII (Colorado, Montana,
  Nebraska, North Dakota, South
  Dakota, Utah, Wyoming)
Executive Tower Building, Suite 2930
1405 Curtis Street
Denver, CO 80202-2349
(303) 844-2671

Region IX (Arizona, California,
  Hawaii, Guam, Nevada, American
  Samoa)
211 Main Street, Room 530
San Francisco, CA 94105-1914
(415) 974-0673

Region X (Alaska, Idaho, Oregon,
  Washington)
Federal Office Building
909 First Avenue, Suite 3039
Seattle, WA 98174-1103
(206) 442-1558

Business Forum on Aging
John Migliaccio, Forum Chair
American Society on Aging
833 Market Street, Suite 512
San Francisco, CA 94103
(415) 543-2617

> An organization for the business community, the Business
> Forum on Aging is a clearinghouse of information on America's
> aging society and the implications of that aging—among which
> is an older work force. The Forum provides an opportunity
> for businesses to learn how other companies are dealing with
> their aging work forces and retirees. Because the Forum is associ-
> ated with the American Society on Aging, keeping abreast of
> aging research of relevance to the business world is one of its
> objectives.

The Displaced Homemakers Network
Jill Miller, Executive Director
1411 K Street, NW, Suite 930
Washington, DC 20005
(202) 628-6767

> Established in 1979, this membership organization "works to
> increase displaced homemakers' options for economic self
> sufficiency." The Displaced Homemakers Network is a grass-
> roots organization with more than 1,000 programs around the
> country. Among its many activities are advocacy on behalf of
> displaced homemakers, work with government agencies to

develop programs for displaced homemakers, public education, and a referral service to direct displaced homemakers to local services. Displaced homemakers are women who, through the death of a spouse, divorce, separation, or disability, have lost their main source of financial support and suddenly find themselves in need of employment. Local groups assist in meeting that need.

Anyone may join the Network; annual dues are $5.00 for displaced homemakers and $15.00 for others. Members receive the publication *Transition Times* twice a year. A quarterly newsletter, *Network News,* is available for a subscription fee of $50.00.

Employee Benefit Research Institute (EBRI)
Dallas Salisbury, President
2121 K Street, NW, Suite 600
Washington, DC 20037-2121
(202) 659-0670

A nonprofit, nonpartisan public policy research organization, the Employee Benefit Research Institute conducts research and provides information on a wide range of employee benefits topics, many of which are likely to be of interest to employers of older workers. A monthly newsletter—*Employee Benefit Notes*—summarizes pending and recent legislation, research, conferences, and other articles on employee benefits. *EBRI Issue Brief* is a monthly periodical in which experts examine a single benefit issue in some detail. A recent edition reviewed Japan's response to a rapidly aging work force; another looked at pension funds and financial markets. EBRI periodically publishes other reports and sponsors forums on important benefit issues.

For subscription information on *Employee Benefit Notes* and *EBRI Issue Brief,* contact EBRI's distribution agent: The Johns Hopkins University Press, 701 W. 40th Street, Suite 275, Baltimore, MD 21211, (301) 338-6964.

Equal Employment Opportunity Commission (EEOC)
1801 L Street, NW
Washington, DC 20507
(202) 663-4264; (800) USA-EEOC

The Equal Employment Opportunity Commission is the federal government agency that has jurisdiction over the Age Discrimination in Employment Act. Older workers who think that they have been discriminated against should contact the EEOC for information on steps that must be taken in seeking redress. District EEOC offices investigate charges and litigate; area offices investigate charges that may lead to litigation. District and area offices are as follows (check the telephone book for local EEOC offices, which are not full-service offices):

Albuquerque Area Office
505 Marquette, NW, Suite 1105
Albuquerque, NM 87102-2189

Atlanta District Office
75 Piedmont Avenue, NE, Suite 1100
Atlanta, GA 30335

Baltimore District Office
109 Market Place, Suite 4000
Baltimore, MD 21202

Birmingham District Office
2121 Eighth Avenue, North, Suite 824
Birmingham, AL 35203

Boston Area Office
JFK Federal Building, Room 409-B
Boston, MA 02203

Charlotte District Office
5500 Central Avenue
Charlotte, NC 28212

Chicago District Office
536 South Clark Street, No. 930-A
Chicago, IL 60605

Cincinnati Area Office
550 Main Street, Room 7015
Cincinnati, OH 45202

Cleveland District Office
1375 Euclid Avenue, Room 600
Cleveland, OH 44115

Dallas District Office
8303 Elmbrook Drive
Dallas, TX 75247

Denver District Office
1845 Sherman Street, 2nd Floor
Denver, CO 80203

Detroit District Office
477 Michigan Avenue, Room 1540
Detroit, MI 48226

El Paso Area Office
700 East San Antonio Street, Room
  B-406
El Paso, TX 79901

Houston District Office
1919 Smith Street, 7th Floor
Houston, TX 77002

Indianapolis District Office
46 East Ohio Street, Room 456
Indianapolis, IN 46204

Jackson Area Office
100 East Capitol Street, Suite 721
Jackson, MS 39269

Kansas City Area Office
911 Walnut, 10th Floor
Kansas City, MO 64106

Little Rock Area Office
320 East Capitol Avenue, Suite 621
Little Rock, AR 72201

Los Angeles District Office
3660 Wilshire Boulevard, 5th Floor
Los Angeles, CA 90010

Louisville Area Office
601 West Broadway, Room 613
Louisville, KY 40202

Memphis District Office
1407 Union Avenue, Suite 621
Memphis, TN 38104

Miami District Office
1 Northeast First Street, 6th Floor
Miami, FL 33132

Milwaukee District Office
310 West Wisconsin Avenue, Suite 800
Milwaukee, WI 53203

Nashville Area Office
404 James Robertson Parkway, Suite
  1100
Nashville, TN 37219-1588

New Orleans District Office
701 Loyola Avenue, Suite 600
New Orleans, LA 70113

New York District Office
90 Church Street, Room 1501
New York, NY 10007

Newark Area Office
60 Park Place, Room 301
Newark, NJ 07102

Norfolk Area Office
200 Granby Mall, Room 412
Norfolk, VA 23510

Oklahoma City Area Office
531 Couch Drive
Oklahoma City, OK 73102

Philadelphia District Office
1421 Cherry Street, 10th Floor
Philadelphia, PA 19102

Phoenix District Office
4520 North Central Avenue, Suite 300
Phoenix, AZ 85012-1848

Pittsburgh Area Office
1000 Liberty Avenue, Room 2038-A
Pittsburgh, PA 15222

Raleigh Area Office
1309 Annapolis Drive
Raleigh, NC 27608-2129

Richmond Area Office
400 North 8th Street, Room 7026
Richmond, VA 23240

St. Louis District Office
625 North Euclid Street, 5th Floor
St. Louis, MO 63108

San Antonio District Office
5410 Fredericksburg Road, Suite 200
San Antonio, TX 78229

San Francisco District Office
901 Market Street, Suite 500
San Francisco, CA 94103

Seattle District Office
2815 Second Avenue, Suite 500
Seattle, WA 98121

Tampa Area Office
700 Twiggs Street, Room 302
Tampa, FL 33602

Washington Field Office
1400 L Street, NW, Suite 200
Washington, DC 20005
(202) 275-7377

Forty Plus
(see regional office addresses that follow)

Forty Plus is a career center for executives and professionals aged 40 and older. A two-week orientation program for new members teaches job applicants about interviewing, networking, and goal setting. Forty Plus offices provide facilities such as telephones, word-processing systems, and a business address for job seekers. Members pay an initial membership fee and monthly dues and must agree to work one day a week in the Forty Plus office while actively looking for work. For information, contact one of the Forty Plus offices.

Forty Plus of New York
15 Park Row
New York, NY 10038
(212) 233-6086

Forty Plus of Buffalo
701 Seneca Street
Buffalo, NY 14210
(716) 856-0491

Forty Plus of Northern California
7440 Lockheed Street
Oakland, CA 94603
(415) 430-2400

Forty Plus of Southern California
3450 Wilshire Boulevard, No. 510
Los Angeles, CA 90010
(213) 388-2301

Forty Plus, Orange County Division
23151 Verdugo Drive, No. 114
Laguna Hills, CA 92653
(714) 581-7990

Forty Plus of Chicago
53 West Jackson Boulevard
Chicago, IL 60604
(312) 922-0285

Forty Plus of Colorado
639 East 18th Avenue
Denver, CO 80203
(303) 830-3040

Forty Plus, Northern Division
3840 South Mason Street
Fort Collins, CO 80525
(303) 223-2470, Ext. 261

Forty Plus, Southern Division
17 North Spruce Street
Colorado Springs, CO 80905
(303) 473-6220, Ext. 271

Forty Plus of Central Ohio
1545 Huy Road
P.O. Box 24405
Columbus, OH 43224
(614) 262-4440

Forty Plus of Dallas
13601 Preston Road, No. 402
Dallas, TX 75240
(214) 991-9917

Forty Plus of Hawaii
126 Queen Street, No. 312
Honolulu, HI 96813-4415
(808) 521-2168

Forty Plus of Houston
3935 Westheimer, No. 205
Houston, TX 77027
(713) 850-7830

Forty Plus of Philadelphia
1220 Ransom Street
Philadelphia, PA 19107
(215) 923-2074

Forty Plus of Utah
1234 Main Street
Salt Lake City, UT 84117-0750
(801) 533-2191

Forty Plus of Washington, D.C.
1718 P Street, NW
Washington, DC 20036
(202) 387-1582

Institute on Aging, Work and Health
Robert Levin, Director
Washington Business Group on Health
777 North Capitol Street, NE, Suite 800
Washington, DC 20002
(202) 408-9320

A resource for businesses and policymakers coping with aging issues, the Institute on Aging, Work and Health collects and disseminates information on older workers and health-related and productivity issues. A two-year grant from the U.S. Administration on Aging enabled the institute to foster collaborative programs between employers and aging agencies at the state and local levels to "advance the interests of older persons both inside and outside the workplace." Seed money went to several programs dealing with caregiving, including one program on the elder-care demands faced by a growing number of workers and another on the long-term care needs of employee caregivers. Other programs dealt with drug and alcohol abuse, health risk appraisal and referral for retirees, seminars for business managers and human resource planners responsible for older workers and retirees, and health care coverage for preretirees.

National Caucus and Center on Black Aged, Inc.
Samuel J. Simmons, President
1424 K Street, NW, Suite 500
Washington, DC 20005
(202) 637-8400

Among its other activities on behalf of the aged, the National Caucus and Center on Black Aged—established to improve the status of black elderly—conducts older worker employment research and training programs. This nonprofit organization also serves as a national Senior Community Service Employment Program sponsor.

National Center for Women and Retirement Research
Christopher Hayes, Director
Long Island University (LIU)
Southampton Campus
Southampton, NY 11968
(516) 283-4809

Though described as the first academic center to focus exclusively on the life-planning needs of women, the National Center for Women and Retirement Research has the very practical goal of using research, education, and training to enhance the economic situation of women as they approach retirement age. It seeks to promote and improve planning that will assure women a secure economic future.

The center grew out of the PREP preretirement and planning program for women at LIU, which produced a series of workbooks to help midlife women plan for the future. The workbooks, available for a small charge from the center, deal with financial planning, employment, health, and social/emotional concerns.

The center also conducts seminars for midlife women around the country on financial planning and employment and retirement concerns, among other topics.

National Clearing House on State and Local Older Worker Programs
Ann Lordeman, Director
National Association of State Units on Aging (NASUA)
2033 K Street, NW
Washington, DC 20006
(202) 785-0707

NASUA was founded in 1964 to provide technical assistance and information on behalf of older persons to State Units on Aging. Staff have particular expertise in the Job Training Partnership Act (JTPA) and JTPA programs. Proceedings of conferences on JTPA and other reports on older worker employment are available for a fee. NASUA's National Clearing House on State and Local Older Worker Programs provides technical assistance to older worker program professionals in a number of areas, such as job development and older worker recruitment, training, and retention. The NASUA Membership Directory follows:

Alabama
Commission on Aging
136 Catoma Street, 2nd Floor
Montgomery, AL 36130

Alaska
Older Alaskans Commission
Department of Administration
Pouch C–Mail Station 0209
Juneau, AK 99811-0209

Arizona
Aging and Adult Administration
Department of Economic Security
1400 West Washington Street
Phoenix, AZ 85007

Arkansas
Division of Aging and Adult Services
Arkansas Department of Human
  Services
1417 Donaghey Plaza South
7th and Main Streets
Little Rock, AR 72201

California
Department of Aging
1600 K Street
Sacramento, CA 95814

Colorado
Aging and Adult Service
Department of Social Services
1575 Sherman Street, 10th Floor
Denver, CO 80203-1714

Connecticut
Department on Aging
175 Main Street
Hartford, CT 06106

Delaware
Division on Aging
Department of Health and Social
  Services
1901 North DuPont Highway
New Castle, DE 19720

District of Columbia
Office on Aging
1424 K Street, NW, 2nd Floor
Washington, DC 20005

Florida
Program Office of Aging and Adult
  Services
Department of Health and
  Rehabilitative Services
1317 Winewood Boulevard
Tallahassee, FL 32301

Georgia
Office of Aging
878 Peachtree Street, NE, Room 632
Atlanta, GA 30309

Guam
Division of Senior Citizens
Department of Public Health and
  Social Services
Government of Guam
P.O. Box 2816
Agana, GU 96910

Hawaii
Executive Office on Aging
Office of the Governor
335 Merchant Street, Room 241
Honolulu, HI 96813

Idaho
Office on Aging
State House, Room 114
Boise, ID 83720

Illinois
Department on Aging
421 East Capitol Avenue
Springfield, IL 62701

Indiana
Division of Aging Services
Department of Human Services
251 North Illinois Street
P.O. Box 7083
Indianapolis, IN 46207-7083

Iowa
Department of Elder Affairs
Jewett Building
914 Grand Avenue, Suite 236
Des Moines, IA 50319

Kansas
Department on Aging
Docking State Office Building
915 Southwest Harrison, No. 122-S
Topeka, KS 66612-1500

Kentucky
Division of Aging Services
Cabinet for Human Resources
CHR Building—6th West
275 East Main Street
Frankfort, KY 40621

Louisiana
Office of Elderly Affairs
4550 N Boulevard
P.O. Box 80374
Baton Rouge, LA 70806

Maine
Bureau of Elder and Adult Services
Department of Human Services
State House, Station No. 11
Augusta, ME 04333

Maryland
Office on Aging
State Office Building
301 West Preston Street, No. 1004
Baltimore, MD 21201

Massachusetts
Executive Office of Elder Affairs
38 Chauncy Street
Boston, MA 02111

Michigan
Office of Services to the Aging
P.O. Box 30026
Lansing, MI 48909

Minnesota
Board on Aging
Human Services Building
444 Lafayette Road, 4th Floor
St. Paul, MN 55155-3843

Mississippi
Council on Aging
301 West Pearl Street
Jackson, MS 39203-3092

Missouri
Division on Aging
Department of Social Services
2701 West Main Street
P.O. Box 1337
Jefferson City, MO 65102

Montana
Department of Family Services
48 North Last Chance Gulch
P.O. Box 8005
Helena, MT 59604

Nebraska
Department on Aging
301 Centennial Mall-South
P.O. Box 95044
Lincoln, NE 68509

Nevada
Division for Aging Services
340 North 11th Street
Las Vegas, NV 89101

New Hampshire
Division of Elderly and Adult Services
6 Hazen Drive
Concord, NH 03301-6501

New Jersey
Division on Aging
Department of Community Affairs
CN807
South Broad and Front Streets
Trenton, NJ 08625-0807

New Mexico
State Agency on Aging
224 East Palace Avenue
La Villa Rivera Building, 4th Floor
Santa Fe, NM 87501

New York
Office for the Aging
New York State Plaza
Agency Building No. 2
Albany, NY 12223

North Carolina
Division of Aging
Kirby Building
1985 Umstead Drive
Raleigh, NC 27603

North Dakota
Aging Services
Department of Human Services
State Capitol Building
Bismarck, ND 58505

Northern Mariana Islands
Office of Aging
Department of Community and
    Cultural Affairs
Civic Center—Susupe
Saipan, Northern Mariana Islands
    96950

Ohio
Department of Aging
50 West Broad Street, 9th Floor
Columbus, OH 43266-0501

Oklahoma
Aging Services Division
Department of Human Services
P.O. Box 25352
Oklahoma City, OK 73125

Oregon
Senior Services Division
313 Public Service Building
Salem, OR 97310

Pennsylvania
Department of Aging
231 State Street
Harrisburg, PA 17101-1195

Puerto Rico
Gericulture Commission
Department of Social Services
Apartado 11398
Santurce, PR 00910

Rhode Island
Department of Elderly Affairs
79 Washington Street
Providence, RI 02903

American Samoa
Territorial Administration on Aging
Office of the Governor
Pago Pago, AS 96799

South Carolina
Commission on Aging
400 Arbor Lake Drive, Suite B-500
Columbia, SC 29223

South Dakota
Office of Adult Services and Aging
700 North Illinois Street
Kneip Building
Pierre, SD 57501

Tennessee
Commission on Aging
706 Church Street, Suite 201
Nashville, TN 37219-5573

Texas
Department on Aging
1949 IH 35, South
P.O. Box 12786, Capitol Station
Austin, TX 78741-3702

Trust Territory of the Pacific
Office of Elderly Programs
Community Development Division
Government of TTPI
Saipan, Northern Mariana Islands
96950

Utah
Division of Aging and Adult Services
Department of Social Services
120 North—200 West
Box 45500
Salt Lake City, UT 84145-0500

Vermont
Department of Rehabilitation and
Aging
103 South Main Street
Waterbury, VT 05676

Virgin Islands
Senior Citizen Affairs
Department of Human Services
19 Estate Diamond Fredericksted
St. Croix, VI 00840

Virginia
Department for the Aging
700 Centre
700 East Franklin Street, 10th Floor
Richmond, VA 23219-2327

Washington
Aging and Adult Services
Administration
Department of Social and Health
Services
OB-44A
Olympia, WA 98504

West Virginia
Commission on Aging
Holly Grove—State Capitol
Charleston, WV 25305

Wisconsin
Bureau of Aging
Division of Community Services
217 South Hamilton Street, Suite 300
Madison, WI 53707

Wyoming
Commission on Aging
Hathaway Building, Room 139
Cheyenne, WY 82002-0710

National Commission for Employment Policy (NCEP)
1522 K Street, NW, Suite 300
Washington, DC 20005
(202) 724-1545

> The National Commission for Employment Policy is an independent federal agency that conducts and sponsors research on national employment issues. While the commission's primary constituents are Congress and the president, much of its work is relevant to policymakers and practitioners at the state and local levels. In the early 1980s, the commission undertook a study of the employment situation of older workers that led to the publication of a number of papers and reports, including *A Practitioner's Guide for Training Older Workers* and *Older Worker Employment Comes of Age.* More recent work has focused on the Job Training Partnership Act. Single copies of the commission's reports are available free of charge.

National Council of Senior Citizens (NCSC)
Lawrence Smedley, Executive Director
925 15th Street, NW
Washington, DC 20005
(202) 347-8800

> The National Council of Senior Citizens is an advocacy organization working on behalf of older persons at the national, state, and local levels. Issues on which NCSC has worked over the years include social security, Medicare, housing, social services, and community employment projects. Expanding job opportunities for persons over 50 is a focus at the national level. NCSC is a national Senior Community Service Employment Program prime sponsor.

National Senior Citizens Law Center (NSCLC)
1052 West 6th Street
Los Angeles, CA 90017
(213) 482-3550

Burton Fretz, Executive Director, Washington office
2025 M Street, NW
Washington, DC 20036
(202) 887-5280

> The National Senior Citizens Law Center was established in 1972 to help older persons live their lives free of poverty. NSCLC attorneys in this nonprofit center practice law on behalf of poor aged clients and client groups. They provide a number of services and work on a variety of legal problems, including age discrimination.

New Ways to Work
Barney Olmsted and Suzanne Smith, Codirectors
149 Ninth Street
San Francisco, CA 94103
(415) 552-1000

> New Ways to Work, a community-based work resource center, was established in 1972 "to increase opportunities for reduced and restructured work schedules and to ensure equity for those who choose them." The organization serves as a clearinghouse on alternative work options, advocates on behalf of the expansion of alternative work options, and assists organizations and individuals interested in such options through consulting efforts, technical assistance, counseling, and workshops. Brochures highlighting publications and other resources are available from New Ways to Work, which publishes *Work Times,* a quarterly newsletter.

9to5, National Association of Working Women
Karen Nussbaum, Executive Director
614 Superior Avenue, NW
Cleveland, OH 44113
(216) 566-9308
Job Problem Hotline (800) 245-9to5 (in Cleveland, 566-5420)

> A nationwide membership group, 9to5 was organized in 1973 to improve the status and working conditions of office workers. The hot line is a national job counseling service that advises callers on their job-related problems; it is not an employment service. Current operating hours are Monday through Thursday from 11 A.M. to 2 P.M. and Wednesday, 6 P.M. to 9 P.M. (Eastern time).

Older Women's League (OWL)
Joan Kuriansky, Executive Director
730 11th Street, NW, Suite 300
Washington, DC 20001
(212) 783-6686

> A national membership organization that strives to improve the status of older women, the Older Women's League is not an employment agency, but it does advocate on behalf of older women workers. Employment discrimination is one of its key agenda issues, and OWL has published educational materials on the subject. Membership in the national organization, which also has local chapters, is open to anyone for $10.00 per year.

Operation ABLE
Shirley Brussel, Executive Director
36 South Wabash, Suite 1133
Chicago, IL 60603
(312) 782-3335

> Operation ABLE (Ability Based on Long Experience) is an umbrella organization of services that helps persons over the age of 50 find employment. Based on the premise that older persons need an intermediary in the job search, the organization seeks to improve general public and employer attitudes about older workers; its three constituencies are job seekers, employers, and older worker employment agencies. Operation ABLE services include a job hot line for older job seekers and access to training and counseling through Job Training Partnership Act funds. It also serves as a clearinghouse for area organizations that train and hire older workers. The success of this organization has spawned similar organizations in several other cities.

POWER
Promoting Older Women's Employment Rights Coalition
Jill Miller, Chair
c/o Displaced Homemakers Network
1411 K Street, NW, Suite 930
Washington, DC 20005
(202) 628-6767

> POWER is a coalition of women's rights and aging organizations "dedicated to promoting the rights of midlife and older women

in all areas of employment and training issues." The coalition evolved out of efforts of the 1986 Roundtable on Older Women in the Work Force, the purpose of which was to bring together organizations concerned about older women's employment issues, human resource managers, business executives, and professionals in aging to examine and try to solve older women's employment problems. One recommendation of the roundtable dealt with the establishment of a coalition to develop job opportunities.

According to its mission statement, POWER will focus its advocacy efforts on public policy, employer attitudes, public opinion, service provision, and constituency or educating midlife and older women about their value as workers and about ways to achieve their employment rights and opportunities.

Prime Time Productivity
Joyce Welch, Director
National Council on the Aging, Inc. (NCOA)
600 Maryland Avenue, SW, West Wing 100
Washington, DC 20024
(202) 479-1200

A program of the National Council on the Aging, Prime Time Productivity offers program development and training services to businesses to help them "mold a workforce that will serve [them] and America well in the year 2000 and beyond." Obviously, making the most effective use of aging employees is a key objective of Prime Time; however, the program acknowledges business's need to remain productive and profitable. Midlife and older workers can contribute to productivity and profits, Prime Time would argue. Consultants offer a range of services designed to maximize the potential of older workers while meeting the needs of individual establishments. Available services include, but are not restricted to, connecting with programs that recruit and train older workers, consultation and analysis to assess the human resource needs of firms, designing in-house training and retraining programs, creating alternative work options, and evaluating firms' human resource strategies over time. Contact Prime Time for additional information on its services and a free introductory issue of *The Aging Workforce* (described in Chapter 10 in the section headed "Publications for the Employer, Practitioner, or Older Worker Adviser").

Senior Community Service Employment Program (SCSEP)
(see national prime sponsor addresses that follow)

> SCSEP is not an organization but a job creation and training program for economically disadvantaged persons 55 and older. Nine organizations and the U.S. Park Service serve as prime SCSEP sponsors. For information on specific programs sponsored by an SCSEP organization, write to "Director, Title V SCSEP" at one of the sponsor addresses listed below.

American Association of Retired Persons
1909 K Street, NW
Washington, DC 20049
(212) 662-4800

Asociación Nacional por Personas
 Mayores
(National Association for Hispanic
 Elderly)
2727 West Sixth Street, Suite 270
Los Angeles, CA 90057
(213) 487-1922

Green Thumb, Inc.
5111 Leesburg Pike, Suite 107
Falls Church, VA 22041
(703) 820-4990

National Caucus and Center on Black
 Aged, Inc.
1424 K Street, NW
Washington, DC 20005
(212) 637-8400

National Council of Senior Citizens
925 15th Street, NW
Washington, DC 20005
(202) 347-8800

National Council on the Aging, Inc.
600 Maryland Avenue, SW, West Wing
 100
Washington, DC 20024
(202) 479-6600

National Indian Council on Aging, Inc.
P.O. Box 2088
Albuquerque, NM 87103
(505) 242-9505

National Pacific/Asian Resource Center
 on Aging
United Airlines Building
2033 Sixth Avenue, Suite 410
Seattle, WA 98121
(206) 448-0313

National Urban League
500 East 62nd Street
New York, NY 10021
(212) 310-9000

USDA Forest Service
P.O. Box 96090
Washington, DC 20090-6090
(202) 535-0927

Service Corps of Retired Executives (SCORE)
National Office
1825 Connecticut Avenue, NW, Suite 503
Washington, DC 20009
(202) 653-6279; (800) 368-5855 (toll-free answer desk)

> SCORE is an association of more than 13,000 businessmen and businesswomen who share their business acumen and expertise

with small businesses around the country. Confidential business counseling is provided by volunteers, most of whom are retired, who receive no recompense but who are reimbursed for authorized travel expenses. SCORE's one-on-one or team counseling services are free of charge. Nominal-fee workshops may also be available.

Established in 1964, SCORE is funded by the U.S. Small Business Administration. The location of the nearest of SCORE's approximately 750 chapters may be obtained by calling the toll-free number above. Anyone contemplating going into business for himself or herself should consider contacting SCORE for assistance; however, SCORE's services are not restricted to new businesses.

U.S. Congress
Senate Special Committee on Aging
G-41 Dirksen Building
Washington, DC 20510
(202) 224-5364

House Select Committee on Aging
House Office Building Annex 1, Room 712
Washington, DC 20515
(202) 226-3375

These nonlegislative congressional committees periodically hold hearings and publish reports on older worker problems amenable to legislative response at the national level. Published materials are made available to the public by the committees themselves until copies are exhausted; some can be ordered through the U.S. Government Printing Office.

Worker Equity Department
Martin Sicker, Director
American Association of Retired Persons
1909 K Street, NW
Washington, DC 20049
(202) 662-4956

Worker Equity was established to assess the societal impact of an aging work force and to promote job opportunities for older workers by assisting both employers and older individuals. It is not an employment agency, but many of its publications are useful to job seekers. These include *Working Options—How To Plan Your Job Search, Your Work Life*; *Look Before You Leap: A Guide to Early Retirement Incentive Programs*; and *A Guide to Understanding Your Pension Plan: A Pension Handbook*. Employers may be interested in *Working Age* (see the listing in Chapter 10 under the heading "Publications for the Employer, Practitioner, or Older Worker Adviser"), *America's Changing Work Force: Statistics in Brief*, and *Using the Experience of a Lifetime*, among other publications. A brochure available from Worker Equity describes the program's activities and publications.

Please note: All Worker Equity publications should be ordered through Fulfillment, AARP, 1909 K Street, NW, Washington, DC 20049. Specify the publication numbers that are cited in Chapter 10.

Chapter 10

Reference Materials

The reference materials in this chapter fall into two broad categories: (1) those designed to assist older workers or job seekers and (2) those designed to inform persons who work with or on behalf of older workers, including employers, practitioners, or older worker advisers. Additionally, students and researchers, as well as business and labor professionals, may find much of this material useful.

Materials have been placed in one of two sections—"Publications for the Older Worker or Job Seeker" or "Publications for the Employer, Practitioner, or Older Worker Adviser"—based on their primary audience. All books, pamphlets, and other printed materials in this chapter have been read in their entirety by the author, who anticipates that many readers will find materials in both sections helpful. Older workers might, for example, wish to examine publications written for employers that include reports on innovative older worker employment opportunities.

Books in this chapter may be ordered directly from the publishers if they are unavailable elsewhere; see *Books in Print* for publisher addresses. Pamphlets, research reports, and other unpublished materials may be ordered from the organizations that produced them (see Chapter 9 for organization addresses). A few of the publications listed are out of print but have been included because they contain useful information; these may be obtained from local libraries or through interlibrary loan.

Every effort has been made to ensure that names, addresses, telephone numbers, subscription charges, and book prices are current and correct. All of these, however, are subject to change and should be confirmed before an order is placed.

Publications for the Older Worker or Job Seeker

Many books are available on how to find a job. Any public library or bookstore provides access to information on such topics as writing effective resumés, doing a skills assessment, getting an interview, and what to wear, say, and do during and after an interview. Job seekers of any age will find many of these books useful. Older applicants, however, face special obstacles and problems when searching for work. Accordingly, most of the publications in this section address the special situation of the older job seeker. Also included are some more general publications that may be of particular interest to older applicants.

Books

Allen, Jeffrey G., and Jess Gorkin. *Finding the Right Job at Midlife.* New York: Simon & Schuster, 1985. 173p. $13.95. ISBN 0-671-53058-5.

> *Finding the Right Job* takes an extremely optimistic and, for the most part, superficial approach to the midlife job search. It generally ignores or glosses over the very real problems faced by persons thrust into the job search in middle age.
>
> Much of the material (e.g., on resumé writing or exercises to identify skills, achievement, and the like) is available in one form or another elsewhere. The book does include a rather extensive list of "positive action" verbs that might, if not overused, be helpful in preparing resumés or writing cover letters, and the reader interested in less than full-time work or in starting a business will find informative sections on those topics. The book is not, however, for everyone.
>
> On the one hand, the self-confident and atypical midlife job seeker might find the suggestions on preparing for an interview—including what to wear, getting through the interview, and negotiating with the prospective employer—to be all that he or she needs to land the perfect job. On the other hand, the employee who has been unexpectedly let go or who is desperate to get out of an unhappy work situation may finish the book with the impression that the right job is his or hers for the asking and thus lacking the tools required for what may well be a long and frustrating search.

The book's case studies of midlife career changes or job searches are in sharp contrast to those in *Forced Out: When Veteran Employees Are Driven from Their Careers* by Juliet Brudney and Hilda Scott (see entry below), which are almost invariably depressing.

Bard, Ray, and Fran Moody. *Breaking In: The Guide to Over 500 Top Corporate Training Programs.* New York: Quill, William Morrow, 1985. 256p. $11.95. ISBN 0-688-05893-0.

> *Breaking In* describes approximately 500 training programs, the information for which was gleaned from 2,000 surveys sent to "the top manufacturing, service, and financial companies in the United States." Each company entry identifies what the company does (and sometimes gives its history), describes the training program, specifies the required qualifications, and provides information on recruitment and placement, salaries, and benefits. The contact person or office is also noted.
>
> Among the book's indices is one that identifies broad training opportunities in such areas as accounting, computer systems, or finance, and the industries in which those training opportunities may be found. A reader could easily locate page references for, for example, management training programs in insurance agencies or engineering training programs in the defense industry. Similarly, readers interested in finding out about training programs in specific industries could locate those in the industry index. Geographic and company indices are also provided.
>
> The programs tend to involve training in a limited number of areas: accounting and auditing, computer systems/programming, credit analysis, engineering, finance, high tech and electronics, management, and sales and marketing. The overall thrust of the training is for entry-level work that will not be of interest to most older job seekers. Nonetheless, the book is a good overview of what several hundred corporations are doing and might provide insights to the midlife worker contemplating a career or establishment switch. Some firms known for their hospitality to older workers, such as Grumman, are included.

Bardwick, Judith M. *The Plateauing Trap.* New York: American Management Association, 1986. $17.95. xi, 209p. ISBN 0-8144-5871-8.

Written by a psychologist, *The Plateauing Trap* deals with the problem of "plateauing," or becoming blocked from further progress. Once seen as a middle-age problem, plateauing increasingly confronts younger workers. Nonetheless, the author feels that the problem is still greatest in middle age, and one chapter is devoted to this age group.

Three kinds of plateauing are the focus of the book: (1) structural, which is the end of work promotions; (2) content, described as becoming bored as a result of knowing too much about a job; and (3) life plateauing (seen as the most serious), where people don't know what to do with their lives.

Each type of plateauing and its impact are described in detail in its own chapter. Final chapters offer suggestions as to how various groups—executives, managers, and readers themselves—should deal with plateauing. An appendix includes questions to ask about plateauing and plateauing symptoms.

Berman, Eleanor. *Reentering: Successful Back-to-Work Strategies for Women Seeking a Fresh Start*. New York: Crown, 1980. ix, 179p. $8.95. ISBN 0-517-539438.

The author of this upbeat book uses individual case studies to frame her discussion of strategies for getting a job later in life. These case studies serve as realistic role models for the types of women likely to read the book. *Reentering* helps readers determine if they even want to go back to work. If they do, the book assists them in deciding who they are and what they can do. It recommends taking advantage of the excellent career planning workshops and courses that are available in many communities. Other specific hints and advice are also provided. For example, the author suggests using professional terms when describing experience: a woman who has been chair of the PTA should call herself a manager or administrator. Many "action" verbs are identified for use in resumés.

Appendices highlight additional sources of information, such as educational programs for mature students and financial aid for education. Also listed are the names and addresses of state sources of professional counseling in setting career goals, which the author thinks is very important. The addresses may well be dated, as are some other parts of the book; nonetheless, much of the advice is as relevant and practical today as it was in 1980, and reentry women should still find this book worth reading.

Birsner, E. Patricia. *The 40 + Job-Hunting Guide.* New York: Arco, 1987. 272p. $8.95. ISBN 0-13-329152-9.

> *40 +,* a job-seeking manual for executives, is the official handbook of the Forty Plus Club, which specializes in helping unemployed midlife and older executives reenter the job market. In contrast to many job-seeking manuals, *40 +* discusses the emotional stages and accompanying feelings of unemployment and offers guidelines for coping with those feelings. One suggestion is to join—or establish, if necessary—a support group of unemployed professionals. In fact, the book sees group support as the key to surviving unemployment and securing subsequent employment.
>
> The book, written in a clear, no-nonsense style, recommends that an individual begin the job search immediately upon losing a job. Birsner also recommends against grasping at straws, making the important point that older job seekers have less time than younger ones do to overcome a mistake in job selection. (Of course, it could also be pointed out that older workers often have fewer choices.)
>
> Chapters on resumé and letter writing are especially good. Birsner identifies words and phrases that may date the applicant and that should consequently be avoided. The book also deals with important topics that are not always covered in manuals of this type; these include time management, image, getting one's finances in order, and recreation and leisure activities.
>
> Although *The 40 + Job-Hunting Guide* is targeted at a specialized audience, portions of it will be helpful to unemployed nonexecutives or workers merely contemplating a job change; such individuals will not be led astray by following the book's advice.

Birsner, E. Patricia. *Job-Hunting for the 40 + Executive: A Handbook for Middle-Aged Managers and Professionals.* New York: Facts on File, 1985. xx, 250p. $16.95. ISBN 0-87196-634-4.

> The four parts to this job-seeking guide for a selected audience address (1) developing a personal job-action plan, (2) the activities a job seeker must go through to set employment goals, (3) the job-seeking activities themselves (e.g., resumé and letter writing, job research), and (4) evaluating whether to accept a job offer. Job seekers are advised that the search should be viewed as problem solving. The author devotes some time to the emotional

traumas associated with job loss, grooming, and personal communications style. A chapter on interviews offers information not generally provided in such detail in books of this type, namely, questions that interviewees should be prepared to answer and to ask. Questions that are illegal under current law are also mentioned.

Bolles, Richard Nelson. *What Color Is Your Parachute?* Berkeley, CA: Ten Speed, 1988. xx, 361p. $8.95. ISBN 0-89815-157-0 (pbk).

What Color Is Your Parachute? may not be targeted specifically at the older market, but its recommendations are as valid for older job seekers as for younger ones. The book's success and popularity, at least as evidenced by its longevity, justify its place in any listing of resources for the unemployed or job changer.

Bolles sets out to assist the reader in identifying what he or she wants to do, locating the appropriate jobs, and determining who has the power to hire. Because Bolles's aim is to help the reader find not just any job but a suitable job, it is a book for job or career changers as well as for the unemployed. The book will also inform reentry women and young people entering the labor market for the first time.

Bolles reviews and generally persuasively debunks common job-seeking methods, but provides many hints to help the seeker along the way. He promises no shortcuts to the job search itself.

Bolles lists and describes references such as the *Dictionary of Occupational Titles* and the *Occupational Outlook Handbook* and explains why they might be helpful to the job seeker. Detailed appendices direct readers to additional resources on job hunting or career changing, sources of special employment-related information and advice (e.g., on alternative work options, volunteer internships, and government and overseas work), and the special problems of minorities and the handicapped. The potential pitfalls of self-employment receive considerable attention.

An effort is made to lighten the tone of the book, which essentially deals with a less than pleasant subject, through the liberal use of amusing cartoons and illustrations, clever graphics, and variations in typeface and page layout that some readers may find distracting. Nonetheless, *What Color Is Your Parachute?* is very definitely packed with useful information. It may not be the only publication an older job seeker will want to take a look at, but it is probably one of the better books of its type.

Although the most recent edition of *What Color Is Your Parachute?* will be the most accurate when it comes to the names and addresses of the many resources, the text itself and exercises seem to change little from year to year, so it should not be necessary to replace an older edition when a new one comes out.

Brodey, Jean Lisette. *Mid-Life Careers.* Philadelphia, PA: Westminster, John Knox, 1983. 248p. $12.95. ISBN 0-664-27003-4.

Written by a journalism professor and career counselor who had to reenter the labor force upon divorce after 17 years as a home-maker, this midlife job-seeking guide recounts some of the author's experiences in obtaining her first job and her eventual return to school to work toward an Ed.D. It is a chatty book that includes a considerable amount of information on the job search, goal setting, strategies for looking for work, and resumé writing. The liberal use of anecdotes to illustrate points makes the book somewhat difficult to skim for specific pieces of advice, but it is a readable book, if perhaps not as substantive as some midlife job-seeking publications.

Brudney, Juliet F., and Hilda Scott. *Forced Out: When Veteran Employees Are Driven from Their Careers.* New York: Simon & Schuster, 1987. 208p. $7.95. ISBN 0-671-64411-4 (pbk).

Letters to the senior author, who was writing a column on work for the *Boston Globe,* served as the impetus for this book. Brudney initially assumed that help would be readily available for her correspondents, who were middle-level older individuals seeking full-time work, but she soon learned, to her disillusionment, that existing agencies were equipped only to serve low-income persons who wanted part-time employment.

Forced Out focuses on the experiences—and they are depressing—of more than 100 50- to 70-year-olds in middle-level jobs who had encountered employment problems since turning 50 that they attributed to age. Reference to surveys of and studies on older worker employment problems is made throughout the book, but the lack of footnotes and citations makes tracking down the originals difficult. The brief bibliography omits some of the cited studies.

The book, which consists largely of anecdotes on the interviewees, is very readable. The authors make it clear that many
traditional job search techniques, such as want ads or employment agencies whose fees are paid by employers, do not lead
to much. They also make the valuable point that job agencies,
even nonprofit ones, are paid for their services; consequently,
seekers turning to job agencies for help should not be made to
feel that the agencies are doing them a favor. Some of the advice
the authors offer is standard and general, for example, "be
assertive." The book includes tips on how to recognize age discrimination and what to do about it, warning that the cost of
suing is high and the wait for a decision long.

While the book includes some successful case studies, the
reader is left with the distinct impression that the employment
prospects of older job seekers are bleak indeed. The authors say
the labor market is generally "unfriendly" to midlevel job seekers and "downright hostile" to those over 50. Seekers with high-
demand skills and a "dogged determination" to pursue goals
may succeed, but even these types did not seem to do especially
well, if the case studies are any guide. The message that comes
through loud and clear is that older midlevel job seekers should
lower their sights.

There can be no doubt about the fact that the job hunt for
older workers is often long and discouraging, and older job
seekers should be prepared for this reality. Nonetheless, they
need some hope, to say nothing of advice, if they are going
to pursue the search, and *Forced Out* is short on both. It is
probably best avoided by older job seekers, although older
worker employment specialists and counselors will find plenty of
ammunition to support expansion of their efforts.

Dychtwald, Ken, and Joe Flower. *Age Wave: The Challenges and
Opportunities of an Aging America*. Los Angeles: Jeremy P. Tarcher,
1989. xix, 380p. $19.95. ISBN 0-87477-441-1.

In this accessible effort to prepare readers of all ages for the
challenges of an aging population, the authors discuss such topics as leisure, love in later life, the maturing market place, and
employment. The 36-page chapter on employment argues that
changes in the way we work can be expected as a result of
changes in other aspects of our lives. It talks about older people's

need and desire to work, as well as their ability to work, given what the authors feel has been an improvement in the health of older workers and a decrease in physically demanding jobs. The chapter touches on new work options, such as phased retirement, flexplace, and flextime, and gives examples of corporations using various types of new employment options. Pension portability is briefly discussed.

Morgan, John S. *Getting a Job after 50*. Princeton, NJ: Petrocelli, 1987. vi, 264p. $27.95. ISBN 0-89433-311-9.

Getting a Job after 50 is an exceptionally informative job-seeking guide for the unemployed and *under*employed mature worker. In fact, it is the attention to this latter group of older workers that distinguishes this publication from many other job-seeking manuals. Morgan's underlying theme is that job hunting is not as hard as older workers may think, but the author does not minimize the problems older job seekers face. A strong emphasis is placed on the abilities and strengths of older seekers—unique experience, multidimensional abilities, self-knowledge, and risk knowledge—and how to parlay those strengths into a job. Morgan delves into the pros and cons of self-employment, pointing out the high failure rate of new businesses, stressing the attributes and assets (such as sufficient capital) that new business owners must possess, and urging readers not to consider self-employment merely to avoid looking for another job.

Morgan warns mature workers of trouble signals that could portend an ultimate firing, but he also points out seemingly troublesome signs that might best be ignored. Similarly, in his focus on the underemployed—who may be the majority of over-50 workers—he discusses when to consider changing careers as well as when not to. He marshals arguments against some of the negative stereotypes about older worker productivity and abilities that might bolster the confidence of the mature job seeker.

The author gives some advice on identifying jobs in aging, which "attract individuals at midcareer." The information may serve as a useful introduction to new opportunities for the reentrant, job loser, or midlife job or career changer.

Myers, Albert, and Christopher P. Anderson. *Success over Sixty*. New York: Summit, 1984. 301p. $15.95. ISBN 0-671-49460-0.

This lively book is an effort to encourage older people to take risks to remain productive as paid employees or volunteers well into old age. It consists primarily of vignettes of successful older people, most of them upper-level corporate executives before they voluntarily retired or otherwise chose to make a job switch. A few—for instance, a housewife who became a cookbook author and a firefighter turned nurse—came from humbler backgrounds.

As in most older worker job-seeking books, the authors assume that post-60 success stories do not just happen. They involve change, curiosity, communication, confidence, and commitment.

The book includes questions and exercises on identifying interests and skills, some dos and don'ts, and some very practical advice on starting a business. General career information, available help for entrepreneurs (including names and addresses), and educational resources (most of them related to owning a business) are highlighted. Also included are a generic list of profitable businesses, a list of specific franchises with addresses, and a chapter on volunteering, with resources for volunteers.

The senior author knows whereof he speaks, having retired after 40 years from the company his father started. He then moved on to other ventures, some of which were successful and some of which were not. His stories may encourage risk taking on the part of other older workers. However, the real virtue of this book lies in its effort to convince readers of the need to think ahead and plan for the future.

Selden, Ina Lee. *Going into Business for Yourself: New Beginnings after 50*. Glenview, IL: Scott, Foresman, 1989. x, 245p. $8.95, regular; $6.50 for AARP members. ISBN-0-673-24882-8.

The author of this guide successfully went into business for herself at the age of 40. She reviews the qualities one should have to start a business (e.g., entrepreneurial characteristics, marketable skills, talents, knowledge, a market for what one wants to sell) and explains how to assess those characteristics. She also asks a number of questions, the answers to which provide insights into whether the reader might be cut out for entrepreneurship.

The book attempts to dispel a number of myths about self-employment, for example, that it requires seven-day weeks or that readers who have not shown an entrepreneurial spirit by age

40 should not consider self-employment now. Successful cases studies of entrepreneurs in a number of fields are included.

Chapters also deal with (1) organizing a business (e.g., the pros and cons of sole proprietorships and partnerships, and such matters as insurance and licensing); (2) the business plan, which describes what the business is, what the owner hopes to accomplish, and how; (3) working at home; (4) start-up money and where to get it; (5) the importance of record keeping; and (6) marketing.

Going into Business may not be the only book an aspiring entrepreneur will need, but it is certainly a well-organized, readable first one.

Stark, Sandra L. *Returning to Work: A Planning Book for Women.* New York: McGraw-Hill, 1983. vii, 151p. $13.95. ISBN 0-07-060887-3.

This book, which can be read alone or used in a group setting, is filled with advice that will give midlife, reentry women the confidence they need to return to work. It focuses on such topics as options, goal setting, finding a job, balancing work and home life, and on-the-job problems. What appear to be very useful chapter exercises should, if completed, aid women in clarifying their thinking, deciding what they want to do, determining the actions that they can now take in pursuit of their goals, and perhaps even getting the job. *Returning to Work* also deals with such standard job-seeking matters as resumés and getting through job interviews successfully.

U.S. Bureau of Labor Statistics (BLS). *Occupational Outlook Handbook.* Washington, DC: U.S. Government Printing Office, biennial. Page numbers vary. $17.00 (1990–1991 ed.).

The *Handbook* is a source of vocational guidance information that lists occupations in the U.S. economy and describes what they entail and pay, the training or education necessary to secure employment in them, and their future outlook. Additional information on the occupations, job hunting, and the labor market is also included. While the handbook is probably most useful to students and younger workers, it might also provide insights to older potential job seekers interested in the requirements of and prospects in entirely new lines of work.

Pamphlets

American Association of Retired Persons (AARP). *The Age Discrimination in Employment Act Guarantees You Certain Rights. Here's How. . . .* Washington, DC: AARP, 1987. 24p. No charge. PW3665/1(887).D12386.

> In clear, precise language, this excellent pamphlet describes the Age Discrimination in Employment Act (ADEA), who and what it covers, exceptions to the law, and discrimination remedies under the act. This last section, which briefly reviews the possible responses to age discrimination, including filing a lawsuit, should be especially useful to workers who wonder whether it might be worth pursuing a grievance, and, if the answer is yes, how to go about doing so. The pamphlet is by no means the only assistance a potential litigant will need, but it is certainly a good place to start.
>
> As this book is going to press, AARP is updating its age discrimination pamphlet. For information of whether the new edition is available, contact the Worker Equity Department of AARP.

American Association of Retired Persons (AARP). *Look Before You Leap: A Guide to Early Retirement Incentive Programs.* Washington, DC: AARP Worker Equity, 1988. 12p. No charge. PW4205(988).D13390.

> *Look Before You Leap* is designed to aid older workers faced with making a decision about early retirement incentive programs, which are inducements to encourage some workers to retire. Many incentive programs are the result of corporate downsizing and represent employers' efforts to avoid layoffs. This pamphlet raises several questions that should be answered before a worker decides to accept or reject an incentive offer.

American Association of Retired Persons (AARP). *Working Options—How To Plan Your Job Search, Your Work Life.* Washington, DC: AARP, 1985. 28p. No charge. PW3671(1186).D12403.

> This brief brochure describes a self-directed job-search plan that, it states, "has a high success rate in finding a job based on [the reader's] needs, interests, skills and abilities" (p. 2). While the

brochure may seem to promise something that similar publications shy away from—that is, a quick fix—it really does not. The plan works because job seekers keep looking until they find the jobs they want. If seekers become frustrated and discouraged and leave the labor market, or if they opt for jobs that they really do not want, they have not followed the plan.

The advice in the brochure also resembles that in other publications: what is required is an intensive but well-thought-out job search. The standard topics are covered: assessing interests and skills, setting goals, evaluating the job market, using contacts to identify job leads (networking), preparing resumés, writing cover letters, and effective interviewing (at almost four pages, one of the longer sections of the brochure). The brochure ends with a short list of resources that might be helpful in the job search and/or in changing careers and lifestyles. At 28 pages, it lacks the detail (much of it unnecessary) of longer publications on the same subject. Examples of what a powerful resumé or eye-grabbing cover letter looks like are missing, but the brochure does highlight most of the issues that job seekers should think about. Best of all, the publication is free.

National Center for Women and Retirement Research. *Employment and Retirement Issues for Women.* Southampton, NY: Long Island University, undated. 40p. $4.00.

This preretirement planning workbook, one of Long Island University's PREP Talk for Women publications, addresses a number of employment issues of concern to midlife women: overcoming assertiveness problems, determining who within a firm has the power, identifying support networks, ensuring a safe and healthy work environment, coping with stress, and postretirement work. Although the workbook does make some specific recommendations and suggestions, these are often embedded in the questions or checklists that shape the publication; for example, "I do not say yes to every request, but first I weigh my present responsibilities and deadlines to see if I can do the task correctly. I am not afraid to say no and explain why it is not possible."

A question and answer format is used to deal with frequently asked questions about gender and age discrimination in employment and about caregiving responsibilities. An appendix lists federal and state agencies that offer assistance on employment rights.

Employment and Retirement Issues for Women is not a job-seeking manual. Rather, it focuses on the problems of currently employed midlife and older women. The workbook can be used by individual readers or as part of a group activity.

Weiss, Francine. *Older Women and Job Discrimination: A Primer.* Washington, DC: Older Women's League, 1984. 14p. $3.00 for members; $5.00 for nonmembers; $7.00 for organizations.

This booklet, prepared by a lawyer who specializes in employment discrimination, is designed to inform older women about "current" sex and age discrimination laws and about how to use those laws on their own behalf. Since it was published in 1984, it is not quite current, given the elimination of mandatory retirement in 1986. That aside, the booklet is an informative overview of what is covered under major laws protecting older women workers (the Age Discrimination in Employment Act and Title VII of the Civil Rights Act). It also points out how to identify discrimination in the form of lower wages, fewer benefits or training opportunities, lack of promotion, and transfer denials.

A valuable section of the booklet deals with signs that a woman may *not* have been discriminated against; for example, age may have been a bona fide occupational qualification; the employee might have had less seniority, or she may have lacked the necessary job qualifications.

The booklet contains a succinct explanation of what to do if discrimination is suspected, what to consider before initiating action, and what steps to take to remedy discrimination. Legal time limits are stressed. The names, addresses, and telephone numbers of EEOC field offices are provided.

Miscellaneous Reports

Crawley, Brenda, and Joseph Dancy, Jr. *Mature/Older Job Seeker's Guide.* Washington, DC: National Council on the Aging, 1984. iv, 126p. $8.00.

The authors of this publication are professional educators and trainers in mature/older person employment and training and have put their combined experiences to use in this easy-to-read, easy-to-follow job-seeking guidebook. A virtue of this publication is that there is very little extraneous or unnecessary material in it. While some of the advice is obvious, the sample forms, sample cover letters, sample resumés, and descriptions of how and when they have been used are an especially helpful and relatively unusual feature of the publication. So is a section on specific questions a mature job seeker might face; possible answers to those questions are included. The authors recommend and guide readers though a pre-job-hunt work-life review and skills (personal, work, and transferable) assessment.

Kahl, Anne. "Careers in the Field of Aging." *Occupational Outlook Quarterly* (Fall 1988): 3–21.

Not only does an aging society pose challenges for employers and employees, but it creates employment opportunities as well. This brief article describes a wide variety of direct service, program planning, administration, and evaluation careers in the aging field. The author explains why degrees in gerontology are not needed for many of the jobs, although experience and/or education generally are. Because the field is growing so rapidly, it is not known what the hiring requirements in the year 2000 will be. It is safe to say, however, that aging is a field with expanding job opportunities, many of which are challenging and rewarding, but often low paying.

Publications for the Employer, Practitioner, or Older Worker Adviser

As a scanning of many college or university library holdings makes abundantly clear, the aging field suffers from no shortage of scholarly publications on the aging work force, older workers, or retirement trends. In fact, employers, practitioners, and older worker advisers in search of the latest research and academic thinking on work and aging can, with relatively little effort, find more than enough to keep them reading for several months or more. However, as important as these publications are to an understanding of, for example, the changing composition of the work force or factors predisposing older workers to retire, their value to people who hire, supervise, work with, or train older workers is sometimes limited.

Therefore, this section concentrates on publications that, while they may be well written, insightful, and, indeed, even "scholarly," seem to have some application or practical relevance for persons engaged in hiring or promoting older workers. But these so-called practical writers are also prolific, and to impose some meaningful limit on the number of annotations, the listing includes mainly recent publications, somewhat arbitrarily defined as works published since 1980.

Reference Tools

American Association for International Aging, in conjunction with Business Publishers, Inc. *U.S. Directory and Source Book on Aging.* Silver Spring, MD: Business Publishers, 1989. xiv, 374p. $69.95.

> This one-volume indexed reference is a compilation of profiles of more than 300 organizations dealing with aging issues. In addition to address and telephone number, entries—which are arranged by state—include such information as a statement of the organization's primary mission, membership constituency, goals or purpose, primary concerns in aging, areas of activity, special services and resources, organization and structure, staffing, and funding sources. Also included is a master list of all major government agencies focusing on the aging.
>
> Although portions of directories are inevitably outdated as soon as they are published, they tend to be extremely useful references. This one can be ordered from Business Publishers, Inc., 951 Pershing Drive, Silver Spring, MD 20910-4464.

Coyle, Jean M. *Women and Aging: A Selected Annotated Bibliography.* Westport, CT: Greenwood, 1989. xxiii, 135p. $35.95. ISBN 0-313-26021-4.

> This annotated bibliography covers 13 broad topics, 3 of which—employment, retirement, and economics—should prove useful to readers interested in older women and work but who cannot keep up with the literature in the field. Chapter annotations are organized around books, articles, films, government documents, and dissertations. All referenced materials should be available through basic library systems.

Department of Health and Human Services. *Social Security Handbook.* 10th ed. Washington, DC: U.S. Government Printing Office, October 1988. 481p. $13.00. ICN 480075.

> Published every other year, the *Handbook* is a thorough reference work on the social security program, including information on virtually all aspects of program eligibility and benefits. It explains, for example, who employees are, who is considered self-employed, who pays payroll taxes, and what the retirement test is. Of primary value to employers and employee benefits specialists, its brief explanations may also help employees of all ages better understand social security.

Gerontological Society of America (GSA). *Data Resources in Gerontology: A Directory of Selected Information Vendors, Databases, and Archives.* Washington, DC: GSA, August 1989. 35p. $2.00.

> *Data Resources* is a useful catalog of the major aging-related databases. The section on information vendors that maintain selected databases gives name, address, telephone number, a brief description, accessing information, and general cost information for each vendor. Similar information is provided on bibliographic or reference databases, which catalog literature citations but not raw data. Information on data archives, or repositories of raw data, such as the Census Bureau, is covered elsewhere in the publication, which also includes the addresses and telephone numbers of regional Census offices and sources of state data on aging.

Hesslein, Shirley B. *Serials on Aging: An Analytical Guide.* Westport, CT: Greenwood, 1986. xx, 176p. $35.00. ISBN 0-313-24709-9.

> This reference book of journals and other serials in aging includes only two serials that focus specifically on employment; however, many others deal with employment-related issues, such as health and fringe benefits. A chapter on statistics and reference tools is very good.

Maddox, George L., editor-in-chief. *The Encyclopedia of Aging.* New York: Springer, 1987. xxv, 890p. $96.00. ISBN 0-8261-4840-9.

> This excellent and comprehensive reference tool provides short and authoritative descriptions of key topics and issues in aging, many of them employment related. An extensive list of references

to aging literature is included. The book's usefulness extends to job seekers as well as to employers, students, researchers, policy-makers, and others.

Sage Publications in cooperation with the National Council on the Aging (NCOA). *Abstracts in Social Gerontology*. Newbury Park, CA: Sage. $98.00 one-year subscription, institutions.

> This quarterly guide to literature on aging (formerly *Current Literature on Aging*) abstracts articles from recent books and more than 75 journals. Items are arranged by subject, for example, "Work and Retirement." Every fourth edition includes cumulative author and subject indices. Order through NCOA, P.O. Box 7227, Ben Franklin Station, Washington, DC 20044.

Wasserman, Paul, Barbara Koehler, and Yvonne Lev, eds. *Encyclopedia of Senior Citizens Information Sources*. 1st ed. Detroit, MI: Gale Research, 1987. 503p. $140.00. ISBN 0-8103-2192-0.

> This reference book was "compiled as a quick and convenient survey of basic information sources" on hundreds of topics in the field of aging. More than 13,000 entries cite publications, organizations, and other information sources, such as conferences, congresses, directories, and on-line databases. Entries are arranged alphabetically by subject and then by type of source and publication or organizational name. If an entry is repeated in a subsequent section, it is repeated in its entirety, precluding the necessity of flipping back and forth to obtain complete citations. This enhances the usefulness of the publication enormously.
>
> Many employment-related topics are covered; sections include "Employment," "Employment Services," "Job Placement," "Part-time Employment," and "Training and Retraining." Although citations are not abstracted, this reference can direct employers, program planners, employment trainers, students, older persons, and virtually anyone with an interest in or need for information on aging issues to a wealth of information sources.

Books

Birren, James E., and K. Warner Schaie, eds. *Handbook of the Psychology of Aging*. New York: Van Nostrand Reinhold, 1985. xvii, 931p. $78.95. ISBN 0-442-21401-4.

This invaluable volume of research in the area of the psychology of aging consists of 32 chapters on such technical subjects as the neural basis of aging, the ecology of aging, vision and aging, and emotion and affect. Parts 5 and 6, respectively, deal with psychological applications to the individual and to society. Of particular interest is Ross Stagner's excellent and practical chapter, "Aging in Industry." The chapter covers in a clear and concise fashion such important topics as job performance, training, mid-career change, work and ability, and motivation. Virtually anyone who deals with older workers in a professional capacity should find this chapter very informative. In fact, probably all professionals in the field of aging should have ready access to the book itself. (The 1990 edition of the *Handbook* does not include Stagner's or a related chapter.)

Boris, Michael E., Herbert S. Parnes, Steven H. Sandell, and Bert Seidman, eds. *The Older Worker*. Madison, WI: Industrial Relations Research Association, 1988. v, 228p. $15.00. ISBN 0-913447-41-2.

> The nine chapters in this publication represent an exploration of "the present state of knowledge about the status, characteristics, and problems of older workers" (p. v). Economists predominate among the authors represented in this book, one in a series of publications by the Industrial Relations Research Association that will probably appeal more to researchers than to other types of readers. Nevertheless, several chapters have a more obviously practical focus, for example, managing an older work force and functioning ability and job performance.

Bureau of National Affairs, Inc. (BNA). *Older Americans in the Workforce: Challenges and Solutions*. Washington, DC: BNA, 1987. ii., 237p. $75.00. ISBN 0-87179-900-6.

> *Older Americans in the Workforce* examines the challenges an aging work force poses for business, labor, government, attorneys, and associations. Case studies—largely corporate and more detailed than those found in some similar books—are the focus of chapters on preretirement planning, early retirement options, training and retraining, flexible work arrangements, rehiring arrangements, age discrimination, health care cost containment, physical accommodations, and dependent care. A resource guide lists and describes a number of public and private

organizations that have some interest—sometimes very tangential—in older worker employment issues and problems. The text of the 1967 Age Discrimination in Employment Act is reprinted in the appendix.

Dennis, Helen, ed. *Fourteen Steps in Managing an Aging Work Force.* Lexington, MA: Lexington, 1988. xi, 245p. $29.95, ISBN 0-669-13206-3.

> A compilation of 14 chapters plus epilogue by some of the country's top experts in the field of aging, this book cuts across academic specialties. Law, business, medicine, psychology, social work, and public policy are brought to bear on issues of concern to employers and human resource personnel who must manage an older work force. Among the chapters that should be especially informative for this audience are those dealing with age discrimination, stress and the older worker, older worker health care issues, older worker performance appraisal, the implications of older worker training and development, and alternative work options. The chapters tend to be concise, informative, and accessible to a nonacademic audience.

Doering, Mildred, Susan R. Rhodes, and Michael Schuster. *The Aging Worker: Research and Recommendations.* Beverly Hills, CA: Sage Publications, 1983. 391p. $29.95. ISBN 0-8039-1949-2.

> The objective of *The Aging Worker* is, in the words of the authors, "to provide background information for the academic researcher interested in pursuing research on aging and work, and for the human resource planner engaged in planning for an aging workforce" (p. 9). The authors have thus conducted a comprehensive literature review of mainly quantitative research that permits comparisons of older and younger workers along a number of dimensions. They have attempted to make their material comprehensible to nonacademic readers; however, the attention paid to methodology and tests of significance—necessary to the scholar who wants to assess the merits of the research—may make the book somewhat heavy going for the human resource planner. A simplified summary helps.
>
> Nonacademic readers might want to start with the final chapter, which summarizes and discusses the organizational implications of the findings. Neither positive nor negative findings

appear to be exaggerated. *The Aging Worker,* which looks at such work-related variables as performance, ability to learn, organizational commitment, job satisfaction, absenteeism, and accident frequency, is an important work, even though an update is probably in order.

Jacobson, Beverly. *Young Programs for Older Workers.* New York: Van Nostrand Reinhold, 1980. xvii, 123p. (Out of print; check library.)

> *Young Programs* is a casebook compiled to meet an apparent need among companies for information on what other establishments are doing for older workers. Written for the "intelligent layperson," the book is a description of some 70 examples of "progressive" older worker policies in effect among a variety of employers at the beginning of the 1980s. It is organized around (1) new work arrangements, which include part-time work, phased retirement, and second career training; (2) reentry women, who are typically women who left the work force to care for families; (3) secondary organizations, or organizations trying to establish data banks to improve the match of annuitants' skills and jobs; (4) redeployment or job displacement; (5) the "new hires," who are generally postretirement workers returning to the work force; and (6) assessing and advising older workers, including performance appraisal, continuing education and training, and preretirement planning.
>
> The number of examples of older worker policies and programs is not very impressive, even for the early 1980s, and many are mentioned in virtually every other compilation of older worker programs. Nonetheless, the book is very readable and, although some programs may have been abolished or substantially modified since the book was written, they may provide employers or human resource personnel just now beginning to worry about older workers with some ideas about what has been done. An advantage of this book is that it addresses a number of issues, such as appraisal, that are often left out of other and more recent publications on company programs for older workers.

Kahne, Hilda. *Reconceiving Part-Time Work: New Perspectives for Older Workers and Women.* Totowa, NJ: Rowman & Allanheld, 1985. xv, 180p. $37.00. ISBN 0-8476-7376-6.

If the employment potential of the population is to be realized fully, part-time employment must be redefined to improve wages, benefits, and job status. So argues Hilda Kahne in *Reconceiving Part-Time Work,* a clearly written, nontechnical overview of part-time employment in the United States. Kahne's "new concept" part-time work would prorate wages and benefits to a full-time equivalent, which would make such employment more attractive to both older workers and mothers caring for children. Various part-time alternatives, such as phased retirement, job sharing, work sharing, and flextime, are examined, as are the conditions under which those alternatives might work to the advantage of employers and employees alike. Both the cost savings and cost increases associated with part-time work are considered. Separate chapters are devoted to older worker interest in part-time work and the particular needs of women workers during various stages of their lives.

Kieffer, Jarold A. *Gaining the Dividends of Longer Life.* Boulder, CO: Westview, 1983. 174p. (Out of print; check library.)

The author of this book, staff director of the 1981 White House Conference on Aging, makes a plea for quick and imaginative action on the part of public and private policymakers to enable older persons, defined as 55 and above, to remain self-reliant beyond current retirement ages. He sees a need on the part of both society and older persons themselves to remain productive; otherwise, the economy and political system will be faced with burdensome dependency costs. *Gaining the Dividends of a Longer Life,* which evolved out of the 1979 report, *Older Americans: An Untapped Resource,* suggests how the goal of continued engagement can be achieved.

Of particular interest is the chapter titled "How To Create and Maintain Needed Jobs." Kieffer shuns make-work and argues instead for "meaningful, cost-effective, and stable jobs." A cost-effective strategy might entail (1) retention of older workers with the same employers, (2) more jobs for retirees, (3) new jobs that focus on unmet community needs, and (4) self-employment in small business. These options are described in considerable detail. Kieffer also suggests that support jobs in the military could be adequately performed by persons 55 and above.

McKee, William L., and Richard C. Froeschle. *Where the Jobs Are: Identification and Analysis of Local Employment Opportunities.* Kalamazoo, MI: W. E. Upjohn Institute for Employment Research, 1985. 175p. $11.95. ISBN 0-88099-029-5 (pbk).

> The objective of this publication is to assist the "nontechnical" reader in using labor market information (LMI) to analyze local labor markets, with an eye toward identifying occupations and industries with job openings. Labor force information, occupational information, and information on where and how to find a job are what LMI is all about. Such information can be used not only by job seekers, but by policymakers to spot employment problem areas, and by education and training planners, job developers, placement personnel, and career counselors, among others. In fact, a chapter on career counseling contains a particularly useful matrix for matching information needs with available resources.
>
> While the nontechnical job seeker can use the book to learn how to evaluate the job market, the book is not an easy read and will probably be left to the professionals whose job it may be to locate employment opportunities. The book explains how to conduct the local area industrial analyses that will identify growth industries and how to identify occupational opportunities within those industries. An appendix defines terms or concepts necessary to conducting the analyses (e.g., *establishment, civilian labor force*) and lists a number of LMI publications. Of particular value is a table of sources of labor market information that details what the sources cover (national or county data, for example), how often they are published, and where they can be found.

Morris, Robert, and Scott A. Bass, eds. *Retirement Reconsidered: Economic and Social Roles for Older People.* New York: Springer, 1988. xii, 258p. $33.95. ISBN 0-8261-5870-6.

> The 16 chapters in this volume, by economists, a psychologist, a lawyer, a Ph.D. in nursing, a political scientist, a philosopher, and a consulting actuary, among others, examine the implications of an aging society and the social and economic roles the elderly do and can play in that society. Although the book—

which looks at such topics as the demographic profile of maturing societies and the aging burden—is likely to be of greater interest to scholars and students than to employers and practitioners, several chapters provide information that might assist people who work with the elderly. These include a short chapter on older worker employment opportunities in the private sector that examines the need for older workers and the barriers to their employment, a chapter that dispels some of the pernicious myths about older workers, and another that focuses on the role of higher education in developing new opportunities for the aged to contribute significantly to society.

Mowsesian, Richard. *Golden Goals, Rusted Realities: Work and Aging in America.* Far Hills, NJ: New Horizon, 1986. $18.95. xxi, 262p. ISBN 0-88282-024-9.

> Since everyone ages, complete objectivity in dealing with aging is impossible, contends the author at the outset of *Golden Goals*. He then goes on to criticize much of the aging literature for treating the subject of aging in an impersonal way, a criticism that cannot be applied to this book. Its "fundamental thesis . . . is that older workers are a grossly overlooked human resource" (p. xiii). The importance of meaningful work to persons of all ages is stressed in a lengthy discussion of work as the core of human existence. Age discrimination, loss of career, and the like remove the elderly from the ranks of the productive, but Mowsesian argues that everyone can be productive. This book may enhance older readers' sense of self-worth and encourage them to stay active, but it is more of a motivational tool than a book of practical job-seeking advice or information.

National Council on the Aging and the Institute of Electrical and Electronics Engineers. *The Aging Workforce: The Challenge of Utilization.* New York: Institute of Electrical and Electronics Engineers, 1986. xiii, 198p. $10.00. Catalogue No. UH-01735.

> In 1986, the National Council on the Aging and the Institute of Electrical and Electronics Engineers cosponsored a conference aimed specifically at engineers and older technical workers. This publication compiles the presentations at that conference, many of which deal with broad work and aging issues (e.g., the "ideal" retirement system, age discrimination), rather than the target population.

A speaker from Aerospace Corporation explains how the utilization of knowledgeable older workers enhanced the productivity of that corporation and describes ways to make use of those workers, while another considers the different challenges—positive and negative—of managing young, middle-aged, and old engineers.

The book may be ordered from the IEEE Service Center, 445 Hoes Lane, Piscataway, NJ 08854; (800) 678-4333.

Nye, David. *Alternative Staffing Strategies.* Washington, DC: Bureau of National Affairs, Inc., 1988. xvi, 203p. $32.00. ISBN 0-8719-548-5.

This book presents a broad overview of various forms of alternative staffing strategies from the perspective of employees and employers, examining several in some detail: (1) temporary work, (2) employee leasing, (3) hiring retirees and older employees, (4) telecommuting, and (5) individual employment contracts. The advantages and disadvantages of each option are clearly spelled out.

The author defines what alternative staffing strategies are and how they depart from permanent, full-time, lifelong employment. Especially informative are the examples of specific companies that have used alternative strategies, why the alternatives originated, and how they worked. The chapter on older workers and retirees examines myths about older workers and strategies for successfully using such workers. Employers and human resource managers, in particular, will find this book a useful reference.

Olmsted, Barney, and Suzanne Smith. *Creating a Flexible Workplace: How To Select and Manage Alternative Work Options.* New York: AMACOM (division of the American Management Association), 1989. xiv, 461p. $49.95. ISBN 0-8144-5919-6.

Written by the cofounders and codirectors of New Ways to Work, this book is a comprehensive and very practical guide to ten alternative work options: (1) flextime, (2) compressed work, (3) regular part-time work, (4) job sharing, (5) phased and part-time retirement, (6) voluntary reduced work time, (7) leave time, (8) work sharing, (9) flexplace, and (10) contingent employment.

Chapters are organized around an easy-to-follow outline that covers the origins of the option, who uses it, when it is most appropriate, its pros and cons, whether an organization should try it, and how to introduce it.

The book has a tremendous amount of very useful information, an extensive "suggested reading" list, and many helpful examples of schedules, forms, and worksheets. It is certainly recommended for employers interested in whether and how to implement a variety of alternative work options.

Rosen, Benson, and Thomas H. Jerdee. *Older Employees: New Roles for Valued Resources*. Homewood, IL: Dow Jones-Irwin, 1985. ix, 201p. $19.95. (Out of print; check library.)

> *Older Employees* is a book for employers and/or their human resource staffs, written by older worker experts whose goal is "to contribute to effective management of older employees"; the authors aim to provide the "concepts and strategies" that will promote effective management.
>
> The book deals with a series of challenges for managers: the development and implementation of comprehensive systems of career management for older workers, the development of accurate and fair systems of assessing older worker performance and potential, the development and implementation of effective systems for maintaining and improving older worker skills, the development and implementation of flexible retirement systems, the achievement of optimal work adjustment for employees and a smooth transition to retirement, and the integration of all of these into a coherent organizational program.
>
> The chapter on the Age Discrimination in Employment Act (ADEA) was written before mandatory retirement was eliminated, but the brief discussions of basic provisions up to the 1986 ADEA amendments and litigation procedures may be helpful. The lack of a bibliography or citations for the research and studies mentioned throughout the book makes it difficult to follow up on some of the important points the authors stress, particularly with regard to issues of crucial concern to employers: older worker absenteeism, work ability, changes in physical conditions with age, and the implications of any age-related physical changes.

Sandell, Steven H., ed. *The Problem Isn't Age: Work and Older Americans*. New York: Praeger, 1987. xiii, 265p. $37.95. ISBN 0-275-92371-1.

In 1982, the National Commission on Employment Policy, an independent federal agency, sponsored research on the aging work force. Experts in the area prepared papers on a range of topics that, in edited versions, form the nucleus of this book. The book's title is a summary of its conclusion: the problems older workers face are not necessarily the result of their age; rather, they stem from (1) "factors unrelated to age, such as racial discrimination or depressed labor markets; (2) factors correlated with age [e.g., poor health, lower educational attainment]; and (3) age discrimination" (pp. xii-xiii).

The book begins with chapters by the editor that review the demographic and economic context within which older worker issues should be examined and employment policies affecting older workers. In the 12 following chapters, work and aging experts look at (1) labor market problems such as the reduced pay of older job losers, age changes and productivity, earnings, part-time employment, and job displacement and employment services; and (2) older worker policies and prospects, including government employment and training programs, state and local employment initiatives, private employment practices, work alternatives, retirement age and social security changes, health plan costs, and volunteer activities. The editor ends with a discussion of the implications of the research.

The chapters in this book are very readable; when the editor says the book was "written for interested people, not only specialists," he is correct.

Shaw, Lois Banfill, ed. *Unplanned Careers: The Working Lives of Middle-Aged Women.* Lexington, MA: Lexington, 1983. viii, 149p. $29.00. ISBN 0-669-05701-0.

In 1967, Ohio State University undertook the National Longitudinal Survey of the Labor Market Experience of Mature Women, which began with personal interviews with more than 5,000 women aged 30 to 44. Interviews were also conducted in 1969, 1971, 1972, and 1977. *Unplanned Careers,* covering ten years of data, is based on the 4,000 women still in the sample in 1977.

Given the significant changes in the lives of women and societal expectations about women's roles over the ten-year period, *Unplanned Careers* is an important book. The editor herself reviews some of the societal changes affecting women in the first Chapter and goes on to examine problems of labor force reentry and the causes of irregular employment patterns in the next two chapters. Other scholars tackle occupational atypicality, attitudes toward work, economic consequences of poor health among mature women, and the economic consequences of mid-life change in marital status.

General readers will find the chapter conclusions informative, but, on the whole, the chapters tend to be rather technical and will be of primary interest to like-minded scholars and researchers.

U.S. Department of Labor. *Opportunity 2000: Creative Affirmative Action Strategies for a Changing Workforce.* Prepared by the Hudson Institute for the Department of Labor. Washington, DC: U.S. Government Printing Office, September 1988. xiv, 181p. $5.00. S/N 029-014-00242-9.

> *Opportunity 2000* provides a review of eight major trends that "will revolutionize tomorrow's workforce." A 12-page chapter on the older work force emphasizes the need business will have for older workers and discusses ways to attract them. These include incentives such as job adaptation, phased retirement, training and retraining, job banks, and volunteer programs. Selected companies using various incentives are mentioned.

Work in America Institute. *New Work Schedules for a Changing Society.* Scarsdale, NY: Work in America Institute, 1981. 128p. $12.00. ISBN 0-89361-025-9.

> Although published in 1981, this book's 50 recommendations to guide employers through the process of making decisions about and implementing new work options are still valid today. Readers interested solely in the recommendations will find them summarized at the beginning of the book. These very specific, almost "micro," recommendations deal broadly with (1) choosing new work schedules, (2) managing new work patterns, (3) seeking new solutions to energy and commuting problems through new work schedules, (4) new work schedules and employment policy, (5) work schedules and family time, and (6) the dangers of overtime abuse. Each of the six issues is discussed in greater detail in subsequent chapters.
>
> The book clearly describes the various types of new work schedules, the pros and cons of various options, and who uses new work schedules. This last information, much of it from the

late 1970s, is now dated, but little else in the book is. Most of the recommendations are targeted at employers; however, the need to involve unions in the decision-making process is reflected in a number of them. Several apply to public policymakers.

While it would be too much to expect that following the recommendations would enable employers to avoid all problems associated with implementing new work schedules, the recommendations seem to cover most contingencies, and heeding their advice would certainly minimize potential problems.

For ordering information, contact the Work in America Institute, 700 White Plains Road, Scarsdale, NY 10583.

Newsletters and Periodicals

Aging Action Alert
Monthly. 8–10p. $105.00 per year.

CD Publications
8204 Fenton Street
Silver Spring, MD 20910
(301) 588-6380

> This monthly newsletter provides news and advice on programs—including those dealing with such issues as job training—for the aged, although employment is not its primary focus. Also included in the newsletter are research updates and reports on relevant legislation. Senior program administrators seem to be the primary intended readership.

Aging Network News
Monthly. $55.00 per year.

P.O. Box 1223
McLean, VA 22101
(703) 734-3266

> *Aging Network News* describes itself as "the only national newspaper dedicated to the entire world of those who are involved in the concerns of aging . . . in the workforce, in health care delivery systems, in politics, in building and product design, in all facets of everyday life." Brief articles highlight such issues as elder care and the corporate sector, age-related issues being debated on

Capitol Hill, and state action on aging that may or may not be relevant to older worker concerns.

Aging Research and Training News
Biweekly newsletter. 8p. $153.50 per year.

Business Publishers, Inc.
951 Pershing Drive
Silver Spring, MD 20910-4464
(301) 587-6300

> *Aging Research and Training News* provides information on re-search funding, grant opportunities, and research awards in the aging field and summarizes recent developments in aging, including research findings, relevant legislative developments, and news on aging. The newsletter is by no means restricted to employment issues, although those issues are covered as appropriate.

The Aging Workforce
Quarterly newsletter. No charge.

National Council on the Aging
600 Maryland Avenue, SW, West Wing 100
Washington, DC 20024
(202) 479-1200

> *The Aging Workforce* is a publication for business leaders produced by the National Council on the Aging's Prime Time Productivity program. It includes readable overviews of developments in the field of aging and work and descriptions of viable older worker programs. A recent eight-page edition highlighted observations at the conference, "Survival in the 90s: Maximizing the Bottom Line, the Older Worker Resource," research findings demonstrating that older people can excel on computers, and the mature worker recruitment effort of Kelly Services.

Monthly Labor Review
Monthly. $20.00 per year.

Superintendent of Documents
U.S. Government Printing Office
Washington, DC 20402
(202) 783-3238

This monthly publication of approximately 100 pages includes a wealth of statistics and articles on topics relevant to an understanding of older workers and their employment behavior and opportunities. Articles occasionally deal specifically with older workers; others often focus on issues relevant to older worker employment, for example, contingent work and alternative work schedules. The publication also includes book reviews, research summaries, and many tables on current labor statistics.

Senior Law Report
Twice-monthly newsletter. $177.00 per year.

8204 Fenton Street
Silver Spring, MD 20910
(800) 666-6380

A publication of eight to ten pages, *Senior Law Report* covers pending and enacted legislation, court rulings, and other developments related to the legal status of the aged. While it does not deal exclusively with work-related topics, this newsletter covers a number of issues likely to concern employers and older worker experts and advocates, such as social security and pension policies and age discrimination.

Social Security Bulletin
Monthly. $19.00 per year.

Superintendent of Documents
U.S. Government Printing Office
Washington, DC 20402
(202) 783-3238

The official monthly publication of the Social Security Administration, the *Social Security Bulletin* provides statistics and analyses on social security and related programs. It is likely to carry articles on issues bearing on older worker employment, such as the impact of raising the full retirement age on older workers in physically demanding occupations, trends in mortality and health status, or the earnings test. A number of articles in recent years have dealt with the employment behavior of new social security beneficiaries.

The subscription includes a copy of the *Annual Statistical Supplement*.

Working Age
Bimonthly newsletter. Free of charge to businesses and organizations interested in older worker issues (use letterhead to request).

Worker Equity Department
American Association of Retired Persons
1909 K Street, NW
Washington, DC 20049
(202) 662-4956

> This AARP newsletter about the changing work force focuses on employment issues affecting midlife and older workers. A recent issue, for example, included a chronology of congressional, judicial, and agency decisions about pension benefits accruals for the post-65 retiree, as well as articles on additional pension benefits accruing to individuals who work beyond age 65, employers and elder care, older worker employment opportunities in Japan, and employer preparation (of which there has been little) for an aging work force.

Pamphlets

American Association of Retired Persons (AARP). *Business and Older Workers: Current Perceptions and New Directions for the 1990's.* Washington, DC: AARP, December 1989. 24p.
PW4428(1189).D13827.

> This is an update of *Workers over 50: Old Myths, New Realities,* a survey conducted for AARP in 1985. The 1985 study focused on human resource executives' positive attitudes toward older workers. Executives were, however, somewhat skeptical about older workers' comfort with new technology.
> In 1989, the Daniel Yankelovich Group again interviewed executives with senior responsibility for human resource decision making in 400 companies of 50 or more employees. *Business and Older Workers* summarizes the major findings of that study, which have disturbing implications for the employment opportunities of senior workers. Although executives still view older workers very positively when it comes to such attributes as loyalty, firm dedication, and quality, and although they are more likely than they were in 1985 to regard older workers as

comfortable with new technologies, the gap between perceived comfort with new technologies and the importance of being comfortable with those technologies has widened substantially. This gap is especially significant in view of the fact that the respondents feel that new technologies will provide most of the future's productivity improvements. Furthermore, in marked contrast to the earlier survey, which found that executives were most concerned about the insurance costs of workers with dependents, in 1989, older male workers were considered more expensive to insure.

American Association of Retired Persons (AARP). *How To Manage Older Workers*. Washington, DC: AARP, Worker Equity Department, 1988. 16p. No charge. PW4162(788).D13288.

> This booklet of advice for managers includes a number of principles designed to motivate older workers by identifying their needs, setting goals, and rewarding achievement. It also examines age stereotypes, how stereotypes affect work relationships, and what can be done about them. Suggestions are offered for dealing with common management problems such as communications breakdowns, status uncertainties, skills obsolescence, resistance to change, and dealing with conflict.

American Association of Retired Persons (AARP). *How To Recruit Older Workers*. Washington, DC: AARP, Worker Equity Department. 1988. 16p. No charge. PW4157(788).D13279.

> Designed to help employers recruit older workers, this booklet is organized around a variety of older worker types: (1) midlife career changers, (2) early retirees, (3) older retirees, (4) displaced workers, and (5) persons—namely, women—who have never worked outside the home. Discussion focuses on who these people are, why they might need to work, and what they want. It offers very specific advice, e.g., be sure to check the local demographic scene and labor market information to ensure that there are enough older people to justify recruitment efforts.

American Association of Retired Persons (AARP). *How To Train Older Persons*. Washington, DC: AARP, Worker Equity Department. 16p. No charge. PW4161(788).D13287.

This guide to the training of mature workers starts from the premise that "effective career management is the first line of defense" against some of the common employment problems of older workers: career burnout, plateauing, and obsolescence. Some practical suggestions for solving those problems are offered, as are steps to take in developing a well-designed career management system that takes full advantage of a firm's older employees. These steps include determining the organization's needs, designing a training program, and motivating older workers to take advantage of training opportunities. Effective training techniques are discussed briefly.

American Association of Retired Persons (AARP). *Using the Experience of a Lifetime*. Washington, DC: AARP, Worker Equity Department, 1988. 40p. No charge. PW4187(888).D13353.

Taken from AARP's computerized data system of older worker employment programs (NOWIS), the examples of employment programs in this publication highlight companies that provide older worker full- and part-time employment opportunities, older worker training, job redesign, and retirement transition assistance. Though brief and lacking specifics as to how programs operate, the examples demonstrate effective utilization of older workers and may also serve as ammunition for older persons who wish to remain in or reenter the work force.

Axel, Helen. *Job Banks for Retirees*. Report No. 929. New York: Conference Board, 1989. viii, 37p. Price varies (see below).

Job Banks reports on the results of interviews with executives from 28 corporations with job banks, which are rosters of internal temporary employment pools. The banks range from relatively informal reemployment programs to well-established pools that have existed for as long as 10 to 15 years. No one model, it is stressed, is suitable for all companies.

Relatively few of the banks consist entirely of retired workers, but retired workers figure prominently in all of them. The report discusses what job banks are, presents profiles of a number of them, and devotes considerable space to the matter of managing job banks. A final chapter highlights management's overwhelmingly positive perspectives on jobs banks.

Job Banks should be a useful resource to employers and managers interested in establishing and managing job banks. For information on ordering, contact the Conference Board, Inc., 845 Third Avenue, New York, NY 10022; (212) 759-0900. The price of the report varies, depending on whether the purchaser is an associate of the Conference Board, a nonprofit organization, or "other."

National Alliance of Business (NAB). *Invest in Experience: New Directions for an Aging Workforce.* Washington, DC: NAB, 1985. 25p. $3.95.

Invest in Experience is based on the premise that corporations should turn their attention to older workers not out of a sense of social responsibility but because it makes good business sense. This report identifies eight reasons that is so and briefly mentions what a number of companies are doing to take advantage of an older labor supply. Such companies are, as the report points out, still more the exception than the rule. Potential barriers to older worker labor force participation and corporate older worker strategies are also discussed.

To order, contact the NAB Clearinghouse, 1201 New York Avenue, NW, Washington, DC 20005; (202) 289-2910.

U.S. Department of Labor. *Older Worker Task Force: Key Policy Issues for the Future.* Report of the Secretary of Labor. Washington, DC: U.S. Department of Labor, January 1989. 30p. No charge.

The Department of Labor's Older Worker Task Force was established to evaluate the work force implications of the maturing of the work force and the drop in young labor force applicants. This report, which provides no answers or recommendations, represents an effort to "guide policy makers toward the key policy issues of the future" (p. i). Its three sections deal with (1) tomorrow's work force, (2) tomorrow's workplace, and (3) public policy conclusions and issues. A key conclusion is that public policy "must enable older workers to remain in or return to the work force without institutional barriers limiting their choices" (p. iv).

To order, contact U.S. Department of Labor, Office of Public Information, 200 Constitution Avenue, NW, Washington, DC 20210.

Miscellaneous Reports

Alegria, Fernando L., Jr., and Ann Lordeman. *Serving Older Individuals under the Job Training Partnership Act: State Initiatives and Practices*. Washington, DC: National Governors' Association and National Association of State Units on Aging, 1988. 19p. $6.75.

> *Serving Older Individuals* highlights state activity on and approaches to administrative arrangements for JTPA 3-percent older worker programs, SCSEP and 3-percent program coordination, dislocated older workers, expenditures, income eligibility, performance standards and goals, training options for older worker programs, entrepreneurial programs for older individuals, state-level older worker media campaigns, and state task forces on older individuals. Given the brevity of this report, each topic is dealt with in only a cursory fashion; relatively little information for specific states is provided.
>
> Order from National Governors Association, 444 North Capitol Street, Washington, DC 20001.

American Association of Retired Persons (AARP). *AARP WORKS*. Employment Planning Program Manuals for Participants and Program Leaders. Washington, DC: AARP, undated.

> *AARP WORKS* is an employment planning program to help midlife and older workers find employment that meets their needs and abilities. The program consists of a series of eight job search workshops led by AARP volunteer teams and community agencies at sites around the country. Among the topics covered are identifying skills and values, taking responsibility for the job search, and implementing a job search plan. Separate manuals for workshop leaders and participants include a variety of activities and exercises, as well as guides and references to other resources.
>
> Workshops are offered around the country. For further information, contact AARP WORKS, Worker Equity Department, American Association of Retired Persons, 1909 K Street, NW, Washington, DC 20049. Please note that the title of the program may be changed.

Beaver, Linda Zane, and Lorraine Lidoff. *Retiree Employment Program Model.* Vol. III. Washington, DC: National Council on the Aging, 1983. 22p. 30+ pages of appendices. $8.00.

> Part of the National Council on the Aging's Developments in Service Delivery for the Aging series, this volume is a guide that companies can use to develop reemployment options for company retirees. The model, based on the Travelers Retiree Job Bank, focuses on temporary or part-time positions filled by capable former employees knowledgeable about the company. Reemployment planning, organization, development, and implementation are discussed, and the specific steps in each stage are spelled out. The publication also includes suggested readings on retiree employment, planning, public relations, and evaluation. The Travelers Pre-Retirement Opinion Survey and Retirement Opinion Survey, reprinted in the appendix, might be used as is or adapted by employers interested in soliciting similar information.

Boyd, Arthur, and Judy Chynoweth. *Increasing Employment for Older Workers: State Leadership.* Washington, DC: Council of State Policy and Planning Agencies, 1987. xi, 76p. $6.00.

> The authors of this report contend that state governors must take the lead in increasing older worker employment because they have both the authority and the resources to do so. The Council of State Planning Agencies' Academy on Increasing Older Worker Employment set out to help six state teams (in Colorado, Florida, Mississippi, Montana, Nebraska, and New Hampshire) define and develop appropriate approaches to dealing with older worker problems and produce two-year plans of action. Boyd and Chynoweth describe what the states did and publish the documents developed by the states to improve opportunities for older workers.
>
> Order from the Council of State Policy and Planning Agencies, Hall of States, 400 North Capitol Street, Suite 291, Washington, DC 20001.

Fretz, Burton W., and Neal S. Dudovitz. *The Law of Age Discrimination: A Reference Manual.* Chicago: National Clearinghouse for Legal Services, Inc., January 1987. xxvi, 89p. $15.00. Clearinghouse No. 42,450.

The Law of Age Discrimination provides a clear and concise description of the Age Discrimination in Employment Act (ADEA) and extensive references to court cases prior to 1987. In addition to an overview of the ADEA and what it covers, the book discusses administrative exhaustion (prior to a civil suit), civil actions, defenses, remedies, and jury instruction. Although it has been several years since this report was published, it still serves as an informative overview of the ADEA and court action on age discrimination for older workers, employers, and older worker advocates, among others.

For ordering information, contact the National Clearinghouse for Legal Services, Inc., 407 South Dearborn, Suite 400, Chicago, IL 60605; (312) 939-3830.

Fyock, Catherine D., and Greg Newton. *Making the Older Worker Connection.* Louisville, KY: Innovative Management Concepts, 1988. 33p. $16.00.

Billed as the "complete guide to facts, figures, names, addresses, and phone numbers to make your older worker program a success," this spiral-bound publication prepared by management consultants consists of tips on how to recruit older workers by word of mouth, media contacts, and advertising in mass transit, shopping malls, and church newspapers. It also includes messages that presumably work in the recruitment effort, a list of employers who hire older workers, and the addresses and telephone numbers of state units on aging.

For ordering information, contact Innovative Management Concepts, P.O. Box 905, Louisville, KY 40059; (502) 228-3869.

Harris, Louis, and Associates, Inc. *Older Americans: Ready and Able To Work.* Report No. 1 in a series; Study No. 884030. New York: Louis Harris and Associates, Inc., undated. 22p. No charge.

In 1989, the Commonwealth Fund, as part of its Older Americans at Work Program, contracted with Louis Harris and Associates to interview over 3,500 individuals between the ages of 50 and 64. The objective of the program was "to improve employment opportunities available to older Americans," and the survey was a step toward that end. It looked at how many older Americans are able and willing to work, whether they are employable, and why some stop working while others continue.

The results will be used to ascertain what government and the private sector can do to keep people working or to get them back into the labor force.

A database has been created with information on such topics as work history, work preferences, reasons for working or not working, retirement decision making, and health. The sample of persons between the ages of 50 and 64 represents about 21.5 million people, 38 percent of whom are not working. This first report presents the major findings on respondents who are ready and able to work. The study identified 1.9 million nonworking Americans who fall into that category; 1.1 million were seen as "most ready and able to work." The report highlights the types of jobs in which respondents would be interested and the conditions under which they would accept employment.

For ordering information, contact the Commonwealth Fund, One East 75th Street, New York, NY 10021; (212) 535-0400.

Lester, Brenda. *A Practitioner's Guide for Training Older Workers.* Washington, DC: National Commission on Employment Policy, undated. 213p. No charge.

This publication is exactly what its title says it is: a guide to aid practitioners in training older workers in Job Training Partnership Act (JTPA) programs. It covers design, implementation, and evaluation of programs and places a particular emphasis on the private sector, since that is where most jobs are. The guide assumes that "JTPA practitioners will act as catalysts for bringing together older workers and private-sector employers" (p. 2).

The four sections of the book deal with (1) the JTPA, (2) program planning and development, (3) program operation, and (4) program evaluation. The longest section, Part II, is divided into three chapters that review older worker employment needs, employment barriers, techniques to increase employment opportunities, job placement strategies, determining the work force needs of employers, older worker employment barriers from the perspective of employers, techniques employers can use to increase older worker employment opportunities, appropriate strategies for marketing older workers in the private sector, and administrative issues in program planning and development.

Recommendations for practitioners, many of which are very practical, are highlighted and easy to locate. JTPA program operators will find a tremendous amount of basic information on older workers that has a bearing on JTPA activities, as well as advice on what to do about specific problems that older workers face. Case examples illuminate with descriptive information. Appendices abstract National Center for Employment Policy older worker studies, describe the National Older Workers Information System, and list the national Senior Community Service Employment Program sponsors and a number of older worker resource organizations. All in all, this appears to be a comprehensive and very valuable resource for JTPA program operators.

Lordeman, Ann, Solomon G. Jacobson, and Susan Coombs-Ficke, eds. *Proceedings of the National Invitational Conference on Older Worker Involvement in the Job Training Partnership Act, May 6–7, 1984.* Washington, DC: National Association of State Units on Aging, July 1984. 94p. $8.00.

In 1984, 145 federal, state, and local officials responsible for developing and implementing the Job Training Partnership Act (JTPA) met to discuss strategies for training and placing economically disadvantaged older workers and to identify older worker opportunities in growth and high-tech jobs. These conference proceedings highlight discussions at that conference. Three key chapters cover (1) planning and measurement, (2) coordination and organization, and (3) recruitment, training, and placement. Briefly summarized is practical information on older worker recruitment procedures, public relations efforts, and supportive service needs such as health care and transportation.

The JTPA was new when the conference was held, so information based on experience, particularly that of trial and error, is limited. However, many of the suggestions and observations would undoubtedly be made at a JTPA conference held today. The proceedings make a very important point that older worker advocates should bear in mind, namely, that "to many employers, the 'older worker' problem is their presence in the work force not [their] training and hiring" (p. 40).

National Association of State Units on Aging (NASUA). *Finding Jobs for Older Workers.* Washington, DC: NASUA, undated. 107p. $26.50.

Many practical suggestions on ways to market older workers to employers can be found in this spiral-bound book, which summarizes observations made at a seminar sponsored by NASUA and the Center for Community Futures. The publication looks at (1) the target market, (2) employer marketing campaigns, (3) how to make sales to employers, (4) marketing materials for employers, and (5) marketing the older individual. Direct mail tips are included, as are guidelines for meeting with small business owners, preparing and distributing a newsletter for employers, and making a sale. The advice is very specific, with a minimum of verbiage. Because the goal of most employment programs is to place workers in the private sector, what works with employers is of utmost importance.

National Caucus and Center on Black Aged, Inc. (NCCBA). *Job Placement Systems for Older Workers.* Volume 1: *Research Findings, Case Studies, Program Models* (ix, 274p.); Volume 2: *A Planning Framework: Placement Tools and Techniques* (v, 125p.). Washington, DC: NCCBA, undated.

> *Job Placement Systems* reports on a study of "successful" job placement systems for older workers funded through the Job Training Partnership Act (JTPA), the Senior Community Service Employment Program (SCSEP), Displaced Homemakers' Program, and some privately funded programs. The first volume begins with a discussion of six key elements of successful older worker placement programs. Major chapters include an introduction to the study of job placement systems for older workers and a review of the JTPA 3-percent set-aside. A total of 23 case studies are described in separate chapters on JTPA programs, SCSEP, displaced homemakers' programs, and "programs for special circumstances."
>
> Volume 2 is the "how-to" volume, with chapters on designing and managing older worker placement systems and on placement tools and techniques.
>
> Copies have been available through the NCCBA, 1424 K Street, NW, Suite 500, Washington, DC 20005.

National Commission for Employment Policy (NCEP). *Older Worker Employment Comes of Age: Practice and Potential.* Washington, DC: NCEP, undated. 94p. No charge.

> In 1982, the National Commission for Employment Policy sponsored 14 research projects on the labor market problems of older

Americans. Findings and observations believed to be of value to local and state governments, program operators, and the private sector are included in this volume. The guide, as it is referred to, reviews the status of older workers and their employment issues and then identifies older worker practices and initiatives that have been or could be undertaken by (1) the public, private, and community sectors; (2) employers and labor; (3) state and local governments; and (4) community groups. A final section deals with developing older worker employment strategies.

The facts and figures cited in this publication may now be dated, as are some of the statements about older workers and the law (e.g., this was written before the 1986 Age Discrimination in Employment Act amendments). For readers unaware of some of the changes in the law, particularly those changes less well publicized than the elimination of mandatory retirement, the publication's now erroneous information could pose problems. That is a shame, because much of the book's content (such as what is involved in assessing the local labor market for older workers or what communities or employers have done on behalf of older workers) is as valid and potentially useful today as it was in the mid-1980s.

9to5, National Association of Working Women. *Social Insecurity: The Economic Marginalization of Older Workers.* Cleveland, OH: 9to5, September 1987. 140p. $7.00 for members; $15.00 for nonmembers.

The basic thesis of this report is that older workers are "shock absorbers for a changing economy"; early retirements and layoffs are pushing older workers out of the labor force and into increasingly marginal statuses. Pervasive age discrimination and the decline of unions are seen as placing older workers, especially women, at a great disadvantage when it comes to getting a job and remaining employed.

Numerous tables and figures document such developments and topics as population and labor force growth, unemployment, earnings, and pension receipt. The report calls for a comprehensive older worker employment policy and provides suggestions as to what that might entail.

Older Women's League (OWL). *Building Public/Private Coalitions for Older Women's Employment: An OWL Guidebook.* Washington, DC: OWL, July 1987. 30p., mimeo. $10.95 for members, $15.95 for nonmembers, $19.95 for institutions.

Based on three demonstration projects, this guidebook explains the dos and don'ts of building coalitions to promote midlife and older women's employment opportunities. Establishing and nurturing coalitions can pay off; however, the report notes that doing this is a "difficult and time-consuming activity." The report discusses a number of principles that should assist in coalition building, for example, "build on existing relationships first," "allow plenty of time," "develop a common understanding of the purpose of [the] coalition." Where relevant, findings from the demonstration projects are included. For example, one demonstration site found that big business lent names and prestige to coalition efforts, while smaller firms had the flexibility to make needed changes. The coalition thus concentrated job development efforts on smaller firms while accepting the type of help big business would provide.

The report ends with a discussion of a number of "action options" for coalition builders, among which are hints or suggestions on how to involve businesses in coalitions and how to utilize businesses reluctant to join job coalitions (i.e., on advisory boards).

Building Public/Private Coalitions is a very well-written report on the advantages and potential pitfalls of coalition building that offers specific suggestions about establishing and maintaining coalitions.

Operation ABLE of Greater Boston. *A Silver Opportunity*. Boston: Operation ABLE, undated. 64p. $7.25 plus $1.50 postage and handling. (Reduced per copy price for multiple orders.)

Successful initiatives taken by employers to hire older workers, obtained from hundreds of interviews with employers and from roundtable discussions with 60 company representatives, form the core of this publication. In addition to presenting company models of such initiatives as part-time work, flexplace, temporary work, and efforts to maintain the productivity of long-tenure employees, the report attempts to counter myths about older worker productivity, training ability, ability to get along with others, attendance, compensation, and benefits costs. A number of older worker employment programs are listed at the end.

Order from Operation ABLE of Greater Boston, World Trade Center Boston, Suite 306, Boston, MA 02210-2004; (617) 439-5580.

Perlman, Leonard G., and Gary F. Austin, eds. *The Aging Workforce: Implications for Rehabilitation*. Alexandria, VA: National Rehabilitation Association, 1987. 83p. $15.00.

> In October 1986, the Eleventh Mary E. Switzer Memorial Seminar brought together 20 individuals from a variety of backgrounds and disciplines, as well as consumers, to discuss the rehabilitation implications of an aging society. *The Aging Workforce* is a collection of seven papers, five of which were written for the seminar. Chapters of particular relevance to employers and human resource personnel include "Challenges for the Older Worker in the Rehabilitation Process," "Aging and Employment: Guides for the Rehabilitation Counselor and Employer," "Options for Equality of Services for the Older Worker with a Disability," and "The Need for Rehabilitation Services among Older Workers." Where appropriate, chapters include an easy-to-locate summary of recommendations for action.
>
> Perhaps one of the most pertinent points made during the seminar was that of Switzer Scholar Malcolm Morrison to the effect that a distinction must be made between permanent medical impairment and disability. Medical information alone, he stresses, is generally not enough to predict an individual's ability to perform. Disability "can be determined only within the context of the personal, social, or occupational demands or statutory or regulatory requirements that the individual is unable to meet as a result of [any] impairment" (p. 2).
>
> This is a practical document for persons involved with aging workers with disabilities, although many of the recommendations and observations apply to older workers in general.

Rothstein, Frances R., ed. *Commitment to an Aging Workforce: Strategies and Models for Helping Older Workers Achieve Full Potential*. Washington, DC: National Council on the Aging, 1988. 194p. $15.00.

> Although its title suggests a focus on older workers in general, *Commitment to an Aging Workforce* is primarily concerned with improving older worker services under the Job Training Partnership Act (JTPA). A chapter on employment-related programs for older workers, therefore, takes a look at the JTPA and programs in which JTPA participants might get involved—those funded

under the Senior Community Service Employment Program, the Vocational Education Act, and the Adult Education Act. The manual, an edited assortment of articles by older worker practitioners, relies heavily on information gleaned from demonstration programs funded through NCOA's Prime Time Productivity program.

Considerable attention is paid to coordination activities at the state and local levels. Readers relatively new to the JTPA might find especially informative a section that spells out the state's role with regard to the JTPA; for example, the governor determines which state agencies will administer JTPA older worker set-asides.

Specific efforts to solve some problems are described in detail, as in the case of an Ohio task force established to deal with the common problem of underexpenditures in the JTPA 3-percent set-aside for older workers. Sections on coordination also deal with such issues as interagency agreements, performance standards, and coordination between JTPA and community colleges.

Older worker recruitment, training, and business outreach and marketing are covered, as is a topic often neglected in publications designed to promote employment—the importance of training older worker program staff. This publication also differs from many others in that it includes advice tailored to special populations that are generally overlooked or ignored in employment publications of this type—refugees and the homeless. It ends with a brief annotated bibliography of older worker resource publications.

Much of the material in *Commitment to an Aging Workforce* should be of value to employers and older worker specialists other than those who hire or attempt to assist JTPA participants. The lack of an index is the volume's major weakness.

Roundtable on Older Women in the Work Force. *Roundtable on Older Women in the Work Force: Proceedings and Recommendations.* Washington, DC: Roundtable, undated. 52p. No charge.

In 1986, 13 organizations concerned with midlife and older women's employment issues cosponsored a conference of representatives of the sponsoring organizations, human resource managers, business executives, and professionals in the aging field to discuss older women's employment issues. This handsomely bound report summarizes the major issues considered at that conference: access to and opportunities for employment, compensation and benefits, and training needs and opportunities. Also included are 65 recommendations to enhance the employment and ultimate economic security of older women and a six-point implementation plan. An appendix categorizes the 65 recommendations according to public policy initiatives, educational programs for older women, educational programs for employers, model/demonstration programs, network/liaison activities, and research needs. This categorization makes it easy for policymakers, program developers, or researchers, for example, to zero in on recommendations relevant to their line of work or interest.

The publication's succinct summary of work force changes, older worker and employer attitudes, and compensation and training issues and programs should prove informative to newcomers to the field of aging, women, and work, but it will be of limited value to those who know the field well. Activists concerned with improving the lot of older female workers will appreciate the scope of the recommendations, one of which led to the establishment of POWER (see Chapter 9).

Copies may be obtained by contacting Business Partnerships Section, Worker Equity Department, American Association of Retired Persons, 1909 K Street, NW, Washington, DC 20049.

U.S. Congress. Senate. Special Committee on Aging. *Developments in Aging.* 2 vols. Washington, DC: U.S. Government Printing Office, annual. Several hundred pages. No charge. (Available while supply lasts.)

This report reviews aging-related developments of the previous year in such areas as social security, employee pensions, taxes and savings, health care, long-term care, and employment. Although the employment chapter in Volume 1 varies from year to year, it generally provides an explanation of a number of important pieces of legislation and programs, such as the Age Discrimination in Employment Act, Title V of the Older Americans Act, and the Job Training Partnership Act. These descriptions, coupled with the legislative update, make the publication a very useful reference. Appendices in Volume 2 present reports from federal agencies on developments affecting the elderly in the previous year.

U.S. Congress. Senate. Special Committee on Aging. *Personnel Practices for an Aging Work Force: Private-Sector Examples.* Washington, DC: U.S. Government Printing Office, 1985. viii, 67p. (Check government repository library or interlibrary loan.)

> *Personnel Practices* describes private sector older worker programs included in the National Older Workers Information System (NOWIS) in the early 1980s. As of September 1984, NOWIS included 180 companies and a total of 369 programs or practices involving part-time work (the most common practice), some full-time work, training, retirement transition, job placement, flextime, job redesign, and appraisal. This Senate report summarizes programs and policies from selected, named companies.
>
> At the time, NOWIS, a computerized retrieval system, was housed at the University of Michigan's Institute of Gerontology; it is now a project of the American Association of Retired Persons (see the section headed "Computer-Based Information" in Chapter 11), which has been updating the system. The value of this Senate publication lies not in its timeliness—for a variety of reasons, many of the programs no longer exist—but in the ideas and encouragement it might give to employers seeking ways to accommodate older workers.

U.S. Department of Labor. *Labor Market Problems of Older Workers.* Report of the Secretary of Labor. Washington, DC: U.S. Department of Labor, January 1989. vii, 73p. No charge.

> Written by Philip Rones and Diane Herz of the Bureau of Labor Statistics, this sharply focused report is a fine overview of older worker unemployment and other labor market problems, such as job discouragement and displacement, and institutional impediments to the employment of older workers, among which are social security regulations and pension plan provisions, the market for part-time jobs, and age discrimination. The special problems of older women are treated separately. The authors also address such issues as what happens to older workers once they lose their jobs or become unemployed, the effects of recession on older workers, and whether older workers are truly disproportionately represented among discouraged workers (they suggest care in concluding that this is the case). Numerous tables provide data to support observations made in the report.

To order, contact U.S. Department of Labor, Office of Public Information, 200 Constitution Avenue, NW, Washington, DC 20210.

U.S. Department of Labor. *Senior Community Service Employment Program Directory.* Washington, DC: U.S. Department of Labor, Office of Special Targeted Programs, Division of Older Worker Programs. iii, 280p. (1988–1989 ed.). No charge.

> This annually revised state-by-state compilation of the location of and number of slots in programs funded under Title V of the Older Americans Act (the Senior Community Service Employment Program [SCSEP]) lists the prime sponsor (e.g., National Council on the Aging or American Association of Retired Persons); the sponsor's local address, phone number, and director; the location, or site, of programs; and the number of participant slots per sponsor. It should be noted that a prime sponsor can oversee more than one program, and a state might have more than one prime sponsor.
>
> The directory is designed to assist SCSEP sponsors "with coordination, equitable distribution and referrals between projects." However, it might be of interest to potential applicants and/or employers seeking to locate SCSEP slots or workers. There is no information about program activities.
>
> For copies, contact the U.S. Department of Labor, Office of Special Targeted Programs, Division of Older Worker Programs, 200 Constitution Avenue, NW, Washington, DC 20210.

Weiss, Francine K. *Employment Discrimination against Older Women: A Handbook on Litigating Age and Sex Discrimination Cases.* Washington, DC: Older Women's League (OWL), 1989. 32p., plus exhibits. $10.95 for members, $16.95 for nonmembers, $19.95 for institutions.

> This handbook was compiled to assist attorneys representing women who are victims of employment discrimination, particularly on the basis of age and sex. It includes a brief overview of laws protecting older women workers, namely, Title VII of the Civil Rights Act, the Age Discrimination in Employment Act (ADEA), and the Employee Retirement Income Security Act (ERISA). The content is limited to federal law; however, the author recognizes that lawyers need to be familiar with state laws as well.

Employment Discrimination reports on the author's study of court decisions on employment discrimination. It also discusses strategy for pursuing Title VII, ADEA, and ERISA cases at the administrative level, filing a lawsuit, and other available remedies. Sample documents, such as the notice of right to sue and notice of deposition, are included.

Although lawyers are the intended audience for this publication, women considering filing discrimination cases will find it readable and worth reviewing.

Chapter 11

Computer-Based Information, Films, and Videos

Computer-Based Information

Only computer-based and related information sources that deal specifically with aging issues are described below. These sources, however, by no means encompass all of the databases that include information on older workers. For example, the U.S. Census Bureau's Current Population Survey (CPS) and Survey of Income and Program Participation (SIPP), both of which ask respondents how old they are, probe extensively about work experience. Data tapes can be purchased, making it possible for anyone with the appropriate computer facilities to answer a wide range of questions about older workers. Public opinion pollsters such as Louis Harris and Associates occasionally conduct employment surveys, and these data sources, when made available, can often answer researchers', employers', and others' questions about older workers. Many of these tapes can be obtained through the National Archive of Computerized Data on Aging (see below).

Age Base
The Brookdale Foundation Group
126 East 56th Street
New York, NY 10022
(212) 308-7355

Age Base, a national clearinghouse of service programs for the elderly, provides information free of charge about programs in its computerized database. A typical printed citation would include current address, phone number, and contact person for each program, a program abstract, funding level and source of funds, current program activities, and information on the population served. Entries are updated periodically. Age Base was established to meet the service information needs of foundations, service providers, policymakers, state and area agencies on aging, program planners, educators, researchers, and other professionals in the field of aging.

To request a search for and receive a printout of programs of a particular type—older worker training programs, for example—contact the Age Base Coordinator at the Brookdale Foundation Group. With a computer and modem, the Age Base Network can be accessed directly by dialing (212) 750-0132 between the hours of 4 P.M. and 9 A.M.

Age Base differs from AARP's AgeLine (described below) in that service programs, rather than publications, form the core of the system. A brochure describing Age Base is available from the Brookdale Foundation Group.

AgeLine Database
National Gerontology Resource Center
American Association of Retired Persons (AARP)
1909 K Street, NW
Washington, DC 20049
(202) 728-4895

AgeLine is an on-line bibliographic database of the American Association of Retired Persons that focuses on documents dealing with the middle-aged and aged. Through AgeLine's computerized information retrieval system, users may retrieve citations on a wide range of aging-related topics in journal articles, books, government documents, reports, chapters, dissertations, and conference papers. The holdings of AARP's National Gerontology Resource Center form the nucleus of AgeLine; descriptions of federally funded aging research projects are also cataloged. Entries of material published before 1978 are described as "selective."

A typical citation from AgeLine would indicate the publication type (e.g., journal, dissertation), author(s), exact title, source and date of publication, key topics, and an abstract. Users can limit publication searches by, for example, requesting only publications issued after 1986.

AgeLine should be an especially useful resource to a variety of people, including researchers, service providers, program directors, policymakers, and older Americans themselves. There is a charge, however. AgeLine can be accessed only through Bibliographic Retrieval Services (BRS), which is available for a fee at many public and university libraries or by subscribing directly to BRS. AARP does *not* provide direct access to AgeLine.

A brochure describing AgeLine may be obtained from AARP's National Gerontology Resource Center. A *Thesaurus of Aging Terminology* provides the terms used in classifying citations and will aid in any search; it is available from the Resource Center for a prepaid postage and handling fee of $5.00.

National Archive of Computerized Data on Aging (NACDA)
Inter-university Consortium for Political and Social Research
P.O. Box 1248
Ann Arbor, MI 48106
(313) 763-5010

This archive, which operates under the auspices of the University of Michigan's Inter-university Consortium for Political and Social Research (ICPSR), is a repository of data collections for researchers. The collections are made available on magnetic tape for the cost of the tape to researchers at colleges and universities that belong to ICPSR. Others may gain access for a fee. Researchers at member institutions should issue their requests through their ICPSR representatives.

A catalog, available at no charge, describes the data sets, which are organized into three general groupings: (1) studies of social and economic status, (2) studies of health and well-being, and (3) studies of the life course. The catalog briefly describes the contents of the collection; technical information on the files is also provided. The archive houses well over 100 government and private data sets, and new ones are added periodically. Not all of them deal with employment, but the major aging and work studies, such as the National Longitudinal Surveys of the Labor Market Experience of Mature Men and Mature Women, are part of the archive. The archive is not for the casual seeker of a few statistics; however, a researcher seeking raw data on the elderly for secondary analyses would do well to start the search here.

National Older Workers Information System (NOWIS)
American Association of Retired Persons
1909 K Street, NW
Washington, DC 20049
(202) 728-4896

> NOWIS is a computerized information retrieval system of private sector programs and practices for older workers. It was developed by the Institute of Gerontology at the University of Michigan to serve as a source of practical information on older worker employment programs and practices actually implemented by companies across the United States. Program types include part-time and full-time employment, job redesign, flextime, job placement, transitional retirement, training, and job appraisal. AARP has acquired NOWIS and has begun updating and expanding the original database. There is no charge for program descriptions or abstracts obtained from NOWIS.

Films and Videocassettes

Films and videos on older workers are in relatively short supply. In fact, a search of the Library of Congress's audiovisual holdings in mid-1989 turned up only a single reference to older workers out of 129 films or videos that had anything at all to do with aging. Robert Yahnke's *The Great Circle of Life: A Resource Guide to Films on Aging* (Owings Mills, MD: National Health Publishing, 1988) includes no films on employment. Bettina Erives's *Audiovisual Resources for Gerontological and Geriatric Education 1987-1988* (Los Angeles: Pacific Geriatric Education Center, 1987) mentions only four. The Ethel Percy Andrus Gerontology Center published several editions of a catalog of aging films, *About Aging: A Catalog of Films,* which cited several "employment" films, but the last catalog was in 1981.

While films and videos of older workers in the 1960s and 1970s might interest researchers or film historians, they can work to the disadvantage of older workers, who have problems enough without appearing visibly dated in dress and style. Furthermore, the older the film or video, the greater the probability that it refers to programs that no longer exist or laws that have been updated. Thus, with one exception, the following films and videos have all been produced since 1980, and even some of these more recent ones may now be out of date.

Able, Stable, and Wise—The Older Worker
Type: 16mm color film
Length: 19 min.
Date: 1977
Cost: Purchase $200.00
Source: Maddron and Maddron
         1949 East 28th Avenue
         Eugene, OR 97403

This video summarizes four decades of research reported in an article on older worker abilities published in a mid-1970s issue of *Industrial Gerontology*. Though dated, the film highlights some of the positive characteristics of older workers—stability, high work quality, less absenteeism, continued ability to learn—and so may be useful to older job seekers needing confirmation of their work ability. Employers who need proof that older workers can perform might also find this film of value. Check film or video rental libraries.

Choices
Type: Video
Length: Varies (see below)
Date: 1988
Cost: Purchase $795.00
Source: BNA Communications Inc.
         9439 Key West Avenue
         Rockville, MD 20850
         (800) 233-6067; in Maryland, (301) 948-0540

Choices is a 12-module, video-based Bureau of National Affairs training program to assist managers in avoiding discrimination in an increasingly diverse work force. Module 10, "Who's Kidding Who?" deals with age issues and includes a two-minute tape that dramatizes the meeting between a plant manager and an older man who had lost his job. The substance of *Choices* lies in printed materials that accompany the tapes; these are to be used during training sessions.

The entire 12-module training program, which includes a trainer's guide and participant manuals in addition to the videos, can be reviewed before purchase for $75.00.

Employment and Aging Linkages

Type: Series of seven videos
Length: Average of 20 min. each
Date: 1989
Cost: Copies available for the cost of duplicating
Source: State of Colorado
           Aging and Adult Services
           1575 Sherman Street, 10th Floor
           Denver, CO 80203
           Attn: Tami Jo Wells

Produced by Colorado Aging and Adult Services and the Governor's Older Worker Task Force, these seven training videos were developed as the product of a number of regional training sessions in 1989. They will be made available to all state units on aging, the Department of Labor, and other aging agencies as well as to anyone willing to pay the cost of duplicating.

The videos are intended primarily to assist program planners in recruiting, assessing, and counseling older workers, although almost anyone interested in older worker issues may find these videos of value. One provides an overview of demographic and economic trends that may highlight the need to encourage older workers to remain in or return to the labor force, while another deals specifically with Colorado resources and, as such, might serve as a model for other states. The shortest video (10.5 minutes) provides employer perspectives on trends, the need for older workers, and techniques for retaining them.

The titles of the seven videos are as follows: *The New Older Workforce: Challenges and Opportunities; Colorado Services for Older Workers; Recruiting Older Workers and Employers; Assessment of Older Workers; Counseling Older Workers; Age Discrimination: Legal Protections and Processes;* and *Older Workers: The Employer's Perspective.*

Fair Employment Practice

Type: Video
Length: Varies (see below)
Date: Early 1980s
Cost: Purchase $850.00

Source: BNA Communications Inc.
9439 Key West Avenue
Rockville, MD 20850
(800) 233-6067; in Maryland, (301) 948-0540

Fair Employment Practice is a five-module video-based training program of the Bureau of National Affairs designed to help managers recruit, select, promote, discipline, and discharge workers according to EEOC regulations. Actual cases of age discrimination in the work force are included in the 40-minute "Preventing Age Discrimination" video. The videos and accompanying materials can be used in training sessions for managers.

The five-module training program, which includes videos and manuals for trainers and participants, is available for review for $75.00.

The Graying of America's Workforce
Type: Video (Beta, VHS)
Length: 60 min.
Date: 1988
Cost: Purchase $95.00
Source: Commerce Clearing House
4025 West Peterson Avenue
Chicago, IL 60646
(800) 248-3248

In 1988, the American Society of Personnel Administration (ASPA) and the Commerce Clearing House (CCH) surveyed ASPA members to learn what organizations are doing to prepare for an aging work force. This video discussion with leading personnel management authorities analyzes survey findings and presents advice on how companies can deal with their senior employees. The video covers, but is not limited to, strategies for productively utilizing senior workers, effective performance assessment, flexible training, a variety of alternative work options, and innovative retirement policies. Included with the videocassette are the ASPA/CCH survey, a "quizzer," and a discussion outline.

Growing Old in America, Part I: The Retirement Dilemma
Type: Video (VHS)
Length: 58 min.
Date: 1985
Cost: Three-day rental $15.00

Source: University of Washington
IMS Film Collection
350 Kane Hall DG 10
Seattle, WA 98195
(206) 543-9909

Narrated by Hugh Downs, this video takes a look at early retirement, age discrimination in employment, retirement income sources, and the utilization of the skills of retirees in the work world.

Older Americans in the Workforce: Asset or Liability
Type: 16mm film and video (Beta, VHS, 3/4″ U-Matic)
Length: 30 min.
Date: 1987
Cost: See below
Source: See below

This color film/video produced by the Bureau of National Affairs deals with corporate older worker policies, the costs and benefits of retaining and retraining older workers, and age discrimination issues. Although the Bureau of National Affairs is no longer distributing it, *Older Americans in the Workforce* may be available through film/video rental libraries.

Partners in Change
Type: Video (VHS)
Length: 17 min.
Date: 1989
Cost: Purchase $20.00 plus $2.00 handling and shipping
Source: Displaced Homemakers Network
1411 K Street, NW, Suite 930
Washington, DC 20005
(202) 628-6767

The aim of this color video, produced by the American Association of Retired Persons in conjunction with the Displaced Homemakers Network and narrated by Edwin Newman, is to encourage employers to give a chance to displaced homemakers, who, with their homemaking and volunteering skills, can and will "do the job." Employers and their new employees can become partners in integrating mature women into the work force, hence the title. Several successful older labor force reentrants are featured; employers relate their experiences. *Partners in Change* is a very persuasive educational tool.

Should I Retire Early?
Type: Video (Beta, VHS, 3/4″ U-Matic)
Length: 57 min.
Date: 1985
Cost: See below
Source: Drake Beam Morin, Inc.
          100 Park Avenue
          New York, NY 10017
          (212) 692-7700

> According to *The Video Source Book* (10th ed., edited by David J. Weiner; Detroit: Gale Research, 1988), this color film/video is designed to help employees decide whether to retire early or continue working until normal retirement age. It is apparently no longer in the catalogs of Drake Beam Morin; however, it may be possible to have copies made. For information, contact Drake Beam Morin, Inc., at the address above.

A Silver Opportunity
Type: Video (Beta, VHS, 3/4″ U-Matic)
Length: 15 min.
Date: 1986
Cost: Purchase $125.00 plus postage and handling; one-week rental $35.00; handbook $7.50 plus postage and handling
Source: Operation ABLE of Greater Boston
          World Trade Center, Suite 306
          Boston, MA 02210-2004
          (617) 439-5580

> This video for employers, accompanied by a handbook, highlights the value of older workers, who are portrayed as an answer to current and future labor shortages. This fact, plus numerous positive characteristics of older workers, makes them a "silver opportunity" for employers.

Using the Experience of a Lifetime
Type: Video
Length: 12 min.
Date: 1988
Cost: Available on loan

Source: **Worker Equity Department**
Business Partnership Section
American Association of Retired Persons
1909 K Street, NW
Washington, DC 20049
(202) 662-4959

This brief color video deals with the experiences that older workers bring to the workplace, focusing on a single large company's older worker retraining efforts and rehiring of its retirees.

Why Should I Hire You? Answers and Ideas for Older Workers
Why Should I Hire You? Information for Employers
Type: **Video**
Length: *Answers and Ideas,* 27 min.; *Information for Employers,* 7 min.
Date: **1989**
Cost: *Answers and Ideas,* purchase $195.00 for community service organizations, $295.00 for corporate customers; *Information for Employers,* purchase $50.00
Source: **The Training Group**
c/o Albert Wilhelm
P.O. Box 13547
Salem, OR 97309
(503) 362-4136

Answers and Ideas for Older Workers was developed to help older workers become successful job seekers, while *Information for Employers* attempts to counter myths about older workers. Nineteen older workers have brief speaking parts in *Answers and Ideas for Older Workers,* produced to motivate viewers who are over 55, out of work, and scared. This video will also help them develop answers to the common question, "Why should I hire you?" After being instructed on the art of job seeking, older workers in the video apply for private sector jobs and return to the training site to discuss their experiences. The two videos have been described as suitable for presentation at job fairs and SCSEP training sessions, among other places.

Work and Retirement
Type: **16mm film and video ($3/4''$ U-Matic)**
Length: **21 min.**
Date: **1981**

Cost: Three-day rental $28.00
Source: Film and Video Library
            University Library
            University of Michigan
            400 Fourth Street
            Ann Arbor, MI 48103-4816
            (313) 764-5360; (800) 999-0424

Intended for a general audience, this color film/video (one in the Aging in the Future series) is described in the library's catalog as "a fast-paced look at the historical achievement of a society that can afford retirement for its workers." Interviews with older people stress the importance of a long work life and continued productivity. Future support issues are also addressed. (A free comprehensive catalog of the holdings of the Film and Video Library, updated periodically, is available from the library.)

Working Late

Type: 16mm film and video (VHS)
Length: 29 min.
Date: 1986
Cost: Film purchase $500.00; video purchase $300.00; five-day rental $150.00; one-day preview $75.00
Source: Woody Clark Productions
            943 Howard Street
            San Francisco, CA 94103
            (415) 777-1668

Produced under a grant from the Administration on Aging and narrated by Elliott Gould, this film/video focuses on age discrimination in the workplace. Victims of age discrimination discuss their experiences, while aging experts talk about the steps that can be taken to remedy age discrimination problems.

Glossary

Age Discrimination in Employment Act (ADEA)   Legislation enacted in 1967 to promote the employment of older persons "based on their ability rather than age" that prohibits discrimination in "compensation, terms, conditions or privileges of employment, because of [an] individual's age." The law covers workers aged 40 and older in establishments of 20 or more employees. With the 1986 amendments, mandatory retirement was eliminated.

alternative work schedule   A work schedule that deviates from the standard five-day, 40-hour workweek.

Carl D. Perkins Vocational Education Act   Legislation enacted in 1984 authorizing monies for sex equity, job training, and special services for adults. The act mandated that 8.5 percent of funds be set aside for vocational education and training for single parents and homemakers, with a special emphasis on displaced homemakers.

chronological age   Age in years.

Comprehensive Employment and Training Act (CETA)   The precursor to the Job Training Partnership Act (JTPA), CETA was designed to provide training and employment opportunities to economically disadvantaged unemployed or underemployed persons. CETA programs differed from JTPA programs in a number of substantial ways, one of the most significant of which involved services. Services provided under CETA were more extensive than those under JTPA.

compressed workweek   The completion of a standard workweek or 40 hours of work in, generally, 4 or 4.5 days.

contingent work   Employment, often less than full-time, that generally involves little job security and variable hours.

delayed retirement credit   An increase in the social security retired worker benefits payable to workers who delay retirement beyond age 65 and up to the age of 70.

discouraged worker   An individual who would like to work but who is not in the labor force because he or she does not believe work is available. Discouraged workers are not technically unemployed because they have not been looking for work. (The official definition of *unemployment* requires a worker to have looked for work within the previous four weeks.)

dislocated worker   A worker unemployed as a result of plant closing, technological change, or skill obsolescence. Dislocated workers typically have little chance of returning to their former industry or occupation. The 1982 Job Training Partnership Act also defined as "dislocated" the long-term unemployed with "limited opportunities for employment or reemployment in the same or a similar occupation in the area in which such individuals reside, including any older individuals who may have substantial barriers to employment by reason of age" (Section 302[a]).

displaced homemaker   An individual who has been out of the labor force for a number of years providing unpaid family care and who loses financial support as a result of divorce, separation, widowhood, or disability of a spouse. In the language of the Carl D. Perkins Vocational Education Act, someone so displaced "has diminished marketable skills."

early retirement   Retirement before an establishment's normal or full retirement age.

early retirement incentive program or plan (ERIP)   Special early retirement incentives, often offered for a limited period of time. To encourage early retirement, an employer might reduce or eliminate any early retirement actuarial adjustment to pension benefits, thus increasing the ultimate benefit. Or an employer might credit additional years of service or reduce retirement-age

requirements. ERIPs are often used to avoid other types of termi-
nations in corporate downsizing efforts. The Age Discrimination in Employment Act requires that the decision to accept these
offers be voluntary; however, there is considerable question as
to whether or not workers always feel they have a real choice in
the matter.

earnings test   See *retirement test.*

economically disadvantaged   For the purposes of eligibility under the
Job Training Partnership Act, an economically disadvantaged
individual is one who "(A) receives, or is a member of a family
which receives, cash welfare payments under a Federal, State, or
local welfare program; (B) has, or is a member of a family which
has, received a total family income for the six-month period
prior to application for the program involved (exclusive of
unemployment compensation, child support payments, and welfare payments) which, in relation to family size, was not in excess
of the higher of (i) the poverty level determined in accordance
with criteria established by the Director of the Office of Management and Budget or (ii) 70 percent of the lower living standard
income level; (C) is receiving food stamps pursuant to the Food
Stamp Act of 1977; (D) is a foster child on behalf of whom State
or local government payments are made; or (E) in cases permitted by regulations of the Secretary, is an adult handicapped
individual whose own income meets the requirements of clause
(A) or (B), but who is a member of a family whose income does
not meet such requirements" (Section 4[8]).

Employee Retirement Income Security Act (ERISA)   Legislation enacted in
1974 to extend and protect the private pension rights of workers.

Equal Employment Opportunity Commission (EEOC)   The federal agency
with responsibility for enforcing laws prohibiting discrimination, including age discrimination.

extended workweek   Five and one-half or more days of work per week.

flextime or flexible work schedule   An alternative to the common early
morning to late afternoon workday that allows workers variability

in beginning and ending their workdays. Generally, a "core time" is established during which all employees are expected to be at work.

full retirement age   The age at which a worker is entitled to collect full pension benefits, or benefits that have not been reduced to account for early retirement. Full retirement age under social security is 65, although that age will gradually increase beginning in the year 2000.

functional age   A definition of age based on individual capacity rather than years.

job bank   A roster or file of the names of persons available at short notice for what is generally temporary or short-term employment.

job sharing   An alternative work option in which two (or conceivably more) workers share one full-time job.

Job Training Partnership Act (JTPA)   Legislation enacted in 1982 that provides job training assistance to economically disadvantaged individuals and others who face serious employment barriers. JTPA programs are federally funded but administered jointly by local governments and private sector agencies. The law requires that most assistance be provided to the young. However, 3 percent of the funds under Title II (Training Services for the Disadvantaged) are to be made available to economically disadvantaged workers aged 55 and older. Older workers may also be assisted under a Title II provision that allows 10 percent of the participants to exceed the income requirements if they face certain employment barriers. Displaced homemakers and older workers are specifically singled out. As of mid-1990, Congress was considering amendments to the JTPA that would eliminate the 3-percent set-aside; however, a certain proportion of funds would still be targeted toward older workers.

labor force participation rate   Proportion of persons of a certain age (e.g., 16 and older, 18–64) who are working or looking for work (i.e., officially unemployed).

long-term unemployed   Generally, individuals who have been unemployed 15 weeks or longer.

National Older Workers Information System (NOWIS)   A database of older worker employment programs maintained by the American Association of Retired Persons. It includes examples of part-time and full-time employment opportunities, job redesign, flextime, job placement, transitional retirement programs, and older worker training programs.

Old-Age, Survivors, Disability, and Health Insurance Program (OASDHI)   The social security program, enacted in 1935 and subsequently amended.

older worker   Definitions vary. For the purposes of protection under the Age Discrimination in Employment Act, a worker or would-be worker aged 40 or older is an older worker. "Older" participants in Job Training Partnership Act and Senior Community Service Employment Programs must be at least 55.

part-time work   As officially defined by the Department of Labor, scheduled work of fewer than 35 hours per week.

phased retirement   A gradual reduction in work time prior to retirement that enables preretirees to ease into retirement. Plans vary, but schedules may be adjusted daily, weekly, monthly, or annually, generally in the months preceding full retirement. Phased retirement helps workers avoid "retirement shock" and, under the best of circumstances, test whether they are really ready for retirement. (May also be referred to as *partial, gradual, or transitional retirement.)*

Private Industry Council (PIC)   One of the key administrative units under the Job Training Partnership Act. A council of nongovernmental representatives in each service delivery area is responsible for policy guidance and planning, implementation of program decisions, and oversight jointly with the local government. (Decisions may involve plan development, selection of grant recipients, and the like.) A majority of PIC members must represent private business; others appointed may be from educational agencies, organized labor, rehabilitation agencies, community-based organizations, economic development agencies, employment services, community education agencies, and other interested organizations.

reentrant A person returning to the labor force after an absence. Reentrants are commonly women who have been out of the labor force for family reasons. Some are also retired workers.

retirement test Also referred to as the *earnings test,* the retirement test is the amount of earnings a worker collecting social security retired worker benefits is allowed before benefits are withheld. In 1990, a worker under age 65 could earn $6,840 per year, and a worker between the ages of 65 and 70 could earn $9,360, without losing any social security benefits. Workers aged 62 to 65 lose $1.00 in benefits for every $2.00 in earnings above the limit; workers aged 65 to 69 lose $1.00 for every $3.00. The earnings limit is increased annually, but considerable pressure is being placed on Congress to eliminate or liberalize it. The rationale for the test is that social security benefits were meant to replace, not supplement, earnings lost to an individual because of retirement.

Senior Community Service Employment Program (SCSEP) A federally funded employment program to "promote useful part-time opportunities in community service activities for unemployed low income persons" 55 and older. Administered by the Department of Labor, the program awards funds to national sponsoring organizations and state agencies. SCSEP is more a job creation program than a job training program. Participants' income level cannot exceed 125 percent of the poverty level. SCSEP is often referred to as Title V of the Older Americans Act.

service delivery area (SDA) The state or one or more units of local government designated by the governor as the area in which job training services under the Job Training Partnership Act program will be provided. Under the act, SDAs may be political jurisdictions or consortia of contiguous units of local governments with an aggregate population of at least 200,000.

standard workweek   A 40-hour workweek, generally over a five-day period. Alternatives to the 40-hour workweek are typically referred to as *alternative work schedules or options.*

telecommuting   Employment in an off-site location (e.g., home or satellite office) linked electronically to another location, such as the corporate headquarters.

3-percent set-aside   The 3 percent of JTPA Title II-A funds targeted to programs for economically disadvantaged older workers.

Title VII of the Civil Rights Act   Legislation enacted in 1964 that prohibits employment discrimination based on sex, race, or national origin.

waiver of rights   The giving up, or signing away, of rights. Employers, who are banned from forcing employees to retire, are increasingly responding to the need to trim their work forces by offering early retirement incentives. The Age Discrimination in Employment Act requires that acceptance of these offers be voluntary. To ensure that workers will not subsequently decide that they were coerced into accepting early retirement offers, employers may ask employees to "waive their [ADEA] rights" to sue.

work sharing   A reduction in work hours and wages occurring during periods of slack work when the available work is spread among all or some of an organization's work force. Work sharing is designed to reduce the need for layoffs.

References

Achenbaum, W. Andrew. *Social Security: Visions and Revisions.* Cambridge: Cambridge University Press, 1986.

Alegria, Fernando L., Jr., and Jose R. Figueroa. *Study of the JTPA Eight Percent Education Coordination and Grants Set-Aside and the Three Percent Set-Aside Training Program for Older Individuals.* Washington, DC: National Governors' Association, 1986.

American Association of Retired Persons (AARP). *Workers over 50: Old Myths, New Realities.* Washington, DC: AARP, undated.

———. *Work and Retirement: Employees over 40 and Their Views.* Washington, DC: AARP, 1986.

———. *The Age Discrimination in Employment Act Guarantees You Certain Rights: Here's How . . .* Washington, DC: AARP, 1987a.

———. "Early Retirement: Boom or Bust?" Conference sponsored by the Worker Equity Department, AARP, Biltmore Hotel, Los Angeles, December 7, 1987b.

———. *Using the Experience of a Lifetime.* Washington, DC: AARP, 1988.

———. *Business and Older Workers: Current Perceptions and New Directions for the 1990s.* Washington, DC: AARP, 1989.

Axel, Helen, ed. *Employing Older Americans: Opportunities and Constraints.* New York: Conference Board, 1988a.

———. "Part-Time Employment: Crosscurrents of Change." In *Flexible Workstyles: A Look at Contingent Labor.* Washington, DC: U.S. Department of Labor, Women's Bureau, 1988b.

———. *Job Banks for Retirees.* Research Report No. 929. New York: Conference Board, 1989.

Barnow, Burt S., and Laudan Y. Aron. *Survey of Government-Provided Training Programs.* Washington, DC: U.S. Department of Labor, Commission on Workforce Quality and Labor Market Efficiency, undated.

Bell, Donald, and William Marclay. "Trends in Retirement Eligibility and Pension Benefits, 1974–83." *Monthly Labor Review* 110 (April 1987): 18–25.

Belous, Richard S. "How Human Resource Systems Adjust to the Shift Toward Contingent Workers." *Monthly Labor Review* 112 (March 1989): 7–12.

Berglind, Hans. *Training of Older Workers in Sweden.* Discussion Paper No. 38. Geneva: International Labor Organization, June 1989.

Berkowitz, Monroe. "Functioning Ability and Job Performance As Workers Age." In *The Older Worker,* edited by Michael E. Borus, Herbert S. Parnes, Steven H. Sandell, and Bert Seidman. Madison, WI: Industrial Relations Research Association, 1988.

Birren, James E. *The Psychology of Aging.* Englewood Cliffs, NJ: Prentice-Hall, 1964.

Brown, Charles. *Empirical Evidence on Private Training.* Paper prepared for the U.S. Department of Labor, Commission on Workforce Quality and Labor Market Efficiency. Washington, DC: U.S. Department of Labor, undated.

Bureau of National Affairs, Inc. (BNA). *Older Americans in the Workforce: Challenges and Solutions.* Washington, DC: BNA, 1987.

Burtless, Gary. "Occupational Effects on the Health and Work Capacity of Older Men." In *Work, Health, and Income Among the Elderly,* edited by Gary Burtless. Washington, DC: Brookings Institution, 1987.

Carey, Max L. "Occupational Tenure in 1987: Many Workers Have Remained in Their Fields." *Monthly Labor Review* 111 (October 1988): 3–12.

Centaur Associates, Inc. *Report on the 502(e) Experimental Projects Funded Under Title V of the Older Americans Act.* Washington, DC: Centaur Associates, Inc., 1986.

Chapman, Steven H., Mitchell P. LaPlante, and Gail Wilensky. "Life Expectancy and Health Status of the Aged." *Social Security Bulletin* 49 (October 1986): 24–48.

Charness, Neil, ed. *Aging and Human Performance.* Chichester, Great Britain: John Wiley & Sons, 1985.

Christensen, Kathleen. "Women's Labor Force Attachment: Rise of Contingent Work." In *Flexible Workstyles: A Look at Contingent Labor.* Washington, DC: U.S. Department of Labor, Women's Bureau, 1988.

Christensen, Kathleen, and Mary Murphree. "Introduction." In *Flexible Workstyles: A Look at Contingent Labor.* Washington, DC: U.S. Department of Labor, Women's Bureau, 1988.

Coberly, Sally, and Mary Jackson. *Promoting Employment Opportunities for Older Workers at the Local Level.* Los Angeles: National Policy Center on Employment and Retirement, Andrus Gerontology Center, 1985.

Commerce Clearing House. *1988 ASPA/CCH Survey: Managing the Aging Work Force.* Washington, DC: Commerce Clearing House, June 28, 1988.

Commonwealth Fund Commission on Elderly People Living Alone. *Old, Alone and Poor.* Baltimore, MD: Commonwealth Fund Commission, 1987.

Conway, Elizabeth. "Women and Contingent Work." In *The American Woman 1990–91,* edited by Sara E. Rix. New York: W. W. Norton, 1990.

Crown, William H., Phyllis H. Mutschler, and Thomas D. Leavitt. *Beyond Retirement: Characteristics of Older Workers and the Implications for Employment Policy.* Waltham, MA: Policy Center on Aging, Heller School, Brandeis University, 1987.

Davies, D. R., and P. R. Sparrow. "Age and Work Behavior." In *Aging and Human Performance,* edited by Neil Charness. Chichester, Great Britain: John Wiley & Sons, 1985.

Day, Jeff S. "Employee Leasing." In *Flexible Workstyles: A Look at Contingent Labor.* Washington, DC: U.S. Department of Labor, Women's Bureau, 1988.

Dillingham, Alan E. "Age and Workplace Injuries." *Aging and Work* 4 (1981): 1–10.

Doering, Mildred, Susan R. Rhodes, and Michael Schuster. *The Aging Worker: Research and Recommendations.* Beverly Hills, CA: Sage, 1983.

Duncan, Greg J., and Saul D. Hoffman. "A Reconsideration of the Economic Consequences of Marital Dissolution." *Demography* 22 (November 1985): 485–497.

Dychtwald, Ken, and Joe Flower. *Age Wave: The Challenges and Opportunities of an Aging America.* Los Angeles: Jeremy P. Tarcher, 1989.

Easterlin, Richard A., Eileen M. Crimmins, and Lee Ohanian. "Changes in Labor Force Participation of Persons 55 and Over since World War II: Their Nature and Causes." In *Aging and Technological Advances,* edited by Pauline K. Robinson, Judy E. Livingston, and James E. Birren. New York: Plenum, 1984.

"Economic Incentives for Retirement in the Public and Private Sectors." *EBRI Issue Brief* 57 (August 1986).

Elias, Penelope Kelly, Merrill F. Elias, Michael A. Robbins, and Paulette Gage. "Acquisition of Word-Processing Skills by Younger, Middle-Age, and Older Adults." *Psychology and Aging* 2 (1987): 340–348.

Executive Office of the President. Office of Management and Budget. *Budget of the United States Government: Fiscal Year 1991.* Washington, DC: U.S. Government Printing Office, 1990.

Feldman, Jacob J. "Work Ability of the Aged under Conditions of Improving Mortality." *Aging and Work* 6 (1983): 197–213.

Fields, Gary S., and Olivia S. Mitchell. "Restructuring Social Security: How Will Retirement Ages Respond?" In *The Problem Isn't Age: Work and Older Americans,* edited by Steven H. Sandell. New York: Praeger, 1987.

Fischer, David Hackett. *Growing Old in America.* Oxford: Oxford University Press, 1978.

Flaim, Paul O., and Ellen Sehgal. "Displaced Workers of 1979–83: How Well Have They Fared?" *Monthly Labor Review* 108 (June 1985): 3–16.

Friedman, Lawrence M. *Your Time Will Come: The Law of Age Discrimination and Mandatory Retirement.* New York: Russell Sage Foundation, 1984.

Fullerton, Howard N, Jr. "New Labor Force Projections, Spanning 1988 to 2000." *Monthly Labor Review* 112 (November 1989): 3–12.

Greenberg, Barbara R. "A Comprehensive Company Approach." In *Employing Older Americans: Opportunities and Constraints,* edited by Helen Axel. New York: Conference Board, 1988.

Harris, Louis, and Associates, Inc. *Older Americans: Ready and Able To Work.* New York: Louis Harris and Associates, Inc., undated.

Hartley, Alan A., Joellen T. Hartley, and Shirley A. Johnson. "The Older Adult as Computer User." In *Aging and Technological Advances,* edited by Pauline K. Robinson, Judy E. Livingston, and James E. Birren. New York: Plenum, 1984.

Herz, Diane E. "Employment Characteristics of Older Women, 1987." *Monthly Labor Review* 111 (September 1988): 3–12.

Herz, Diane E., and Philip L. Rones. "Institutional Barriers to Employment of Older Workers." *Monthly Labor Review* 112 (April 1989): 14–21.

Horvath, Francis W. "Work at Home: New Findings from the Current Population Survey." *Monthly Labor Review* 109 (November 1986): 31–35.

Howe, Wayne J. "Temporary Help Workers: Who They Are, What Jobs They Hold." *Monthly Labor Review* 109 (November 1986): 45–47.

Humple, Carol Segrave, and Morgan Lyons. *Management and the Older Workforce: Politics and Programs.* New York: Management Associations, 1983.

Iams, Howard M. "Jobs of Persons Working after Receiving Retired-Worker Benefits." *Social Security Bulletin* 50 (November 1987): 4–18.

ICF Incorporated. *The Impact of Increased Employment of Older Workers on the National Economy.* Report prepared for the Commonwealth Fund. Fairfax, VA: ICF Incorporated, 1989a.

———. *Why Workers Retire Early.* Report prepared for the Commonwealth Fund. Fairfax, VA: ICF Incorporated, 1989b.

Jablonski, Mary, Larry Rosenblum, and Kent Kunze. "Productivity, Age, and Labor Composition Changes in the U.S." *Monthly Labor Review* 111 (September 1988): 34–38.

Jacobson, Beverly. *Young Programs for Older Workers.* New York: Van Nostrand Reinhold, 1980.

Jamieson, G. H. "Age, Speed, and Accuracy: A Study in Industrial Retraining." *Industrial Retraining* (Summer 1969): 50–51.

Jessup, Denise, and Barbara Greenberg. "Innovative Older-Worker Programs." *Generations* (Summer 1989): 23–27.

Johnson, Terry R., Katherine P. Dickinson, and Richard W. West. *Job Displacement and the Assistance Provided by the Employment Service.* Washington, DC: National Commission on Employment Policy, 1983.

Kahne, Hilda. *Reconceiving Part-Time Work.* Totowa, NJ: Rowman and Allanheld, 1985.

Kalet, Joseph E. *Age Discrimination in Employment Law.* Washington, DC: Bureau of National Affairs, 1986.

Kearsley, Greg. *Introducing New Technology into the Workplace: Retraining Issues and Strategies.* Washington, DC: U.S. Department of Labor, Commission on Workforce Quality and Labor Market Efficiency, undated.

Keating, Norah, and Barbara Jeffrey. "Work Careers of Ever Married and Never Married Retired Women." *Gerontologist* 23 (August 1983): 416–421.

Kelleher, Carol H., and Daniel A. Quirk. "Age, Functional Capacity and Work: An Annotated Bibliography." *Industrial Gerontology* 19 (Fall 1973): 80–98.

Knowles, Daniel E. "Auditing the Company for Age Discrimination." In *Employing Older Americans: Opportunities and Constraints,* edited by Helen Axel. New York: Conference Board, 1988a.

———. "Dispelling Myths about Older Workers." In *Employing Older Americans: Opportunities and Constraints,* edited by Helen Axel. New York: Conference Board, 1988b.

Kovar, Mary Grace, and Andrea Z. LaCroix. "Aging in the Eighties: Ability to Perform Work-Related Activities." In *Advance Data from Vital and Health Statistics* 136. DHHS Publication No. (PHS) 87-1250. Hyattsville, MD: Public Health Service, May 8, 1987.

Kutscher, Ronald E., and James F. Walker. "Comparative Job Performance of Office Workers by Age." *Monthly Labor Review* 83 (January 1960): 39–43.

Levitan, Sar A., and Elizabeth A. Conway. *Part-Time Employment: Living on Half Rations*. Washington, DC: George Washington University, Center for Social Policy Studies, 1988.

Libassi, Peter. Remarks presented at the Second Annual Conference and Membership Meeting of the National Academy of Social Insurance, Washington, DC, January 26, 1990.

McConnell, Stephen R., Dorothy Fleisher, Carolyn E. Usher, and Barbara Hade Kaplan. *Alternative Work Options for Older Workers: A Feasibility Study*. Los Angeles: Ethel Percy Andrus Gerontology Center, University of Southern California, 1980.

McFarland, Ross A. "The Need for Functional Age Measurements in Industrial Gerontology." *Industrial Gerontology* (Fall 1973): 1–19.

Mangum, Stephen L. *Evidence on Private Sector Training*. Paper prepared for the U.S. Department of Labor, Commission on Workforce Quality and Labor Market Efficiency. Washington, DC: U.S. Department of Labor, undated.

Meier, Elizabeth L., and Elizabeth A. Kerr. "Capabilities of Middle-Aged and Older Workers: A Survey of the Literature." *Industrial Gerontology* (Summer 1976): 147–156.

Mellor, Earl F. "Shift Work and Flexitime: How Prevalent Are They?" *Monthly Labor Review* 109 (November 1986): 14–21.

Mercer, William M., Inc. *Employer Attitudes: Implications of an Aging Work Force*. New York: William M. Mercer, Inc., November 1981.

Miller, Jill. "Displaced Homemakers in the Employment and Training System." In *Job Training for Women: The Promise and Limits of Public Policies,* edited by Sharon L. Harlan and Ronnie J. Steinberg. Philadelphia: Temple University Press, 1989.

Mitchell, Kenneth. "The Aging Work Force and the Politics of Incapacity." In *The Aging Workforce: Implications for Rehabilitation*. Alexandria, VA: National Rehabilitation Association, 1987.

Mitchell, Olivia S. "The Relation of Age to Workplace Injuries." *Monthly Labor Review* 111 (July 1988): 8–13.

Modjeska, Lee. *Employment Discrimination Law,* 2nd edition. Rochester, NY: Lawyers Co-Operative, 1988.

Moloney, Thomas W., and Barbara Paul. "Enabling Older Americans to Work." In *The Commonwealth Fund 1989 Annual Report*. New York: Commonwealth Fund, 1989.

Monge, Rolf H. "Learning in the Adult Years: Set or Rigidity." Summary in *Industrial Gerontology* (Spring 1970): 36–38.

Moody, Harry R. "Education as a Lifelong Process." In *Our Aging Society*, edited by Alan Pifer and Lydia Bronte. New York: W. W. Norton, 1986.

Morgan, Leslie A. "Continuity and Change in the Labor Force Activity of Recently Widowed Women." *Gerontologist* 24 (October 1984): 530–535.

Morrison, Malcolm H. *The Transition to Retirement: The Employer's Perspective*. Washington, DC: Bureau of Social Science Research, 1985.

———. "Work and Retirement in an Older Society." In *Our Aging Society*, edited by Alan Pifer and Lydia Bronte. New York: W. W. Norton, 1986.

Mullan, Cathal, and Liam Gorman. "Facilitating Adaptation to Change: A Case Study in Retraining Middle-Aged and Older Workers at Aer Lingus." *Industrial Gerontology* 15 (Fall 1972): 20–39.

National Alliance of Business (NAB). *Invest in Experience: New Directions for an Aging Workforce*. Washington, DC: NAB, 1985.

National Commission on Social Security. *Social Security in America's Future*. Washington, DC: National Commission on Social Security, 1981.

National Committee on Careers for Older Americans. *Older Americans: An Untapped Resource*. Washington, DC: Academy for Educational Development, Inc., 1979.

National Council on the Aging (NCOA). *Aging in the Eighties: America in Transition*. Washington, DC: NCOA, 1981.

National Research Council. Committee on National Statistics. *The Aging Population in the Twenty-First Century: Statistics for Health Policy*. Washington, DC: National Academy Press, 1988.

"New Findings on Work Force Trends Challenge Common Perceptions." *Employee Benefit Notes* 11 (February 1990): 3–5.

Newquist, Deborah D. "Toward Assessing Health and Functional Capacity for Policy Development on Work-Life Extension." In *Age, Health, and Employment*, edited by James E. Birren, Pauline K. Robinson, and Judy E. Livingston. Englewood Cliffs, NJ: Prentice-Hall, 1986.

Newsham, D. B. "*The Challenge of Change to the Adult Trainee*, reviewed by R. M. Belbin." *Industrial Gerontology* 3 (October 1969): 32–33.

9to5, National Association of Working Women. *Social Insecurity: The Economic Marginalization of Older Workers*. Cleveland, OH: 9to5, 1987.

Older Women's League (OWL). *Failing America's Caregivers: A Resource on Women Who Care*. Washington, DC: OWL, 1989.

Opinion Research Corporation (ORC). *Report of a National Survey of Women 45 and Older Who Work Part-Time*. Princeton, NJ: ORC, 1989.

Osler, William, quoted in Stanley G. Hall. *Senescence: The Last Half of Life*. New York: D. Appleton, 1923.

Panek, P. E., Alexander Barrett, and Harvey L. Sterns. "Age and Self-Selected Performance Pace on a Visual Monitoring Task." *Aging and Work* 2 (1979): 183–191.

Parnes, Herbert S. "The Retirement Decision." In *The Older Worker*, edited by Michael E. Borus, Herbert S. Parnes, Steven H. Sandell, and Bert Seidman. Madison, WI: Industrial Relations Research Association, 1988.

Paul, Carolyn. "Work Alternatives for Older Americans: A Management Perspective." In *The Problem Isn't Age: Work and Older Americans*, edited by Steven H. Sandell. New York: Praeger, 1987.

Personick, Valerie A. "Industry Output and Employment: A Slower Trend for the Nineties." *Monthly Labor Review* 112 (November 1989): 25–41.

Peterson, David, and Sally Coberly. "The Older Worker: Myths and Realities." In *Retirement Reconsidered,* edited by Robert Morris and Scott A. Bass. New York: Springer, 1988.

Plewes, Thomas J. "Understanding the Data on Part-Time and Temporary Employment." In *Flexible Workstyles: A Look at Contingent Labor*. Washington, DC: U.S. Department of Labor, Women's Bureau, 1988.

Polivka, Anne E., and Thomas Nardone. "On the Definition of 'Contingent Work.'" *Monthly Labor Review* 112 (December 1989): 9–16.

Poon, Leonard N. "Learning." In *Encyclopedia of Aging,* edited by George Maddox. New York: Springer, 1987.

Quinn, Joseph F. "The Extent and Correlates of Partial Retirement." *Gerontologist* 21 (December 1981): 634–643.

Rhine, Shirley. *Managing Older Workers: Company Policies and Attitudes*. New York: Conference Board, 1984.

Riley, Matilda White, and John W. Riley, Jr. "Longevity and Social Structure: The Potential of the Added Years." In *Our Aging Society,* edited by Alan Pifer and Lydia Bronte. New York: W. W. Norton, 1986.

Robinson, Pauline K. "Age, Health, and Job Performance." In *Age, Health, and Employment,* edited by James E. Birren, Pauline K. Robinson, and Judy E. Livingston. Englewood Cliffs, NJ: Prentice-Hall, 1986.

Rosen, Benson, and Thomas H. Jerdee. "The Nature of Job-Related Age Stereotypes." *Journal of Applied Psychology* 61 (April 1976): 180–183.

———. *Older Employees: New Roles for Valued Resources.* Homewood, IL: Dow Jones-Irwin, 1985.

Roundtable on Older Women in the Work Force: Proceedings and Recommendations. Report of a roundtable held in Columbia, MD, September 30–October 2, 1986. Washington, DC: Roundtable on Older Women in the Work Force, undated.

Rowland, Diane. *Help at Home: Long-Term Care Assistance for Impaired Elderly People.* Baltimore, MD: Commonwealth Fund Commission on Elderly People Living Alone, May 1989.

Ruhm, Christopher J. "Why Older Americans Stop Working." *Gerontologist* 29 (June 1989): 294–299.

Rupp, Kalman, Edward C. Bryant, Richard E. Montovani, and Michael D. Rhoads. *Eligibility and Participation Rates of Older Americans in Employment and Training Programs.* Washington, DC: National Commission for Employment Policy, Spring 1983.

———. "Government Employment and Training Programs, and Older Americans." In *The Problem Isn't Age: Work and Older Americans,* edited by Steven H. Sandell. New York: Praeger, 1987.

Sandell, Steven H. "Public Policies and Programs Affecting Older Workers." In *The Older Worker,* edited by Michael E. Borus, Herbert S. Parnes, Steven H. Sandell, and Bert Seidman. Madison, WI: Industrial Relations Research Association, 1988.

Sandell, Steven H., and Kalman Rupp. *Who Is Served in JTPA Programs: Patterns of Participation and Intergroup Equity.* Washington, DC: National Commission for Employment Policy, 1988.

Schulz, James H. *The Economics of Aging.* 4th edition. Dover, MA: Auburn House, 1988a.

———. *Job Matching in an Aging Society: Barriers to the Utilization of Older Workers.* Paper presented at the annual meeting of the Gerontological Society of America, San Francisco, November 1988b.

Schuster, Michael, Joan A. Kaspin, and Christopher S. Miller. *The Age Discrimination in Employment Act: An Evaluation of Federal and State Enforcement, Employer Compliance and Employee Characteristics.* Syracuse, NY: All-University Gerontology Center, Syracuse University, 1987.

Schuster, Michael, and Christopher S. Miller. "An Empirical Assessment of the Age Discrimination in Employment Act." *Industrial and Labor Relations Review* 38 (October 1984): 64–74.

Shank, Susan E. "Preferred Hours of Work and Corresponding Earnings." *Monthly Labor Review* 109 (November 1986): 40–44.

Shaw, Lois B. *Older Women at Work.* Washington, DC: Women's Research and Education Institute, 1985.

———. "Special Problems of Older Women Workers." In *The Older Worker,* edited by Michael E. Borus, Herbert S. Parnes, Steven H. Sandell, and Bert Seidman. Madison, WI: Industrial Relations Research Association, 1988.

Sheppard, Harold L. "Work Continuity Versus Retirement: Reasons for Continuing Work." In *Retirement Reconsidered,* edited by Robert Morris and Scott A. Bass. New York: Springer, 1988.

Sherman, Sally R. "Reported Reasons Retired Workers Left Their Last Job: Findings from the New Beneficiary Survey." *Social Security Bulletin* 48 (March 1985): 22–30.

Shilkoff, Marilyn Leader. *Type of Work: Its Impact on the Productivity of Older Workers.* Paper presented at the 31st Annual Scientific Meeting of the Gerontological Society, Dallas, TX, November 1978.

Siemen, James R. "Programmed Material as a Training Tool for Older Persons." *Industrial Gerontology* 3 (Summer 1976): 183–190.

Silvestri, George, and John Lukasiewicz. "Projections of Occupational Employment, 1988–2000." *Monthly Labor Review* 112 (November 1989): 42–65.

Smith, Shirley J. "The Growing Diversity of Work Schedules." *Monthly Labor Review* 109 (November 1986): 7–13.

Stagner, Ross. "Aging in Industry." In *Handbook of the Psychology of Aging,* edited by James E. Birren and K. Warner Schaie. New York: Van Nostrand Reinhold, 1985.

Stecker, Margaret L. "Beneficiaries Prefer to Work." *Social Security Bulletin* 14 (January 1951): 15–17.

Sterns, Harvey L. "Training and Retraining Adult and Older Workers." In *Age, Health, and Employment,* edited by James E. Birren, Pauline K. Robinson, and Judy E. Livingston. Englewood Cliffs, NJ: Prentice-Hall, 1986.

Sterns, Harvey L., and Dennis Doverspike. "Training and Developing the Older Worker: Implications for Human Resource Management." In *Fourteen Steps in Managing an Older Workforce,* edited by Helen Dennis. Lexington, MA: Lexington, 1988.

———. "Aging and the Training and Learning Process in Organizations." In *Training and Development in Work Organizations,* edited by I. Goldstein and R. Katzell. San Francisco: Jossey-Bass, forthcoming.

Stewart, J. S. "Retraining Older Workers for Upgraded Jobs." *Industrial Gerontology* (Summer 1969): 26–31.

Sum, Andrew, Christopher Ruhm, and Peter Doeringer. *Work, Earnings, and Retirement*. Boston: Boston University Center for Applied Social Science/Institute for Employment Policy, 1988.

Treas, Judith. "The Historical Decline in Late-Life Labor Force Participation in the United States." In *Age, Health, and Employment,* edited by James E. Birren, Pauline K. Robinson, and Judy E. Livingston. Englewood Cliffs, NJ: Prentice-Hall, 1986.

Treat, Nancy J., Leonard W. Poon, and James L. Fozard. "Age, Imagery, and Learning in Paired Associate Learning." *Experimental Aging Research* 7 (1981): 337–342.

U.S. Bureau of the Census. *The Statistical History of the United States from Colonial Times to the Present*. Stamford, CT: Fairfield, 1965.

————. *Lifetime Work Experience and Its Effect on Earnings*. Current Population Reports, Series P-23, No. 136. Washington, DC: U.S. Government Printing Office, June 1984.

————. *Projections of the Population of States by Age, Sex, and Race: 1988–2010*. Current Population Reports, Series P-25, No. 1017. Washington, DC: U.S. Government Printing Office, October 1988.

————. *Labor Force Status and Other Characteristics of Persons with a Work Disability: 1981 to 1988*. Current Population Reports, Series P-23, No. 160. Washington, DC: U.S. Government Printing Office, July 1989.

U.S. Congress. House. *American Attitudes toward Pensions and Retirement*. Hearing before the Select Committee on Aging, House of Representatives. 96th Congress, 1st Session, February 28, 1979. Washington, DC: U.S. Government Printing Office, 1979.

U.S. Congress. Senate. *Toward a National Older Worker Policy: An Information Paper*. Washington, DC: U.S. Government Printing Office, 1981.

————. Senate. *Aging and the Work Force: Human Resource Strategies: An Information Paper*. Washington, DC: U.S. Government Printing Office, 1982.

————. Senate. *The Costs of Employing Older Workers: An Information Paper*. Washington, DC: U.S. Government Printing Office, 1984.

————. Office of Technology Assessment. *Displaced Homemakers: Programs and Policy—An Interim Report*. Washington, DC: U.S. Government Printing Office, 1985a.

————. Senate. *Health and Extended Worklife: An Information Paper*. Washington, DC: U.S. Government Printing Office, 1985b.

————. Senate. *Personnel Practices for an Aging Work Force: Private-Sector Examples*. Washington, DC: U.S. Government Printing Office, 1985c.

————. Senate. *Developments in Aging: 1986.* Vol. 1. A Report of the Special Committee on Aging. Washington, DC: U.S. Government Printing Office, 1987.

————. Senate. *Developments in Aging: 1987.* Vol. 1. A Report of the Special Committee on Aging. Washington, DC: U.S. Government Printing Office, 1988.

————. Senate. *Developments in Aging: 1988.* Vol. 1. A Report of the Special Committee on Aging. Washington, DC: U.S. Government Printing Office, 1989.

U.S. Department of Education. Center for Education Statistics. *Trends in Adult Education 1969–1984.* Washington, DC: U.S. Government Printing Office, undated.

U.S. Department of Health and Human Services. Social Security Administration. "Increasing the Social Security Retirement Age: Older Workers in Physically Demanding Occupations or Ill Health." *Social Security Bulletin* 49 (October 1986): 5–23.

————. Social Security Administration. *Annual Statistical Supplement, 1987.* Washington, DC: U.S. Government Printing Office, 1987.

————. Social Security Administration. *Income of the Population 55 or Older, 1986.* Washington, DC: Social Security Administration Office of Policy, Office of Research and Statistics, June 1988.

U.S. Department of Labor (DOL). Bureau of Labor Statistics. *Comparative Job Performance by Age: Large Plants in the Men's Footwear and Household Furniture Industries.* Bulletin 1223. Washington, DC: U.S. Government Printing Office, 1957.

————. Bureau of Labor Statistics. *Handbook of Labor Statistics.* Washington, DC: U.S. Government Printing Office, June 1985.

————. Employment and Training Administration. *Training and Employment Report of the Secretary of Labor.* Washington, DC: U.S. Government Printing Office, 1988.

————. Bureau of Labor Statistics. *Employment and Earnings.* Washington, DC: U.S. Government Printing Office, January 1989a.

————. Commission on Workforce Quality and Labor Market Efficiency. *Investing in People.* Washington, DC: DOL, 1989b.

————. *Labor Market Problems of Older Workers.* Report of the Secretary of Labor, prepared by Philip L. Rones and Diane E. Herz. Washington, DC: DOL, 1989c.

————. *Older Worker Task Force: Key Policy Issues for the Future.* Report of the Secretary of Labor. Washington, DC: DOL, 1989d.

————. Bureau of Labor Statistics. *Employment and Earnings*. Washington, DC: U.S. Government Printing Office, January 1990.

U.S. Equal Employment Opportunity Commission (EEOC). *20th Annual Report, FY1985*. Washington, DC: EEOC, undated.

U.S. General Accounting Office (GAO). *The Equal Employment Commission Has Made Limited Progress in Eliminating Employment Discrimination*. HRD-76-147. Washington, DC: GAO, September 1976.

————. *Information on the Senior Community Service Employment Program and the Proposed Transfer to the Department of Health and Human Services*. GAO/HRD-84-42. Washington, DC: GAO, March 12, 1984.

————. *Retirement before Age 65 Is a Growing Trend in the Private Sector*. GAO/HRD-85-81. Washington, DC: GAO, July 15, 1985.

————. *Dislocated Workers: Local Programs and Outcomes under the Job Training Partnership Act*. GAO/HRD-87-41. Washington, DC: GAO, March 1987a.

————. *Pension Plans: Many Workers Don't Know When They Can Retire*. GAO/HRD-87-94BR. Washington, DC: GAO, August 1987b.

————. *Job Training Partnership Act: Participants, Services, and Outcomes*. GAO/T-HRD-88-31. Statement of Lawrence H. Thompson before the Committee on Education and Labor, U.S. House of Representatives. Washington, DC: GAO, September 29, 1988a.

————. *Equal Employment Opportunity: EEOC and State Agencies Did Not Fully Investigate Discrimination Charges*. GAO/HRD-89-11. Washington, DC: GAO, October 1988b.

————. *Job Training Partnership Act: Information on Training, Placements, and Wages of Male and Female Participants*. GAO/HRD-89-152FS. Washington, DC: GAO, September 1989.

Wade, Alice. "Social Security Area Population Projections: 1987." *Social Security Bulletin* 51 (February 1988): 3–30.

Weiss, Francine K. *Older Women and Job Discrimination: A Primer*. Washington, DC: Older Women's League, 1984.

————. *Employment Discrimination Against Older Women: A Handbook on Litigating Age and Sex Discrimination Cases*. Washington, DC: Older Women's League, 1989.

Weitzman, Lenore J. *The Divorce Revolution: The Unexpected Social and Economic Consequences for Women and Children in the United States*. New York: Free Press, 1985.

Williams, Harry B. "What Temporary Workers Earn: Findings from New BLS Survey." *Monthly Labor Review* 112 (March 1989): 3–6.

Index